Cambodia

REPORT FROM A STRICKEN LAND

ALSO BY HENRY KAMM

Dragon Ascending: Vietnam and the Vietnamese

Cambodia

REPORT FROM A STRICKEN LAND

Henry Kamm

ARCADE PUBLISHING • NEW YORK

FIRST EDITION

Library of Congress Cataloging-in-Publication Data

Kamm, Henry
 Cambodia : report from a stricken land / Henry Kamm. —1st ed.
  p.   cm.
 Includes index.
 ISBN 1-55970-433-0
 1. Cambodia—History—Civil War, 1970–1975. 2. Cambodia—History 1975–1979. 3. Cambodia—History—1979– I. Title.
 DS554.8.K3832 1998
 959.604'2—dc21   98–22707

Published in the United States by Arcade Publishing, Inc., New York
Distributed by Little, Brown and Company

10 9 8 7 6 5 4 3 2 1

Designed by API

PRINTED IN THE UNITED STATES OF AMERICA

For my Children,

Alison, Thomas, and Nicholas,

and Theirs

Contents

Preface

It began with a letter from the consul general of Cambodia in Hong Kong, K. R. L. Wongsanith. It was the only funny rejection that I ever received in a long career of often being found unacceptable by one or the other country for the purpose of reporting from it. This is what Mr. Wongsanith wrote he had been instructed by the secretary of state for information to tell me:

"For the moment we are obliged to admit no journalist to our country as, in November, we shall be celebrating our National Day 'en famille' and the entry of journalists to our country is submitted to very strict rules which cannot be twisted."

The letter was dated November 6, 1969. The moment I received it, I reached a firm decision. To make a possible visit to a country that worked such innocent wonders with the English language, a country that refused to "twist" its visa rules to protect the family character of its version of the Fourth of July, I would even stoop to lying. And so I called on a Cambodian consulate that I had not yet badgered for a visa having truthfully laid my journalistic cards on the table. I was an unknown quantity at the consulate in Vientiane, the sleepy capital of Laos. The friendly lady accepted my self-description as a "company representative," not quite a lie, and immediately stamped my passport to allow me two weeks of tourism in her country.

PREFACE

It was with amusement that I first saw Cambodia, and the sign on the Royal Palace grounds to "Beware of the Naughty Elephant!" did not diminish that feeling. Above all, Cambodia was a country in Indochina that remained at peace, and one could enjoy its pleasures — a lovely, well-tended capital, people who much preferred smiling to scowling, the absence of uniformed men, barbed wire, traffic jams, neon signs, or masses of tourists, and, of course, the marvels of Angkor — without feeling that at any moment a grenade would prove it all to be an illusion. The war that was ravaging Vietnam and Laos touched Cambodia only along its border with Vietnam.

But less than a month after I had left, the Indochinese tragedy engulfed the last country to have been spared. The war that America to this day calls "the Vietnam War" had spread to the third and last of the countries that until the mid-1950s had formed French Indochina. The falsely limiting misnomer ignores the fact that next door to Vietnam, in Laos, the United States Air Force and contingents of Central Intelligence Agency "advisers" had since the early 1960s been participating in extensive fighting by the government army against the Laotian Communists and the North Vietnamese Army. And it continued to be "the Vietnam War" in American parlance even after March 1970, when Cambodia also became part of the Indochinese battleground and remained embattled until 1975. Then all three countries fell under Communist rule.

And as the insouciant Khmer smile continued to beam when there was nothing to smile about, my sense of Cambodia began to change. The Khmer habit of smiling innocently even at casual passersby whose eyes met theirs had beguiled Western visitors and writers since France's colonization in the nineteenth century began drawing occasional travelers to the reclusive land. (The Khmers are its dominant indigenous ethnic group.) The coming of full-scale war, which Cambodia had been spared until 1970 and for which it was utterly unprepared, warranted anything but smiles. With every passing day it seemed to me more that Cambodia was a country so alien in our world, so unfamiliar with its harsh ways, that the clash with the brutal reality of a pitiless war, which it had not wanted and would have little say over, would crush it.

With the encouragement of my editors at the *New York Times*, I became a regular attendant at Cambodia's deepening tragedy. The sense of amusement that had first drawn me there was as short-lived as the few weeks that separated my two-week experience of Cambodia in its last days of peace from its descent into war and its appalling sequels. It has been my painful privilege to observe from close up all the phases of what increasingly I came to feel was the doom of a nation ill-used by outside forces and betrayed by most of those of its own who arrogated to themselves power over their people. Nothing that I saw or heard on my most recent visit, at the end of 1997, lightened that sense.

What follows is an attempt to retrace the events of nearly three decades as seen by a reporter who was granted the privilege of being taken into the confidence of many Cambodians, men and women whom I admired and whose hopes for their country I shared, as well as others. I recall with infinite sadness those among them who paid with their lives for staying when they could have fled, before total darkness enveloped Cambodia for four years that have known no equal in history.

My thanks go to those, too numerous to mention, who over the years filled me with sympathy for Cambodia and compassion for its ever-suffering people, as well as to those who suffered at the hands of Cambodians. And I thank my publishers, Jeannette and Dick Seaver, for inviting me to try to explain a country whose ultimate secret, I confess, continues to resist my understanding.

Phnom Penh, Cambodia, and Lagnes, France
1997–98

Chronology

First century of the current era — Chinese chronicles tell of the existence of the Kingdom of Funan, precursor of the Khmer (Cambodian) Empire. It covers the south of the Indochinese Peninsula and the north of the Malay Peninsula.

Seventh century — The Kingdom of Chenla, north of Funan, conquers Funan. The first stone inscriptions in the Khmer language appear. Toward the end of the century, marauders from Java and other islands establish positions of power in Chenla, which is torn by rivalries and internecine conflicts.

Ninth century — King Jayavarman II establishes stability and secures Chenla's independence from Java. He founds his capital north of the later site of Angkor.

889 — King Yasovarman moves the capital to the present site of Angkor. His enlarged realm reaches from what is now southern Laos to the Gulf of Thailand.

1002–50 — In the reign of Suryavarman I, the Khmer Empire expands to include much of today's Myanmar (formerly Burma) and reaches farther into the Malay Peninsula in the south and Laos in the north.

1113–50 — Suryavarman II has Angkor Wat built in his honor and further extends the empire's sway.

1177 — The Kingdom of Champa, in today's central Vietnam, conquers and sacks Angkor.

1181 — Jayavarman VII subjugates Champa. He builds Angkor Thom and the Bayon, the last of the great royal capitals. His reign is the summit of Cambodia's greatness.

1218 — Jayavarman VII's death marks the beginning of the end of Khmer glory. The rise of the Siamese and Vietnamese kingdoms reduces the Khmers' hold over the realm.

Fourteenth century — Siam (now Thailand) twice conquers and sacks Angkor.

Fifteenth century — A third Siamese conquest in midcentury causes the Khmers to abandon for good their royal capital to the jungle.

1594 — Siam conquers Lovek, the new capital.

Seventeenth to nineteenth centuries — The fatally weakened Khmer Kingdom, rent by unending internecine struggles, turns alternately to Siam and Vietnam for aid and protection. The price is great loss of territory, especially to Vietnam, which progressively annexes what is today's southern Vietnam, including Saigon.

1864 — France, having colonized Cochin China (now southern Vietnam), obliges King Norodom to sign a treaty making Cambodia a French protectorate.

1884 — France further reduces the king's power, making Cambodia, in effect, a colony.

1941 — France enthrones Prince Norodom Sihanouk, believing it will easily manipulate the eighteen-year-old's kingship to its advantage. Japan occupies Cambodia as part of its conquest of Southeast Asia.

1945 — Japan is defeated. Political conflict arises between France, which desires to restore its former colonial hold, and radical Cambodian nationalists, who wish by force to prevent France's return. Sihanouk chooses the political course of not risking an anticolonial war but negotiating with France for eventual independence. He outmaneuvers both the French and the Cambodian nationalists.

1953 — Sihanouk dramatically steps up his independence campaign, launching a "royal crusade for independence." France, preoccupied by its losing war against the Vietnamese Communists, grants independence.

1954 — The Geneva Conference ratifies the Vietnamese Communist victory and divides independent Vietnam into Communist North and pro-Western South. Cambodia's undivided independence and its right to accept foreign military assistance are recognized. The United States becomes the principal supplier, but Sihanouk rejects American pressure to abandon neutrality and join an American-led anti-Communist alliance.

1955 — To take the leading role in the agitated political scene, divided over Cambodia's role in the civil wars continuing in Vietnam and Laos, King Sihanouk abdicates in favor of his father, Norodom Suramarit, and forms a broad political movement, which wins all seats in Parliament.

1958 — In new elections, Sihanouk wins more than 99 percent of the popular vote. Opposition is strong among the small educated minority, divided between pro-Westerners, neutralists and Communists. Sihanouk calls the Communists "Khmers Rouges," or Red Cambodians, and the name Khmer Rouge sticks. Under his increasingly authoritarian and arbitrary rule, all opponents are persecuted. The Communists seek refuge in the countryside and form the nucleus of an underground resistance movement.

1960 — On King Suramarit's death, Sihanouk names himself Chief of State.

1963 — Fearful that the intensifying American involvement in the wars of Vietnam and Laos will engulf Cambodia, Sihanouk cuts off American aid.

1965 — As American troops enter the war in Vietnam, Sihanouk breaks diplomatic relations with the United States.

1965–70 — Taking advantage of Cambodia's military weakness, the Vietnamese Communists install extensive "sanctuaries" for their troops along the Cambodian side of their border. Sihanouk reluctantly tolerates the incursions but urges the Vietnamese to limit their implantation. He also yields to demands that international Communist military aid to Vietnam be received in the port of Sihanoukville and transported across Cambodia to the sanctuaries. American and South Vietnamese troops also violate Cambodia's neutrality by staging raids against North Vietnamese troops based there. Conflicting foreign pressures contribute to increasingly tense domestic politics.

1969 — Worried over the mounting Vietnamese Communist presence and its internal fallout, Sihanouk resumes diplomatic relations with the United States. America begins secret bombing of sanctuaries. Sihanouk forms a Salvation Government under Prime Minister Lon Nol and Deputy Prime Minister Prince Sisowath Sirik Matak, Sihanouk's cousin. Both are strongly anti-Vietnamese and favor rapprochement with the United States.

January 6, 1970 — Sihanouk leaves for an extended trip to France for "health" reasons. He expects that this implicit challenge to Lon Nol and Sirik Matak to solve Cambodia's mounting problems on their own will cause them to beg him to return to solve the crisis and thus restore his earlier authority.

March 18, 1970 — The Salvation Government deposes Sihanouk after having issued an unenforceable ultimatum to the militarily superior North Vietnamese Communists to withdraw their troops from Cambodia. In defiance, the Vietnamese advance more deeply into Cambodia, whose small, ill-equipped army is incapable of resistance. At the same time, South Vietnamese troops pursue their Communist enemy into Cambodia. Cambodia's neutrality is destroyed and it becomes part of the Indochinese theater of war.

March 23, 1970 — Sihanouk meets in China with the Vietnamese and Laotian Communist leaders and makes common cause with them in their struggle against the American-backed regimes in their countries. He heads a united front with his former enemies, the Khmers Rouges, dedicated to defeating the Lon Nol government.

April 30, 1970 — President Nixon announces that American troops have invaded Cambodia with the aim of eliminating the Vietnamese Communist bases. The invasion is limited in space — thirty kilometers from the South Vietnamese border — and in time — withdrawal before June 30. Lon Nol, after initial hesitation, endorses the invasion, of which Nixon did not inform him in advance. To avoid a battle with the American forces until their withdrawal, the Vietnamese Communist troops move out of their thirty-kilometer reach and more deeply into Cambodia. They conquer Angkor, the symbol of Cambodia's past greatness, in June. At the end of the month, American ground forces withdraw to Vietnam, but the air force continues bombing throughout Cambodia.

October 9, 1970 — The Lon Nol government transforms the kingdom into the Khmer Republic. By then, Communist forces, nominally led by Sihanouk, occupy half of Cambodia's territory. The Khmers Rouges rapidly build up their forces, with the aim of eventually replacing their Vietnamese allies, and conduct their own war.

September to December 1970 — In the first of its only two offensives in the five years of war, the Lon Nol army fails to drive the Communist troops from the road from Phnom Penh to Angkor.

February 1971 — Lon Nol suffers a stroke and leaves for two months of treatment in Hawaii. Sirik Matak runs the government in his absence. Lon Nol returns in April, his health and ability to work lastingly impaired, but remains the country's uncontested leader.

October 20, 1971 — Lon Nol declares a state of emergency and assumes power to rule by decree.

October to December 1971 — The government stages its second and last major offensive. Once more the aim is to clear the road to Angkor. It is routed by the Vietnamese Communists.

March 10, 1972 — Lon Nol names himself president, prime minister, defense minister, and marshal of the armed forces. In a subsequent series of rigged votes, he eliminates all legitimate opposition.

January 27, 1973 — The United States and North Vietnam sign an agreement in Paris. Both undertake to end military action in Cambodia. American forces withdraw from South Vietnam, and the U.S. Air Force halts bombing in Cambodia.

February 8, 1973 — Both the United States and North Vietnam violate the Paris agreement. Some North Vietnamese troops remain in Cambodia, and the United States resumes bombing throughout the country.

June 30, 1973 — Congress orders bombing to halt by August 15. With its termination, Lon Nol's forces are on their own against the Khmers Rouges, who have recruited sufficient forces to carry forward their war without the aid of Vietnamese Communist troops.

1973–75 — Fighting on its own, Lon Nol's army loses all initiative and is reduced by the Khmers Rouges to holding Phnom Penh and other towns, while most of the countryside and its people come under Khmer Rouge domination. Continued American arms and food shipments are Lon Nol's lifeline.

April 1, 1975 — With Phnom Penh besieged and Khmer Rouge victory certain, Lon Nol resigns and flees to the United States.

April 12, 1975 — The United States abandons its embassy in Phnom Penh.

April 17, 1975 — The Khmers Rouges capture Phnom Penh and complete their victory. They drive the population out of cities, towns, and villages, and under a plan of unprecedented ultra-Communist social engineering, turn Cambodia into a country of large agricultural communes condemned to unattainable self-sufficiency. They abolish money and prohibit all private property, Western medicine, education, and religious practice. The existence of the ruling Communist party and the names of its leaders are kept secret for years. Power is in the hands of a nameless "organization." Its four years of rule result in the deaths of at least hundreds of thousands (estimates range as high as two million) of Cambodians — by arbitrary execution, starvation, exhaustion from unending overwork, and denial of medical care. The Khmers Rouges no longer need Sihanouk to boost their image and imprison him in the Royal Palace in Phnom Penh. When the existence of the ruling Communist party is finally disclosed, its leader is identified as Pol Pot, nom de guerre of Saloth Sar.

April 30, 1975 — North Vietnamese Communist troops capture Saigon (renamed Ho Chi Minh City), ending the war in Vietnam. Shortly thereafter, the Communists also seize power in Laos, completing the Communist victory in the Indochina War.

1976 — Vietnam is reunified.

1977 — Reports from Vietnamese refugees in Southeast Asia tell of Cambodian military incursions into Vietnam, nominally a brotherly Communist country. Vietnam retaliates with a limited invasion into the border area.

December 31, 1977 — Cambodia breaks off diplomatic relations with Vietnam, the first such act between two Communist countries. It accuses Vietnam of aggression. A year of local skirmishes and mutual vituperation between the former allies follows.

December 1978 — Vietnam establishes the Kampuchean United Front for National Salvation in the "liberated zone" — Cambodian territory occupied by Vietnam. The front consists of Khmer Rouge soldiers captured by Vietnam, Khmer Rouge leaders who escaped to Vietnam during extensive purges in their ranks, and civilian refugees from Khmer Rouge rule. Under the cover of the front, Vietnam mounts a full-scale invasion of Cambodia by its army.

January 7, 1979 — The Vietnamese Army captures Phnom Penh. Pol Pot and his government escape to the Thai border, where they establish themselves with Thai and Chinese support and under the benevolent eyes of the United States and the West in general. The Khmers Rouges send Sihanouk to the United Nations to argue their case, but he defects. Most of the world considers Vietnam's invasion a greater evil than the Pol Pot regime it overthrew. Vietnam installs a Communist puppet regime of Khmer Rouge defectors and changes the name of the country to the People's Republic of Kampuchea.

February 17, 1979 — The Chinese Army invades northern Vietnam in a limited but destructive punitive strike in retaliation for Vietnam's action against Cambodia, China's ally. It withdraws sixteen days later. Vietnam, closely allied with the Soviet Union, is viewed as a hostile force by China.

September 3, 1981 — Under pressure from China and their Southeast Asian neighbors, Sihanouk and the principal anti-Communist resistance movement, headed by a conservative former prime minister, Son Sann, agree reluctantly to join with their Khmer Rouge enemy in a united front of opposition to Vietnam and its Cambodian puppet regime. In 1982 they form the Coalition Government of Democratic Kampuchea. Sihanouk is named as its head.

1985 — Mikhail S. Gorbachev becomes Soviet leader and cuts Soviet military and economic aid to Vietnam, which depended heavily on it. As a result, Vietnam decides to reduce its costly occupation of Cambodia.

1986 — Vietnam and Thailand, on behalf of non-Communist Southeast Asia, begin informal talks on a peaceful settlement of the Cambodian issue.

1987 — Sihanouk on behalf of the Coalition Government and Prime Minister Hun Sen of the pro-Vietnamese regime in Phnom Penh begin negotiations.

1988 — Negotiations open between all the partners in the Coalition Government and the Vietnamese-installed Phnom Penh regime.

1989 — The Phnom Penh government nominally renounces communism and changes the country's name from the People's Republic of Kampuchea to the State of Cambodia. Vietnam withdraws its last occupation troops.

September 10, 1990 — The Supreme National Council is formed. It unites the pro-Vietnamese government of Hun Sen and the partners in Sihanouk's Coalition Government — the Khmers Rouges, Sihanouk's supporters, and the anti-Communist and anti-Vietnamese Son Sann movement. In 1991 Sihanouk is appointed as its head.

October 23, 1991 — Seventeen nations and all the Cambodian factions of the Supreme National Council sign in Paris an "Agreement on a Comprehensive Political Settlement of the Cambodia Conflict." It provides for an end to the fighting between the Phnom Penh government and the Khmers Rouges and other anti-Vietnamese forces, disarmament of all factions, and creation of "a neutral political environment conducive to free and fair general elections." It establishes a United Nations Transitional Authority (UNTAC) with civilian and military components to implement the Paris Agreement.

March 1992 — Yasushi Akashi and Lieutenant General John Sanderson take up their posts, respectively, as head of UNTAC and its military commander. UNTAC deploys a multinational force of six thousand officials and sixteen thousand troops throughout Cambodia to oversee implementation of the Paris Agreement of 1991.

May 30, 1992 — Akashi and Sanderson bow to a Khmer Rouge refusal to let them pass through territory near the Thai border under Khmer Rouge control. As the Khmers Rouges progressively renege on their obligations under the Paris Agreement, the Hun Sen government, which controls most of the country, follows suit. UNTAC implicitly accepts that the proposed cantonment of troops and disarmament are a dead letter and concentrates all efforts on organizing free elections. The Hun Sen regime, through its long-established hold over most of Cambodia, sabotages creation of a neutral political atmosphere. It instigates widespread political violence, mainly against the pro-Sihanouk royalist party headed by Sihanouk's son, Prince Norodom Ranariddh.

May 1993 — Royalists win elections, gaining 45 percent of the vote despite the intimidation of voters by Hun Sen's ex-Communist People's party. They obtain a plurality of Parliament seats. Hun Sen refuses to accept the result and stages a secession of the eastern provinces. Sihanouk bows to pressure, fearing civil war, and assures Hun Sen that despite his election defeat he will be given equal power to govern, together with Ranariddh.

September 24, 1993 — Sihanouk is chosen as king. He names Ranariddh first prime minister and Hun Sen second prime minister. The king, ill with cancer, avoids Cambodia, presumably because of a growing sense of futility over his incapacity to direct Cambodia's course. He spends most of his time in China and North Korea, the countries that gave him asylum during his years in exile in the five years of war against Lon Nol, from 1970 to 1975.

1996–97 — The Ranariddh–Hun Sen coalition, which had become frayed, breaks apart, making government ineffective. Open political warfare by numerous factions opposes both leaders. Hun Sen, who has maintained his control over the countryside and administration that was conferred on him under the Vietnamese occupation, is in a position of superior strength. Both sides seek the support of elements of the Khmers Rouges, whose long years of unity have given way to factional rivalries. One of their principal leaders, Ieng Sary, defects. The government rewards him with personal rule over the rich Pailin region on the Thai border, long under Khmer Rouge control. Khmer Rouge dissension erupts into factional fighting. Pol Pot has his defense minister, Son Sen, and his family murdered. He, in turn, is seized by his top military commander, Ta Mok, "tried," and sentenced to life imprisonment in a Khmer Rouge jungle encampment on the Thai border.

March 30, 1997 — Grenades are thrown at a rally in front of Parliament called by former finance minister Sam Rainsy, the most outspoken opposition leader, a royalist. At least fifteen are killed; evidence points to Hun Sen's responsibility.

July 5–6, 1997 — After both prime ministers, Ranariddh and Hun Sen, bolster their personal military forces in Phnom

Penh, Hun Sen stages a military coup d'état against all his opponents and their leaders — Ranariddh, Sam Rainsy, and Son Sann. Many of their principal aides are murdered. Their headquarters and personal residences are pillaged. They seek safety in exile, although Sam Rainsy returns several months later. Hun Sen reestablishes the status quo that existed before the Paris Agreement: he and his People's party, the renamed pro-Vietnamese Communists, are in full control of Cambodia, except for small encampments on the Thai border of Khmer Rouge and forces loyal to Ranariddh. Hun Sen postpones the elections due in May 1998.

April 1998 — Pol Pot dies after Hun Sen troops capture the last Khmer Rouge stronghold. His body is incinerated without verification whether he died of natural causes.

Cambodia

REPORT FROM A STRICKEN LAND

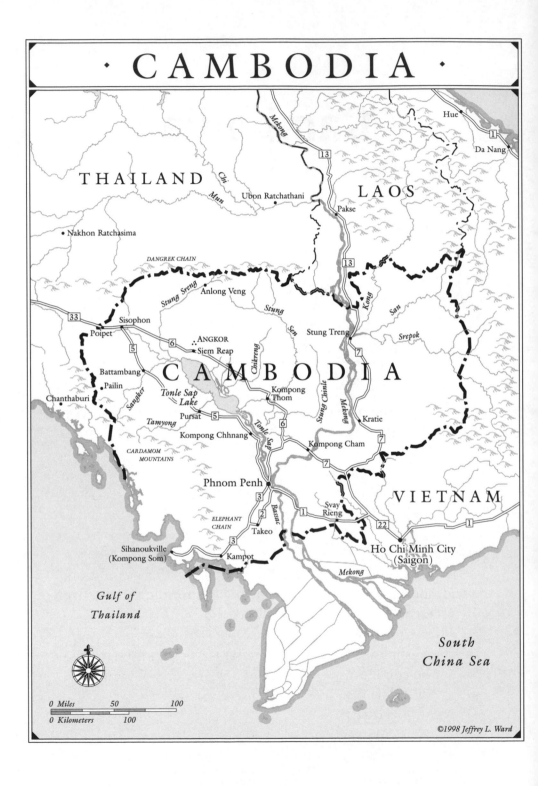

1

Hope Is for the Unborn: 1998

*U*NITED NATIONS officials stationed in the poorest countries of the world share an understandable inclination to work themselves into a constant state of determined optimism about their mission. Without persuading themselves regularly that a brighter future lies ahead, they could hardly face the misery that surrounds them and go about their endeavors to relieve it. Andrew Morris, head of the Cambodian health services of the United Nations Children's Fund (UNICEF), was taking the most hopeful possible view of Cambodia as the year 1997 was drawing to a close.

"I don't think there is a good outlook for this generation," he said, speaking deliberately. "The hope is for the Cambodians not yet born."

Thus the understating Englishman was writing off with pained realism hope for a decent life for today's Cambodians, including the youngest, the generation that is his professional concern at the UNICEF. What is true for today's children in this grossly misgoverned country surely applies with even greater validity to their elders in a nation of more than ten million, half of whom are under eighteen years old. And yet, not long ago the world was hypocritically congratulating itself on having halted Cambodia's distress and set Southeast Asia's stepchild on a course toward peace and recovery.

Since 1970, when it was plunged into the Indochina War, which had begun with the Vietnamese rising against French colonial rule and lasted until the Communist victories in Vietnam, Laos, and Cambodia in 1975, Cambodia has suffered the worst that this callous century has devised. It struggled through five years of bloody civil conflict with the destructive intervention of bellicose foreign powers, four years of a genocidal revolutionary regime, then liberation through invasion and a decade of military occupation by Vietnam, a hated and feared big neighbor, and throughout these years unceasing internecine warfare on its soil, continuing to this day.

Then came the promise of decisive change; at last better days seemed ahead. As the final decade of the century opened, the mightiest powers of the world were rearranging their conflictual mutual relationships. They agreed with considerable fanfare at a drawn-out conference in Paris in 1991 to help ease tensions among themselves by removing the irritant of a small Indochinese country of low intrinsic importance to any of them. At a cost of about two billion dollars, which was spent mainly to transport to Cambodia and maintain there for eighteen months twenty-two thousand aliens — soldiers, police, administrators, diplomats, and experts in varied fields from all corners of the globe — the big powers and Cambodia's neighbors charged the United Nations with implementing the Paris Agreement.

How the warring Cambodian Communist leaderships — Pol Pot's Khmers Rouges and the Vietnamese-installed government of Hun Sen — retaining their crude methods of rule even after forswearing their old doctrines, subverted the very notions of peace and reconciliation to which they agreed in Paris will be related later. So will the sequels of this sabotage: how the international community, determined to rid itself of the Cambodian bone of contention at any cost, pronounced to be a success a mission that had largely failed, and how Cambodia's politicians of all persuasions undermined the single substantial achievement of the international enterprise, the surprisingly popular and clean elections. Following the adoption of a constitution by the newly elected National Assembly, the aliens left. In September 1993, for the first time since war began in March 1970, Cambodians were on their own, relying on the actions of their own elected political leaders.

The leaders betrayed them, much as earlier leaders had done. The incompetence and venality of most of Cambodia's political class has been an unfortunate constant since the country regained its independence from French colonialism in 1953.

Cambodia today is still governed by Second Prime Minister Hun Sen, the same pugnacious leader who ruled thuggishly before the elections, which he and his party lost. The winner yielded to his threat of force. The country has regained a king, who under the constitution adopted by the National Assembly is to serve as the ultimate arbiter of the political process. But Norodom Sihanouk, who represented most Cambodians' hopes for a restoration of normality in their stricken land, is a futile, ailing, absentee monarch, alternately condemning or cajoling, largely by fax from Beijing, the three, yes, three, competing prime ministers of Cambodia.

Political opponents have been murdered, detained, tortured, or have fled into exile, with predictable effect on free political expression and the outlook for future honest elections. The powers that rule are openly criticized largely from the safety of exile or, at far higher risk, by Cambodians who enjoy the limited protection of dual nationality. Freedom of the press survives shakily, often at the cost of unsolved murders and attempted murders of critical journalists. Many provincial and district leaders, as well as military commanders, act as independent warlords, using troops as criminal gangs. These men of power are protected by a totally political judiciary, always at the service of the executive. Lawlessness is the rule. The National Assembly is dormant. Corruption flourishes from the highest to the lowest level of office-holders. And as the rich proudly flaunt their wealth and power, Cambodia's patient and passive people watch their country's treasures vanish into criminal hands, while their leaders mock the people's rights and ignore their needs.

All this may be written off as politics as usual in a country of low political culture, stemming from the harrowing history that Cambodians alive today feel in their bones. It may be reversible. But Cambodia is not just an underdeveloped, misruled country like so many others. It is afflicted with the catastrophic cumulative effects of the destruction of its society in the four years of Khmer Rouge tyranny. These years of horror were preceded by the authoritarian regime of Sihanouk, the once and present king, and five years of war, from 1970 to 1975, between the manic Khmers Rouges and the incompetent, American-supported Lon Nol. There followed a Vietnamese-imposed puppet government that has held, in effect, uninterrupted power since 1979, despite the United Nations operation and the elections of 1993.

Cambodia is a puppet no longer; it gained national independence when Vietnamese occupation troops voluntarily withdrew in 1989. But the Hun Sen regime has never obtained legitimacy in the eyes of Cambodians. It was not the government that they elected when for the first time in their history they were allowed to vote honestly and freely in 1993. It imposed itself, with the complicity of King Sihanouk. Nor have Cambodians forgotten that their present rulers were not victims of the Khmers Rouges, like the overwhelming majority of their generation, but men who held positions of regional or local command in Pol Pot's machine until that paranoiac monster began devouring its own, and they fled to Vietnam for their lives. And some did not convert to less murderous politics until after the Vietnamese invaders drove the Khmers Rouges from power.

So the reflections that made Andrew Morris, the UNICEF

official, deliver so pessimistic a verdict for the chances of today's Cambodians, basing his judgment on the disastrous state of health and education of their children and their mothers, are only a part of Cambodia's enduring crisis. But his diagnosis of a gravely incapacitated country affects the very basis of the chances for recovery and is substantially shared by doctors, midwives, nurses, and educators working in the towns and villages of Cambodia and by educated Cambodians and resident foreigners who view the country with sympathy and compassion. Not all foreigners do. Many are led to unsympathetic and harsh judgments by their impatience with the Cambodians' prevalent passivity before the challenges of life, and by their "imperfect understanding" of modernity as viewed by non-Cambodians. This understanding leads to responses that outsiders view as erratic or irrational. There is also antagonism over the high level of insecurity, corruption, the bureaucracy's dilatory ways and devious business practices. Much of this was also true in the past.

A great deal of the Cambodian tragedy is visible to the naked eye. The capital city of Phnom Penh, before 1970 the trimmest and most cared-for in the region, is today reflective of a society that has been battered and overturned. "Phnom Penh is a lot dirtier, but I still recognize it," said a woman, back from France for her first visit in more than twenty years. "But the faces! They are no longer the same people." She did not mean that, like all Cambodians, she is reminded wherever she turns of family members, friends, and acquaintances whose lives were extinguished in the years of genocide. That goes without saying and applies, to a lesser degree, also to foreigners like myself, who have been witnesses to Cambodia's travails over many years. What the woman remarked on was the profound change that has taken place in Phnom Penh's population, which has nearly doubled from the 600,000 who lived there in 1970. It is no longer the urban mix of roughly equal numbers of Cambodians, Chinese, and Vietnamese of prewar Phnom Penh that made it a city of considerable civility. It collapsed only when in 1970 the Lon Nol regime unleashed a fearful pogrom against the Vietnamese population.

The capital has become a city of country folk. The Khmers Rouges emptied it in 1975, and in their genocidal madness they killed city dwellers even more readily than peasants. Under their draconian regime, few Cambodians succeeded in escaping to foreign asylum. The outflow of refugees that followed the Vietnamese invasion four years later contained a disproportionate share of educated city dwellers who had somehow survived and who understandably had given up hope of being able to rebuild their lives in their country. At the same time, rural people headed into the city from the blighted, war-torn countryside. They hoped to find security, paid jobs, food, shelter, and medical care dispensed by the international aid organizations centered there. They found instead the same poverty that they left behind, but in a setting totally unfamiliar to them.

In their overwhelming majority the rural settlers in Phnom Penh never became urbanized. It takes family links in the city, a level of education never available to them, and urban employment to change the families of subsistence farmers into city dwellers. Phnom Penh has become a city whose residents live rural lives of the most restricted horizons in an urban setting. This is desperately difficult. They no longer belong to a larger community and are separated from their extended families, which gave cohesion to Cambodia's villages. They no longer grow their own food, draw water from a well or a stream, or gather their firewood near their houses. In the city, they must pay for these necessities or do without, and they have very little to pay with. What they can do, wherever they are, is raise household animals. Pigs, chickens, or ducks were as uncommon in prewar Phnom Penh as in New York. Today they are part of city life, along with an occasional lumbering water buffalo for good measure. The Tuol Sleng concentration camp, a former school close to the city center, was a site of torture and death for an estimated total of sixteen thousand men, women, and children in Pol Pot's days. Now its chambers of horror are a stop on the conducted-tour circuit. The pigsties of its neighbors encroach upon the grounds of the memorial.

The center of the city and its surrounding residential quarters have taken on an air of superficial, unhealthy, robber-baron development — bank buildings, hotels, office blocks, and the pompous villas of the newly rich, but no housing for those whose ill-paid labor serves them. A day of rain makes the poorly maintained and overburdened drainage system overflow and leaves deep, stagnant pools and puddles that make streets impassable for days. The farther one goes from the center, the denser become the shantytown slums, rickety huts leaning precariously one against the other. The reek of poverty announces the lack of sanitation and the prevalence of ever-mounting heaps of rotting garbage long before its festering source comes into sight. The vast slums of Phnom Penh make even the low official estimates of the availability of safe drinking water and toilets seem optimistic indeed.

"Most poor Cambodians, whether in rural or urban areas, use water from unprotected wells and springs and have no access to toilets of any kind," said the Cambodia Human Development Report, issued at the end of 1997 by the government and the United Nations Development Program. Children, often naked and almost always barefoot, abound, cheerful despite it all, and women outnumber men by far. "In some regions as many as 50 per cent of all families are headed by women; in other regions the proportion is 20 per cent, but nowhere is it lower," UNICEF has found. In a society in which upheavals and poverty have broken traditional extended-family and village links of mutual caring and substituted an "every man for himself" way of life, it is a severe handicap to have no man in the house.

"A Cambodian child is more likely to die before the age of 1 year than a child in any other country in the East Asia and Pacific Region," the latest UNICEF report states. In numbers, this means that 110 of 1,000 Cambodian children die before reaching their first birthday. The regional average is 42. And 181 children in 1,000 do not live until the age of 5. Pregnancy for a Cambodian woman is a condition of maximum risk. Between 650 and 900 die of complications, accidents in labor, or abortions per 100,000 births, one of the highest rates in the world. Among foreign health workers in the cities and the countryside, there is a strong belief that official statistics underestimate reality. In Cambodia, the gloomiest estimates have always proved closer to the truth.

Florence Beauvilliers is a French midwife who has worked for more than two years on behalf of Médecins Sans Frontières in the remote northern province of Stung Treng, which borders on Laos. There she married a Cambodian doctor. "We have no idea of the mortality rate of mothers or babies, but it must be enormous," she said. "Pregnant women die if there is the least complication. The educational level is very low, and almost all births take place at home with traditional midwives. They don't know how to spot difficult births in advance. The women are taken to town by oxcart or boat at the last moment, and they arrive too late. Hygiene? They don't know what that is in Stung Treng." Dr. Beat Richner, a Swiss pediatrician who runs an exemplary children's hospital that he created virtually single-handedly in Phnom Penh, said, "There is a vicious cycle of diarrhea and malnutrition, the consequence of the hygiene of poverty."

Poverty accounts for the poor state of health and nutrition. About one-half of all children under five are either stunted in growth or underweight. There is little "wasting" of bodies from acute famines, as in the disaster-prone sub-Sahara belt in Africa. The stunting of Cambodia's children stems from long-term, chronic undernourishment, the consequence of unrelieved poverty. The illnesses that give Cambodians born today a poor life expectancy of little more than fifty years (sixty-six and sixty-nine years, respectively, in neighboring Vietnam and Thailand) are those of poverty and wretched living conditions. Tuberculosis, respiratory infections, and diarrhea, as well as malaria, inherent in a land of forests, take a heavy toll. "The TB problem is one of the worst in the world," said Dr. Georg Petersen, a Norwegian who directs the Phnom Penh office of the World Health Organization.

The AIDS scourge has not spared Cambodia. After an encouragingly slow start, due to the country's comparative isolation until the 1990s, the spread of the illness has more than caught up. A 1997 report issued jointly by the government and a number of aid donors states succinctly: "The Kingdom of Cambodia has the most serious HIV/AIDS epidemic in Asia with many contributing factors which suggest that the epidemic has the potential to cause Cambodia to become one of the worst affected countries in the world."

The most reliable estimates put the number of cases of HIV-positive patients at 70,000 to 120,000 in late 1996, and the yearly number of new infections at 17,000 to 25,000. The spread of this illness, too, is a result of poverty and the unraveled social fabric, which has driven more Cambodian women than ever before into prostitution. The illness is due in more than 90 percent of cases to heterosexual transmission, largely by prostitutes, in a country where terminating an evening out among men with a visit to a brothel is not uncustomary. More than 40 percent of the prostitutes in Cambodia's plentiful brothels tested HIV-positive in late 1996. As many as 35 percent of the prostitutes are minors.

Cambodians receive little medical care, and care badly for themselves. Public health services were destroyed in the Khmer Rouge reign and haltingly restored with very limited means under Vietnamese occupation. The frail structure collapsed completely when communism was officially abolished in 1989 and greed in the name of economic liberalism became the official creed. A slow rebuilding began after the 1993 elections, largely through the efforts of foreign donors and nongovernmental aid organizations. A plan for a rational system has been adopted by a willing Health Ministry, but Dr. Petersen emphasized that "a tremendous improvement for delivering health services" now exists "on paper." The Human Development Report states that for the time being, "Cambodia has one of the lowest rates of utilization of health services in the world . . . a Cambodian has only 0.35 medical contacts with the organized health services each year."

Dr. Petersen described the effect of the abandonment of Communist ideology. "Between 1989 and '93 everything collapsed," he said. "Since '93 there is unchecked capitalism. Medicines are sold everywhere in open shops. Even the poorest people spend 7 to 8 percent of their earnings on their health. There are all the side effects of the explosive development of a totally unchecked system. There is incredible misuse of drugs."

Dr. Natacha Prandy, who came to Cambodia as a pediatrician for the Russian community, which was large in the days of the Soviet Union, and stayed on as a general practitioner for Médecins du Monde, a private French relief organization, summarized the fatal link between lack of education and bad health. "They don't know how to take care of themselves," she said. "First they go to the traditional doctor. Most are charlatans. The illness gets worse. Then they go to the pharmacist, most of whom are not pharmacists but drug-sellers. They say they have a stomachache, and he sells them what he wants. They have been to a fake doctor and a fake pharmacist, and often they have been given a fake medicine. They take any drug that they are given. Then, when they are so sick they can no longer work they come to a hospital. And often they arrive too late. The public health system hardly exists. Doctors are very badly trained. They overprescribe dangerously, four antibiotics at a time, why not? They are ignorant of the most elementary things. I know of a fifteen-year-old girl who went blind because of a prescribed massive overdose of quinine."

The effect of chronic malnutrition, stunting, and frequent illnesses on the low state of education is evident. Prolonged absences are common. The average village child suffers four to six

episodes of respiratory infections and the same number of attacks of long-lasting diarrhea a year, Andrew Morris said. There
is also a "tremendous impact on learning ability from severe and
widespread goiter," resulting from iodine deficiency, according to the UNICEF health official. Of the country's twenty provinces, nine have a goiter rate of more than 20 percent among
schoolchildren, four of them surpassing 30 percent. "The goiter
can be undone, but the children can't catch up unless iodine is
introduced while they are very young," according to Morris, who
is a pharmacist. Only 15 percent of the salt used in Cambodia is
iodized; it is sold mainly in the border regions that are supplied
from Vietnam or Thailand.

How much can be expected from an education system that
started from zero in 1979? After the Pol Pot years, in which
schools were abolished, only three hundred Cambodians with a
higher education were left in the country. Most were employed
in the varied tasks of recreating a national administration. A
handful were gathered to recruit teachers — almost anybody
able to read, write, and do simple sums — and write new text-
books, relying on their own memories from school days and on
the political guidelines laid down by the Vietnamese Communist
party. The books were astonishingly ideological, dedicated to
the nigh-impossible tasks of making enthusiastic Communists of
an inert population, people who had just emerged from martyr-
dom under a Communist regime, and of making Cambodians
admire Vietnam. Many are still in use while new texts are being
prepared and distributed, said Jean-Michel Le Pecq, who heads
a European Community program to rebuild primary education.
A program of deletion of political content has left pupils with
many pages more white than black and befuddling breaks in con-
tinuity.

The French educator said that of the 47,000 primary school
teachers, half had been recruited without having completed their
own primary education of five or six years. Less than 1 percent
have finished the eleventh grade. By their own definition, 69

percent of Cambodians over fifteen years old consider themselves literate. The claim meets with incredulity; a 1996 report by the Asian Development Bank found 48 percent of women and 22 percent of men over fifteen to be illiterate. UNICEF expects this problem to grow at least over the next decade because of the high dropout rate in elementary schools and the low levels of achievement of those who stay the course.

The United Nations agency expects that of 1,000 Cambodians born today, 290 will never go to school, 390 will repeat the first grade, and 500 will not complete the primary education that they begin. Only 27 out of 1,000 who enter primary school will graduate from high school, the Human Development Report estimates.

Some more discouraging statistics: teachers' contact with pupils averages less than three hours a day. The average Cambodian adult has had only three and one-half years of schooling. The repeat and dropout rates are chilling. Of those who started first grade in 1989, only 34 percent entered fifth grade five years later. Many repeat the first grade two or three times and drop out by the second grade, particularly girls, said Anne H. Dykstra, who was a UNICEF project officer. "This is a lethal combination," she said. "They can't build an economy on that, not even agrarian."

Not that parents are indifferent to the education of their children. Great hope for the future lies in the fact that in one of the world's poorest countries, families assume two-thirds of the cost of maintaining a public school system, possibly the highest rate of such contributions in Asia. But for that and foreign aid, the system would collapse. The government contribution, a rock-bottom 8.1 percent of the national budget, barely covers the paltry teachers' wages of about fifteen dollars a month. Such low salaries mean that almost all teachers hold second and third jobs. A widely used and tolerated practice is for teachers to keep their classes beyond the regular hours. They call the extra time "private lessons," for which parents must pay about five hundred riels, or sixteen cents, a day. The sacrifice that this represents for the average family can be measured by the fact that the teachers' salaries represent the national average for regularly employed Cambodians, and untold numbers in Phnom Penh and other towns are day laborers who on many a day find no work.

Parents also pay for school repairs and building projects and offer gifts in kind to teachers. Sadly, those who can afford it also offer substantial sums to teachers to assure their children's success in exams. Practiced at all levels of education, this widespread bribery has greatly devalued the reputation of school certificates and diplomas.

It is not only in the vital fields of physical health and education that Cambodians continue to suffer from the effects of the Khmer Rouge whirlwind that blighted society and the traditional civilization that bonded it, and that deprived its members of the comforting certainties of mutual support. A system in which every single person's survival was threatened tore out by its roots a village culture of mutual help of ancient standing. Even today, when 85 percent of Cambodians continue to live in villages, men and women are left feeling alone and threatened in what has changed into an aggressively competitive human environment.

Sociological studies have shown a drastic decline in *sammaki*, a once widely used word denoting solidarity and community spirit. "There is no more mutual help among people," said Florence Beauvilliers, the midwife. "The nurses in the Stung Treng provincial hospital do only the minimum. They hand out pills and meals, but they don't help those who can't feed themselves. They sit on an empty bed and play cards. Maybe you can expect no more from women who earn ten dollars a month." And very often, she added, the nurses deprive patients of the pills that they are to take and sell them for private gain. "It is not the same country," an elderly woman told her daughter-in-law who was on her first visit back from exile in France. "Today your neighbor makes you pay for helping you out with a pinch of salt."

The tradition of *sammaki* today extends only to members of the immediate family, and even there bonds have loosened.

Loyalty between husbands and wives is much looser than before the war years, particularly since economic hardship has split families. Many men leave the village to go where they might find work. The scarcity of men, who suffered greater ravages in the wars and the years of Pol Pot, has made polygamy and deserted wives and children a common social illness. Prostitution and the selling of children into prostitution at home and in Thailand are the results of a general deterioration in a traditional morality that had held fast through the centuries.

Cambodia today is also a ward of untreated psychiatric illnesses that have their principal origin in the four years of the genocide. Twelve psychiatrists practiced in Cambodia before 1975; none were left after the despot's fall. A first group of ten physicians were receiving psychiatric training in 1997. No Cambodian hospital provides in-patient psychiatric care, said Dr. Lavrantz Kyrdalen, a Norwegian specialist who heads the training program. As a result, even violent patients live with their families, sometimes chained up for years.

The causes of widespread mental illness are complex, said Dr. Kyrdalen, a soft-spoken man who delivers opinions precisely, after long thought. He finds the causes in the severe losses under the Khmers Rouges, aggravated by the hardships of today and compounded by the absence of any treatment for twenty years. Severe depressions are the most common disorders: the mood is low, thinking pessimistic, often suicidal, and there are frequent complaints about physical symptoms for which there is no physical cause. Alcoholism, rare in the days of peace, has become common. Many Cambodians suppress their anxieties, deny them to avoid conflict until they cannot manage anymore. Then they may become violently aggressive or suicidal.

"The permanent level of anxiety among Cambodians is unbelievable," Dr. Kyrdalen said. He witnessed two examples. A controlled explosion of a mine found in Phnom Penh brought panic, and when a coup d'état in July 1997 brought street fighting between troops of two rival prime ministers in the capital, previous traumas re-erupted explosively. "They thought the Khmers Rouges were back," the psychiatrist said. "There is a collective pessimism in this country regarding the future. The Cambodian perspective is very short-term. They can't believe in peace; they believe most conflict must lead to violence."

It is difficult to believe in peace in a country where vast regions remain seeded with land mines planted by all the armies and factions that have made war in Cambodia. One-legged men, women, and children draw almost no attention in the streets of Phnom Penh, so common is this terrible mutilation. Despite the continuing, dangerous work of demining, carried out with the help of foreign organizations, no day goes by without making new victims. It is estimated that one of every 243 Cambodians has been maimed by a mine.

Tioulong Saumura is a French-educated economist and was vice governor of the National Bank until Hun Sen's 1997 coup d'état drove her and her husband, opposition leader and former finance minister Sam Rainsy, temporarily into exile. For her, the Pol Pot years "completely destroyed the moral values of Cambodians." She said that even the deeply anchored Buddhist religion has lost its moral content and no longer has roots. "It has become merely a superstition on which you call for protection against misfortune," she said.

"What there is today is a cult of the present and a cult of 'myself.' It shows in the economy. There is no savings and no investment. Even our fruit trees are no longer cared for and pruned. It shows in the poor fruit that you buy in the market. It is the fruit of trees that have been allowed to degenerate. Nothing is maintained any more. It shows in the irrigation system. When a canal gets silted over, forget about it. Wells that are no longer yielding water are abandoned, not repaired. It shows in the beautiful villas that the nomenklatura of Hun Sen's Cambodian People's party has built for itself. They don't maintain the streets on which they stand, even if the rainy-season flooding damages their Mercedeses."

2

Brief Greatness, a Decline without End: From the Beginnings until 1970

*F*OR CENTURIES CAMBODIA, the Khmer Empire, was a great nation, bestriding continental Southeast Asia. Cambodians prefer to call themselves by the name of the dominant ethnic group, the Khmers.

Much of the earliest and some of the later history of Cambodia remains hidden in darkness, legends, conflicting accounts of outsiders, and contradictory chronicles. Chinese historians relate that, starting in the first century A.D., the Kingdom of Funan, the precursor of the Khmer Empire, grew along the Gulf of Siam (now Gulf of Thailand) and the plains of the lower Mekong River, encompassing today's southern Cambodia and the Mekong Delta of Vietnam, as well as parts of Thailand and the Malay Peninsula.

Two great religions that have their origins in India, Hinduism and Buddhism, molded Funan's civilization and carried over into the realm of the Khmers, which succeeded it. Indian merchants were their principal carriers into Southeast Asia. In the region called Indochina, the crossroads of the great civilizations of India and China, Cambodia and Laos were mainly influenced by India, and Vietnam by China. North of Funan there developed the vassal Kingdom of Chenla, whose area corresponded to today's northern Cambodia and southern Laos. Chenla rebelled against Funan, and by the beginning of the seventh century the vassal had conquered his master's realm. The earliest inscriptions in the Khmer language, which is of the Austroasiatic group, date from that period.

Isanavarman, who reigned until 635, completed the conquest of Funan and extended the realm of the Khmers into the region of the Great Lake of the Tonle Sap River, the seat of what was to become the Angkor civilization. Chenla was an unstable state. It first split early in the eighth century into northern and southern kingdoms; by the end of the century there were at least five competing Chenla kingdoms in existence. Seafaring marauders from Java, Sumatra, and the Malay Peninsula raided many parts of the Indochinese mainland and put them under their dominion. It was King Jayavarman II, who had lived at the Javanese court, who ended the anarchy that had riven the Kingdom of Chenla and declared its independence from Java. He ascended the throne in 802 and established his capital on Mount Kulen, north of Angkor. He reigned until 850.

Jayavarman II was the first in the line of god-kings of Cambodia, monarchs who combined divine status with temporal rule, and the founder of the Angkor dynasty. Each Angkor king established his divine status by erecting a temple mountain of stone that aspired to the heavens like the spires of medieval European cathedrals. Their imposing remains confer majesty on the plain of Angkor. Jayavarman centered the kingdom on the region of the Great Lake. Rich in fish and fertile of rice on the lake's alluvial plain, the area was capable of sustaining a large population, the basis of the rise of the dynasty that he founded. It lasted to the beginning of the thirteenth century.

Angkor kingship drew on a cosmology that centered on the worship of a divine being, first Siva, later Vishnu or Buddha. Siva was represented by a phallic symbol in stone called a linga. Each king built a pyramid temple, a holy mountain made of stone, at whose summit was enshrined, for those whose divinity was Siva, a linga representing him. On the king's death, the temple became his mausoleum, where he was believed to unite with Siva. In this Brahman view of god and the world, the temple represented the divinity of the king as well as the center of the material world, the source of all life-giving riches. The king and his court formed a sacred caste, far removed from the ordinary people but seen by them as the providers of all that made life possible.

Indravarman I, who succeeded Jayavarman's son on the throne in 877, was the first to build as a temple to his divine status a stone pyramid similar to the majestic Borobudur in central Java. The Bakong, composed of five superimposed terraces of diminishing size and crowned by a sanctuary, is a precursor of Cambodia's most sacred monument, Angkor Wat, and the first great monument of classical Khmer art and architecture. Indravarman was also the first to construct a large irrigation basin outside his capital, Hariharalaya, near the site where Angkor was to rise. The water stored there during the monsoon season was used to irrigate the paddy fields in the dry months. The ingenious irrigation systems, which were carried forward by his successors, are just as much as the sublime architecture a glory of the Angkorian civilization and a source of its strength.

Indravarman's son, Yasovarman, who became king in 889, founded as his capital the first city of Angkor. Yasovarman was a great builder. His ambition, in the phrase of D. G. E. Hall, the noted historian of Southeast Asia, was "to crown nearly every hill near his capital with a shrine." He went even farther afield by building, on today's Thai-Cambodian border, the great sanctuary of Preah Vihear in the Dangrek Mountains. (After a long dispute, the World Court in 1962 adjudged that this major monument of Khmer architecture belonged to Cambodia, although the easiest access is from the Thai side of the border. Pol Pot's last headquarters, and the place of his subsequent imprisonment by his comrades and death, is in the vicinity.) Other than the evidence of his great architectural feats, little is known of Yasovarman's achievements. Whether the expansion of the realm over which he ruled until his death early in the tenth century was by his hand or that of his predecessors is not known, but inscriptions to his glory have been found over a wide swath of territory between southern Laos and the Gulf of Thailand.

The tenth century was one of conflicts between rulers and usurpers. Six kings reigned during its course. The century's long conclusion was the reign of its most illustrious monarch, Jayavarman V. Hall describes his kingship, from 968 until 1001, as "an age of learning and of brilliant ministers. . . . No Cambodian reign was more distinguished for learning." An age of expansion followed under Suryavarman I, who ruled from 1002 to 1050, at the expense of the kingdom of the Mon, a people closely related to the Khmers and Burmans, in the west, of a Malay realm to the south, and northward in today's Laos.

One of Cambodia's greatest kings, Suryavarman II, the founder of Angkor Wat, ascended the throne in 1113 and ruled until his death, sometime around 1150. He greatly extended the Khmer Empire's sway in wars against the Indianized state of Champa in today's central Vietnam and against the Mon state in western Thailand and today's Myanmar (formerly Burma). He sent several embassies to China and established good political and commercial relations. But his fame is linked above all with the construction of the great temple of Angkor Wat, the apogee of Khmer art. Marvelously preserved despite centuries of depredation by invaders, vandals, temple robbers, and a hostile monsoon climate, the huge central sanctuary of gray sandstone, 130 feet high, stands on a massive square terrace forty feet high. A tower marks each corner of the base, and the towers are connected by galleries decorated with bas-reliefs of grand battle scenes. Covered passages lead from each corner tower to the central shrine. The whole conception is of a breathtaking grandeur rivaled in Southeast Asia only by Borobudur on Java.

Troubled times, marked by unsuccessful wars and internal rebellions, followed Suryavarman's death. They reached their nadir with the conquest and sack of Angkor by the Chams in 1177. The reigning monarch, Tribhuvanadityavarman, was killed, and anarchy followed. Jayavarman, the son of an earlier king, came to the rescue as military commander. He defeated the Chams in a great naval battle, which after his ascension of the throne in 1181 he had depicted in the great bas-reliefs around the base of the temple-mountain built for his glory, the Bayon of Angkor Thom, near Angkor Wat. He pacified the internal rebellions and was crowned king as Jayavarman VII. He put an end to the Cham menace by the conquest of that kingdom to Cambodia's east. After triumphs followed by reverses, Champa, the Chams' territory, was reduced to vassal status in 1203. In the north and south, too, Jayavarman extended the Khmer Empire. His power reached as far north as Vientiane, today's capital of Laos, and southward into the Malay Peninsula.

Jayavarman's lasting achievement was the construction of Angkor Thom, with its astonishing central Bayon. The vast temple is dominated by a perplexing assemblage of countless huge sculptures of the same, faintly smiling human face, facing all the points of the compass. It is a representation of Jayavarman himself as Lokesvara, one of the manifestations of Buddha.

Jayavarman VII was the last of the great rulers of Angkor. After his death, believed to have occurred in 1218, his main realizations were reversed. Champa drove out the Khmer occupier, and a strong Hindu revival replaced Buddhism as the dominant belief. Historians conclude that the succession of pharaonic building projects and costly wars against all neighbors so drained the substance of the state and the strength and energy of the Khmer people that the subsequent decline and demise of their empire were foreordained. On Cambodia's west, the Siamese rose strongly against Khmer overlordship and established their kingdom. As Siamese power rose, Khmer might declined, and Cambodian history becomes a permanent defensive struggle against Siam on its west and Vietnam to the east, and against the nation's incapacity to cope with the modern world.

The power of the god-kings weakened with the spread from the middle of the thirteenth century of the Hinayana school of Buddhism. It had its origins among the Sinhalese of today's Sri Lanka and reached Cambodia with Mon monks from Myanmar. Its monkhood preached and practiced austerity and self-abnegation, the very opposite of the religious regimes that made gods of earthly kings. The Hinayana monks lived among the people, and their teaching was direct, a fundamental break from the separation of king and court hierarchy, living in sumptuous isolation from the population, principles derived from the Indian caste system. "From the day when the sovereign ceased to be Siva descended to earth, or the living Buddha, as Jayavarman VII had been, the royal dynasty failed any longer to inspire the people with the religious respect which enabled it to accomplish great enterprises," wrote George Coedès, the remarkable French scholar. "Under the threat of the anarchical spirit of Sinhalese Buddhism, his prestige diminished, his temporal power crumbled away, and the god-king was thrown down from his altar." By the end of the thirteenth century, Hinayana Buddhism had become the state religion.

Khmer history entered a dark era after the immediate successors of Jayavarman VII. In the decades that followed, the empire began to shrink under Siamese and Vietnamese pressures. The names of rulers are known, but doubts surround the years of their reigns. Jayavarman VIII, who ruled from 1243 until 1295, had the longest reign of any Khmer king, but it was not an era of distinction. Unlike his predecessors, he left no monument of note, nor is he credited with any notable achievement of statecraft or conquest. On the contrary, the Siamese kingdom was erected largely on territory seized from the control of Jayavarman VIII. The realms of Chiang Mai in the north and Sukhothai in the south were created in his time. He was deposed by his son-in-law, Indravarman III.

Little is known of the reigns of the kings who succeeded him. The last monarch whose name appears on contemporaneous inscriptions on stone is Jayavarman Paramesvara, who became king in 1327. Subsequent history has only the Cambodian chronicles, compiled long after the events, as a guide, and much scholarly debate revolves around their reliability, particularly datings. They cover the period until the end of the fifteenth century, times of heavy Siamese pressure. Angkor was conquered by the Siamese for the first time in the middle of the fourteenth century, and for a second time toward its end. Much booty and thousands of prisoners were taken to the Siamese court on each occasion. The third Siamese conquest of the royal capital and its abandonment in favor of Phnom Penh, founded at the site where the Mekong and Tonle Sap Rivers meet, came in the middle of the fifteenth century, the exact date depending on the interpretation of the Cambodian chronicles. The eastward advance of Siamese power had exposed Angkor to easy Siamese attack and made the establishment of a capital more centrally situated in the shrinking kingdom a strategic necessity.

The majestic city that since its founding in the tenth century had risen to become the capital of Southeast Asia's mightiest realm was left to the jungle, rarely visited until French explorers reopened it to the world.

The obscurity of Cambodian history continues after the abandonment of Angkor. Conflicting Khmer and Siamese annals make it difficult to separate history from legend, and Siamese from Cambodian versions of the facts. The sixteenth century produced Cambodia's last king of great stature, Ang Chan. In his reign of a half-century, ending around 1566, he turned back a Siamese invasion that threatened to subjugate the entire Khmer Kingdom to Siamese rule. Instead, Ang Chan mounted continued raids into Siam, reaching at one point close to the gates of Ayutthaya, the capital, only to find it already occupied by the Burmese, who were also at war with Siam. At Ang Chan's death, Cambodia seemed at peace and in prosperity. But his successors continued warring against Siam, to their disadvantage. In 1594 Siamese troops occupied Lovek, then the capital. The fall of Lovek marks the beginning of the unending decline of Cambodia, of its struggle to do no more than to maintain what it has.

In the seventeenth century Cambodia became the object of mounting rivalry between Siam and Vietnam over domination of the weakened, thinly populated country that lay between them. Under Siamese threat, King Chey Chettha II turned for help to the Nguyen dynasty ruling at Hue, in central Vietnam. In return for an anti-Siamese alliance, the king granted Vietnam the right to establish settlements in the region of Saigon, then called Prey Kor. Cambodia never regained control over Saigon. Following endless court intrigues, usurpations of the throne, palace massacres, and mounting internal instability, a usurper king, Batom Reachea, again called for Vietnamese assistance, and in return paid the price by becoming a tributary to Hue and bolstering the privileges of Vietnamese settlers. After three more kings had died violently, a war between brothers brought a Vietnamese army into occupation of the capital, then situated at Oudong, south of Lovek. The Vietnamese were driven out, and the victor became king as Chey Chettha IV in 1674.

His reign continued until 1706. In unceasing internecine warfare, Chey Chettha called at different periods for Siamese or Vietnamese help, in the end accepting Vietnamese suzerainty. Southern Cambodia fell under the increasing domination of Vietnamese settlers steadily pushing southward under the pressure of a large population on scarce land. A Vietnamese was appointed as governor. In 1698 Vietnam created two provinces in Cambodian lands in the Mekong Delta and methodically settled on their lands villages of its creation.

Rival pretenders to the throne played the dangerous game of calling on Siam or Vietnam for help, and Cambodia's two neighbors often met in battle. In the 1720s and '30s, Cambodia had at the same time a ruling king, Satha II, and three former monarchs. All solicited help from their entirely selfish neighbors. The price was the loss of further large areas in the Mekong Delta to Vietnam. As power slipped into foreign hands, dynastic quarrels among kings, ex-kings, sons of kings and ex-kings, and other claimants to the throne threw the country into enduring chaos. The upshot was the definitive loss of what later became the French Vietnamese colony of Cochin China. The result today is a minority of around one million Cambodians in southern Vietnam. Vietnam was the principal beneficiary of its neighbor's weakness; Siam was preoccupied throughout the period with internal troubles and fending off inroads on its territory from Burma. The Siamese found it easier to strike political bargains with Cambodia, because of closer ethnic, cultural, and religious links. The Vietnamese, then as now, were seen as demons, avid for the lands of the Khmers and the extinction of their "race."

Desperately feeble, Cambodia sought to save its sovereignty by submitting to both its powerful neighbors. In 1794 Ang Eng was crowned king in Bangkok, where he had grown up at the royal court, and returned to Cambodia under the protection of a Siamese army. Its commander was a Siamese mandarin who governed the Cambodian provinces of Battambang and Angkor, which had fallen under Siamese rule. Ang Eng died two years later, and his son, Ang Chan II, became heir to the throne at the age of four. On reaching maturity, he paid tribute to Vietnam in 1803 and was crowned king three years later in Bangkok. The following year he requested and received investiture as a vassal of the Vietnamese emperor Gia Long at the court of Hue.

Dynastic rivalry again raised its head, to the great detriment of the nation. Ang Chan II's brother, Ang Snguon, demanded to be named second king, with control over part of the kingdom. In 1812, with a Siamese army, he advanced toward Oudong, once more the capital. King Ang Chan II fled to Saigon after a losing battle and was reinstated the following year with the support of Vietnamese troops. The Siamese fled, taking their pretender with them. To prevent a recurrence, Gia Long installed a Vietnamese garrison in Phnom Penh. Bangkok, at least formally, agreed to recognize what amounted to Vietnamese overlordship over eastern Cambodia and from its strong position in the west looked forward to a day when it might seize what Vietnam held. It tried in 1830. Its invading force defeated the Cambodian army, and the king once again fled. But its advance stalled in eastern Cambodia. King Ang Chan II returned to Oudong and died there in 1834.

To prevent a rise to the throne of one of Ang Chan's pro-Siamese sons, Vietnam elevated one of his daughters, Ang Mey, to be Cambodia's queen. In considerable maneuvering between the two covetous neighbors, Vietnam showed a heavy hand at the court of Oudong, eliminating, usually by murder, the pro-Siamese mandarins. These brutalities provoked a rising in collaboration with Siam, and Ang Duong, the prince who had sided with Bangkok, was carried to the throne in 1842 by a Siamese army. Vietnam reacted with a military offensive that laid siege to Oudong. A peace was signed in 1846, and Ang Duong was crowned with Siamese and Vietnamese consent. He was a popular king, renowned for his sense of justice, but he could halt neither Siamese nor Vietnamese encroachments on his country. He died in 1860 and was succeeded by his son Norodom.

The new monarch was soon confronted by a revolt led by his younger brother, Si Votha. He fled to Battambang and on to Bangkok, where he requested Siamese aid to recover his throne. When the situation calmed, Siam restored Norodom in Oudong, once again gaining the upper hand over Cambodia. This raised the suspicion of France, which was by then solidly installed in Cochin China and its capital, Saigon, and was looking with mercantile eyes at the Mekong River. It saw it as a principal trade route with China. In French eyes, Siam was about to fall prey to British designs of similar character. The great river traverses the full length of Cambodia, entering in the north from Laos and leaving in the south into Cochin China. The idea of establishing a protectorate over weak and embattled Cambodia took hold.

Pretending that it had inherited with its colonization of Cochin China a Vietnamese claim to suzerainty over Cambodia, France exerted great pressure on the unwilling Norodom. Its argument was that to submit to France would secure Cambodia's independence from Siam. Norodom welcomed the idea but feared the possibility that one day France would leave Cochin China, which would expose him to both Vietnamese and Siamese enmity. The king eventually yielded and signed a protectorate treaty in 1863. Siam protested that Cambodia was its vassal and France could deal with Norodom only through Bangkok. Britain, for obvious reasons, supported this view. In fact, Siam insisted, Norodom was no more than its viceroy in Cambodia. King Mongkut of Siam insisted that Norodom come to Bangkok to be crowned. He started in royal procession from Oudong, over French protests, but had not gone far when French troops occupied his palace and planted the tricolor on it. The king made a quick U-turn, Napoléon III ratified the protectorate treaty, and from April 17, 1864, Cambodia's sovereignty resided in Paris.

Three years later, France and Siam struck a deal under which France gave up any Cambodian claim for Siam to restore to Cambodia the annexed regions of Battambang and Angkor in return for Siamese abandonment of its assertion of suzerainty over its neighbor. Cambodia had kept its king but lost its right over Angkor, the most royal territory. In 1884, after Norodom had shown signs of independence, France tightened its hold by reducing the king's powers to ceremonial functions, appointing a French *résident supérieur* as the real holder of executive power and a *résident* for each province. The action, in effect, made the notion of a protectorate nominal and reduced Cambodia to colonial status. A bloody revolt followed; it took France eighteen months to quell it. In 1907 Cambodia regained its lost western provinces in a treaty between Paris and Bangkok.

France's colonization of Cambodia was of a most condescending and patronizing kind. Hardly any Cambodian was trained to perform functions of authority. Little was undertaken to educate Cambodians to take their place in the modern world. Significant administrative functions were held by Frenchmen; economic life in the largely agrarian country was dominated by Sino-Khmers in commerce and imported Vietnamese as skilled artisans and office personnel. Education was not encouraged. As late as 1941, only 22,280 pupils attended 192 state-run primary schools, where French was the language of instruction. In Buddhist pagoda schools, 35,000 pupils received an elementary education. There was only one high school; 537 students attended. The choice of the king was manipulated by France. At Norodom's death in 1904, his brother, Sisowath, was placed on the throne, disregarding the claims of Norodom's sons. When the throne fell vacant with the death of Sisowath's son Monivong in 1941, France passed over his independent-minded son, Monireth, and enthroned Monireth's nephew, Norodom Sihanouk, then an eighteen-year-old high-school student in Saigon, whom they felt they could easily make pliant to their will. It was an error.

The young king outmaneuvered the Cambodian nationalists, led by Son Ngoc Thanh, and the French, who returned in 1945 after the Japanese occupation during World War II with the aspiration of restoring the prewar status quo. Sihanouk opened negotiations for gradual independence, because he believed Cambodia at the outset to be ill-prepared, by lack of education and material means, to stand on its own without French aid. Son Ngoc Thanh, who had been trained in Japan during the war, wanted to prevent France's return and to maintain the independence that Japan had forced Sihanouk to declare in the final stage of its occupation. The king and his uncle, Monireth, persuaded the French and British to remove Thanh from the scene by arresting the able nationalist leader as a threat to the security of their forces. Thanh was tried for treason in Saigon and exiled. The protectorate was replaced by nominal autonomy within the French Union, which did not prevent France from running all essential aspects of Cambodian government. In 1946 Paris obtained the return of Battambang and Angkor's province, Siem Reap, which Thailand had reannexed following France's defeat by Germany in 1940.

Sihanouk liberalized political life by reducing the absolutist powers of the monarchy, which France had reconferred on him with the grant of autonomy. In a series of cunning, often dramatic political moves, the king outwitted both the parliamentary opposition to his conduct of affairs and the French, who resisted his growing demands for independence. In January 1953, Sihanouk dissolved Parliament, declared martial law, and set out on what he called his "royal crusade for independence." After visiting Paris, Washington, and Tokyo to seek support for independence and making frequent public statements accusing France of making the Vietnamese Communists appear to be the only nationalists in Indochina, he spectacularly exiled himself to Bangkok, later to Battambang. He declared that he would not return to Phnom Penh until France had ceded. France, preoccupied with its losing war in Vietnam, capitulated to this coup de théâtre. In November 1953 Sihanouk returned triumphantly to his palace in independent Cambodia.

The independence was assured by the Geneva Conference of 1954, in which Cambodia obtained the withdrawal of the Vietnamese Communist troops from its soil and recognition of its sovereign right to accept foreign military assistance and even bases for its defense and to form alliances. The United States became the biggest supplier of such aid, but Sihanouk steadfastly rejected the pressures of the Eisenhower administration and its secretary of state, John Foster Dulles, to abandon its proclaimed neutrality and join the Southeast Asian Treaty Organization (SEATO), an American brainchild that never got off the ground. To this day, Dulles stands high on Sihanouk's list of his least favorite persons.

Meeting resistance to his program of reforms to give the king strong executive powers, Sihanouk stepped down from the throne in favor of his father, Norodom Suramarit, to enter political life unrestricted by kingship. The move did not lessen his dominance over the government, and his father contented himself with ceremonial functions. Sihanouk formed a broad political movement, the Sangkum, which won all seats in the National Assembly. In elections in 1958, in which only a thinly disguised Communist party opposed the Sangkum, Prince Sihanouk's movement won all but 409 of the 1.6 million votes cast. Sihanouk's authoritarian rule, although deeply resented by educated men and women of the left and right, faced no effective opposition. His opponents were kept under strict surveillance, and Sihanouk's secret police was ruthlessly effective. When the king died in 1960, Sihanouk assumed the title of chief of state.

Sihanouk was deeply disturbed by the conflict that had engulfed Vietnam and Laos. He was convinced from the outset that the determined and highly disciplined Vietnamese Communists could not but eventually vanquish the "softer" and more corrupt governments supported by the United States. He saw Cambodia's only chance of staying out of Hanoi's orbit — and his own best chance of staying in power — in a neutrality that the North Vietnamese would see as favorable to their cause. He was pessimistic about this policy's success but saw no other way. He told me in 1964 that the Vietnamese, who then considered him "progressive," would turn against him as soon as they had won their struggle. With this in mind, Sihanouk in 1963 announced his rejection of any further American assistance.

There were other reasons for his downfall seven years later, notably the erosion of an overlong rule and the glaringly visible corruption of his courtiers. But his turning off the tap of the principal source of economic and military assistance sealed his fate. From then on, Sihanouk's power began to slip visibly. It was Cambodia's tragedy that there were no potent or competent hands that could take over. Sihanouk had done little to encourage those of competence around him, and much to make them his enemies. It was a desperate gamble on his part when in 1969 he formed a Salvation Government under the ever-loyal

Lon Nol, a mediocre bureaucrat of mystic imagination, and Sihanouk's cousin, Prince Sisowath Sirik Matak. Sihanouk committed the ultimate error when he left for medical treatment in France in January 1970. He plainly hoped that his absence would make clear to Cambodia's elite that only he could guide the country out of its drift toward disaster and that its members would beg him to return to resume full power.

Instead, those most aggrieved by what they considered his anti-Western and pro-Communist, or worse, pro-Vietnamese, policies let themselves be carried beyond their original intentions, which were to confront Sihanouk upon his return with a Cambodia that stood up to the Vietnamese Communists. In March 1970 they overthrew Sihanouk. Cambodia began its descent into the abyss from which it has not yet emerged.

3

Tripping into Disaster: 1970

C AMBODIA WAS AT THE VERY BRINK of the abyss when I
first visited it in 1970, but I didn't suspect the catastrophe
that was so near. I knew the seemingly tranquil country
was poised on a tightrope; the war in neighboring Vietnam and
Laos had long spilled over their borders and was steadily height-
ening internal political tensions in the neutral country. But
Norodom Sihanouk, the spectacular chief of state, had through
the years proved a supreme tightrope walker, and he appeared in
not much greater danger of tripping and falling in February of
1970 than in the past. He fell the following month.

No one I met seemed to see disaster around the corner either. Few Cambodians dared criticize the prince to a foreigner,
but even they were confident that Sihanouk was the only source
of real power in Cambodia, and no change could happen against
his will. Whatever occurred or was to occur, it was he, *Samdech
Euv*, or Mylord Daddy, as he was commonly called in public,
who made it happen. The face that Cambodia projected was of a
country as much at ease with itself as was possible in the seething
Indochinese cauldron. Cambodians did not know that they were

teetering at the edge of a calamitous descent into an unending succession of disasters from which it has not recovered.

What remains as my first memory of this most tragic of lands is the miracle of a country in Indochina that enjoyed peace and was pleased with its good fortune. I had just come from unhappy Vietnam and Laos. The contrast was heartening, and as though to point up how delicately balanced stood the scales of peace and war in the one nation of Indochina that had been spared, fate staged a small show for my benefit.

It happened late one afternoon on the terrace of the small hotel in the indolently sleepy fishing village of Kep. Only a vermouth cassis on a small, round French café table stood between me and the calm expanse of the Gulf of Thailand, which filled the view in front of me. The soft lapping of small waves onto an empty beach was the loudest sound that I heard. Nothing could have been more serene, and the arenas of war seemed far off. Suddenly the waiter, grinning and gesticulating in gleeful excitement, pointed to the sky. *"Regardez, Monsieur! Regardez là-haut!"* He pointed to the left. There was the war, another country's war. Two planes — American? South Vietnamese? — were diving at sharp angles, firing rockets or their machine guns at an invisible target on the ground. The sound of the act of war reached Kep only faintly, as though the nearby border muffled the laws of acoustics. Were they aiming at Vietcong guerrillas? Peasants mistaken for the enemy? I hoped whoever it was was not being killed or hurt while I was relaxing over a quiet aperitif after a day's road travel.

"Vietnam," said the waiter reassuringly, as though to calm any fear on the part of his only guest that such disturbances could happen in Cambodia.

I knew that acts of war were indeed occurring in Cambodia, and so did urban Cambodians and the villagers living along the long frontier with Vietnam. The Vietnamese Communist armies had established on the Cambodian side of the border base camps, supply depots, hospitals, and much of the command structure for their forces making war in South Vietnam. The Ho Chi Minh network of trails, over which North Vietnam sent troops and supplies into battle in the South, traversed the jungles of Cambodia's sparsely populated, mountainous northeast. The port of Sihanoukville on the Gulf of Thailand was the point of entry for a significant part of the military aid that China and European Communist countries were furnishing to their Vietnamese allies. These goods were carried across the neutral country to their recipients mainly on a highway built by American aid in the 1950s — such are the ironies in which the three countries that once formed French Indochina abound. The Cambodian Army organized and protected the transport, and General Lon Nol, the defense minister and soon-to-be leader in a war against those to whom he delivered arms, profited handsomely — one more irony. So did his family. The rice trade flourished in the border zones, with Cambodian farmers and merchants obtaining better prices from the Vietnamese Communists than on the local market. Much of this was common knowledge, denied only by those in the United States and elsewhere who made an article of faith of believing that all the right and no wrongdoing whatever in the complex Indochinese conflict lay on the Communist side.

With astonishing frankness, Prince Sihanouk acknowledged to me in 1973, at the height of the war and his alliance with the Communist Vietnamese, the truth of what he had always described as calumnies against Cambodia and himself. After cutting off American military assistance in 1963 he had to placate his military. "Either I accepted all the compromises with American imperialism or I accepted to help the Vietcong," he said. He said he allowed Sihanoukville to be used by Chinese ships delivering arms for the Vietnamese Communists and ordered his army to transport them, to become what he called "the Vietcong's coolies." His voice rose to angry shrillness as he blamed this trade for his downfall. "There was two-thirds for the Vietcong and one-third for my army. That way I didn't have to provide in my budget for military equipment, arms, and ammunition. Two-thirds for the Vietcong, one-third for yourself, two-thirds for the Vietcong, one-third for yourself — at that rate one sells oneself. So that was my end, that was my end. There is the truth, Monsieur."

The American and South Vietnamese military responded to attacks launched from Cambodian soil with raids of their own, which equally violated the sovereign country's neutrality. With Prince Sihanouk's secret consent, obtained from him in 1968 by the liberal Democrat Chester Bowles, President Johnson's ambassador to India, the American military in Vietnam had been mounting what they asserted were retaliatory ground and air raids across the border. Some were. Perhaps without the prince's express agreement, and certainly without public announcement, the United States Air Force had begun in 1969 to send its mammoth B-52s to bomb systematically a much wider swath of Cambodia, aiming at the Communists' transport and supply system. Cambodia protested routinely over specific violations, and equally routinely, from 1969 on, the United States made pathetic relief payments on a fixed scale to victims or their survivors. The rate was $400 for a Cambodian killed, $150 for serious injuries, and $100 for lesser wounds. By February 1970, the American chargé d'affaires told me he had paid out $24,850 in such relief since diplomatic relations, which Sihanouk broke in 1965, were restored in 1969 and an embassy reopened.

Cambodians believed that these concessions to all the combatants in Vietnam were enough to keep the bulk of their country out of war. The waiter laughed happily after the planes had swooshed out of sight. *"Ici c'est la paix,"* he said ("Here we are at peace").

Wherever I went during those two weeks of my first 1970 visit, in which Prince Sihanouk's ban on journalists obliged me to play the part of a tourist, I encountered a smiling insouciance that charmed me. The beatific, guileless Khmer smile — which suggests that the smiler is serenely happy, whatever sad emotion

it may hide — has enchanted Westerners since the French colo-
nizers opened the reclusive country to the world at large in the
second half of the nineteenth century.

Phnom Penh in February 1970 was a tranquil, well-tended
capital of mixed French colonial and Chinese shophouse architecture amid much greenery. Most of the foreign diplomats I visited shared, or for professional reasons pretended to share, the
Cambodians' assumption that there was little to worry about. "If
there was any real danger," Her Britannic Majesty's ambassador
said, exuding certainty, "do you think Prince Sihanouk would be
staying in France for so long?" The chief of state had gone on an
extended vacation the previous month — for medical treatment,
he said. Only the French ambassador, by far the best-informed
diplomat because of the two countries' postcolonial links of inti-
mate familiarity, left open the possibility that graver troubles
than usual lay ahead.

I flew out of Phnom Penh persuaded that I had seen a country in relative contentment, despite the nearness of the Vietnamese and Laotian civil wars, escalated to far higher magnitude
by American intervention. I had seen endemic rural poverty and
backwardness in a country predominantly agrarian. The nation
was run by an absolute ruler, intolerant of criticism, repressive of
opposition and cruel in his punishment of it. He surrounded
himself only with sycophants, to whose corruption and greed he
turned a benevolently unseeing eye. Prince Sihanouk was fully
absorbed in his masterful diplomacy, which had preserved his
country from the worst of the war, and in the production of ex-
travagantly bad movies. He wrote and directed them, composed
their music, and often cast himself, family members, and nor-
mally august public figures in starring roles. He organized international film festivals in his capital, whose pampered juries didn't
fail their generous host in awarding him the top prize, a statuette
of pure gold. Sihanouk sustained his one-man show of statecraft
by an aggressive cult of his charismatic personality. But measured by the sad standard of their former companion countries of

what had been French Indochina, Cambodians were right to consider themselves lucky.

Because I had violated his ban on reporters, Sihanouk was certain to put my name on his blacklist as soon as my first article appeared and never allow me to revisit his country, I thought as I left. And I assumed, like those far more knowledgeable about Cambodia than this one-time visitor, that the man who had led his nation to independence — despite his abdication in 1955 he was still regarded as a god-king by most of his subjects — was there to stay.

And yet less than one month later I found myself once again aboard a plane flying from Bangkok to Phnom Penh. Rioters, clearly organized by shadowy people with larger aims, had sacked the embassies of North Vietnam and the South Vietnamese Provisional Revolutionary Government. With Sihanouk still absent, Cambodia was in turmoil. The Burmese stewardess had just announced our impending landing when the pilot's voice took over the microphone. "We are obliged to return to Bangkok because the airport is closed," he said, and nothing more. Back in Bangkok I learned that at the very moment of our approach to Pochentong Airport, the National Assembly had unanimously deposed Sihanouk and named a political nonentity as chief of state. For five days the airport remained closed. On the sixth, I was on the first plane that was allowed to land in Cambodia. Smiles greeted the handful of previously unwelcome journalists, without visas, at the airport. We were the only passengers.

There were insouciant smiles all over town. Meanwhile, the government had issued an absurd, unenforceable ultimatum to the Vietnamese Communists to withdraw their troops instantly from Cambodian soil. Cambodia's army was 35,000 or so men strong. The soldiers were organized, trained, and equipped mainly for combating permanent, small-scale leftist and rightist insurgencies. They were also used for royal ceremonies, costarring with representatives of the Buddhist clergy and the Royal

Ballet, and for minor public works, but they were totally incapable of backing up the challenge that the new leaders had
thrown out to the toughest and most war-hardened army in the
region. Phnom Penh was lethargically jubilating at the downfall
of the prince, with the same apparent conviction with which it
had until a few days earlier venerated him. Smiles were worn on
the officials' faces in all government offices, including the Defense
Ministry, especially for Americans. How soon will the Americans
come to help us? I was asked by ministers and pedicab drivers.

Didn't they know that their timing was completely off?
That in March 1970 the Nixon administration was well along in
the process of "Vietnamization" — letting Asians fight against
Asians with American equipment — and desperately seeking a
way of getting all American troops out of Vietnam without
appearing to concede that the United States had lost its most unpopular war? Wasn't it clear to Cambodia's leaders that President Nixon was searching for a face-saving formula to allow him
to abandon to its fate the Vietnamese regime that America had
created and not to deploy American forces in a new theater of
war for a fight to the finish?

Surely Prince Sisowath Sirik Matak, who had long wished
for Sihanouk's downfall and was the brains of the regime headed
by Prime Minister Lon Nol, acted with a clear plan and would
explain what was behind the seemingly harebrained ultimatum, I
assumed. Had he obtained prior American assurances of sufficient assistance to make real his challenge to the Vietnamese?

I met Sirik Matak, the principal plotter and first deputy
prime minister, who was Sihanouk's cousin and archrival, in his
office. The courteous, well-educated aristocrat had just received
notes from the two sacked Vietnamese embassies that they were
closing shop. Yes, he agreed, that amounts to a rejection of the
ultimatum and a declaration of war. So what will the new leaders
do to ward off their foes? He replied, his voice gentle, his smile
innocent: They had requested the Soviet Union and Britain, as
cochairmen of the 1954 Geneva Conference that sealed France's

military defeat in Indochina, to activate the stillborn International Control Commission of Canada, Poland, and India to enforce the ultimatum. Yes, he agreed, this body had consistently been impotent throughout Indochina and was quite unlikely to make the Vietnamese give up their bases. So then? "We will appeal to the United Nations," the prince continued. "Since Cambodia is a member, I think the United Nations will help us." The prince's sincerity seemed unfeigned. How? I asked. Sirik Matak said Cambodia had no specific measures in mind. And if neither of these approaches removes the threat, Your Highness? "I am sorry I cannot reply to this question," the prince said, exuding calm confidence and taking leave with a gentle Khmer smile.

And with smiles all around and boundless confidence in a challenge to the Vietnamese Communists that it could not enforce, Cambodia tripped guilelessly into the Indochina War. Few prisoners were taken by either side, and the United States Air Force bombed massively, often without the benefit of forward air controllers to choose targets that were not largely civilian. The war ended five years later with the march into Phnom Penh of the Khmers Rouges, Cambodia's Communists, and Pol Pot's genocidal folly. Until that horrid day, April 17, 1975, the smiles continued. The smiles hesitantly returned when Vietnam, which Cambodians regard as their archenemy, invaded and liberated them from their murderous rulers in 1979. Vietnam reduced the Khmers Rouges to a few redoubts at the edges of Cambodia. The incongruous liberators imposed military occupation and a Soviet-style puppet dictatorship that continued without significant change until 1992. War continued unabated between the Phnom Penh government and its Vietnamese allies facing their ill-assorted foes, who ranged from Pol Pot and his surviving remnants of savages to a variety of anti-Vietnamese and anti-Communist forces. Then, after Mikhail Gorbachev came to power in 1985 and limited his country's international ambitions, the Soviet Union, on its last legs, cut off its life-giving economic support to its Vietnamese client and hence its Cambodian puppet. Vietnam could no longer afford to continue its hold over Cambodia and withdrew.

There followed in 1992–93 the largest United Nations "peacekeeping" mission ever. A daunting armada of more than twenty thousand foreign soldiers, police, diplomats, administrators, and "experts" in all fields descended on a country that had lived in a tight Communist cocoon since 1975, first under the Khmers Rouges, then under the Vietnamese. To put these foreign bodies and their voluminous gear into a country whose complexities few of them understood cost the wealthy nations about two billion dollars, the greatest sum the world at large had ever laid out for attempting to restore peace in one country. But the peacekeepers failed to daunt the rival Cambodian factions, who refused to disarm their troops and put them in cantonment under international control. The peacekeeping mission brought no more than an edgy, incomplete pause in war-making and ended without peace.

Its proudest achievement was a free parliamentary election in 1993, which was boycotted by the Khmers Rouges. Its results, cheered throughout the world as a triumph of democracy, were betrayed immediately, as the Communist losers, Vietnam's former puppet regime headed by Prime Minister Hun Sen, forced the royalist winners to share power with them. The results were fully nullified when Hun Sen, whose party had never surrendered physical dominance over most of the country, shot his way back into full control four years later. Flare-ups of fighting continue.

I know no other country like Cambodia. Its glory was great, its suffering enormous. With the backbreaking toil of millions of men and women, aided by vast herds of beasts of burden, the Khmers constructed between the ninth and thirteenth centuries the great royal capital of Angkor, one of the wonders of the world. But in the fifteenth century, at the sight of invaders, they abandoned this marvel of art and architecture to the jungle. A mighty nation, a master in its region, became almost helpless fodder for covetous neighbors until the nineteenth century. Then France, the colonizer, subjected the faltering kingdom to its rule. Independence was restored in 1953. There followed an interlude of seventeen years of relative peace, the only "good" years that Cambodians of our time have experienced, before the Indochina War and its aftermath of Pol Pot's genocide made their country's name a synonym for incomprehensible horror.

I have returned to Cambodia — or as close as I could get to it during the Khmer Rouge period of total isolation — through all the depressing phases of its recent history. I have listened to many of Cambodia's leaders and to my Cambodian friends, many of whom perished at the hands of the Khmers Rouges. I have heard and read what foreign scholars and diplomats of long experience in Cambodia and its region have said. Psycho-historic constructions that try to penetrate the mystery that envelops a once powerful and creative nation are familiar to me. My mystification at the curse that seems to have singled out one luckless nation from all its neighbors persists. An irresistible impulse has made me return, again and again, to try to comprehend and bear witness. This is a record of my journeys.

4

The Prince and the Chauffeur: 1964 and 1970

S IHANOUK AND SOUPHON were my first mentors in matters Cambodian. I was lucky; both were marvelously vivid communicators, intelligent and interesting. One was the head of state, the other the driver of a rented car. Both taught me much that proved valuable for understanding a people to whose fate I was to draw closer than I ever imagined at these first encounters.

The prince presented for me, in a magisterial private lecture in Paris years before I even thought of setting foot in his country, his conception of Cambodia's place in its imperiled region and the world at large and the motivation for his policies. With deep pessimism and surprising candor, he forecast a gloomy future. I have known few heads of state who, on a first, casual encounter with a reporter, would describe their country as doomed because it is weak and endowed with only hypocritical, self-serving friends.

Souphon was, for the first ten days that I spent in Cambodia (where I had to play the part of a tourist because journalists were not allowed), the man who chauffeured me across the country in a black Mercedes. The car belonged to a wealthy merchant who hired out Souphon and the Mercedes as a team. Quickly my impulsive and talkative driver became my guide, not only to Angkor and other places on the typical tourist's itinerary that formed part of my camouflage, but much more importantly, my link to people of all stations wherever we went. He was the key that first opened doors for me to the minds of Cambodians. Souphon knew no hesitation at striking up conversations on my behalf with anyone we encountered — Buddhist monks, fishermen on the Great Lake in Cambodia's center, district officers, peasants in the fields, their wives and children in front of their thatch-roofed, banana-leaf-walled huts. Having struck up a chat, Souphon would tactfully choose the moment to introduce me into its flow and let me direct it to any subject of interest. Souphon spoke only the most rudimentary French, learned during service in the preindependence colonial army, but he made it go a long way. Graphically descriptive gestures and vivid mimicry tellingly filled in the gaps.

By the end of our cross-country journey we had become friends. I called him *caporal-chef*, a rank he had never attained, and he, in mock deference, appointed me, equally gratuitously, *mon capitaine*. When we returned to Phnom Penh and our passenger-driver relationship came to an end, friendship took over. Souphon invited me to be his guest at an international soccer game in the Olympic Stadium and an elaborate Chinese dinner afterward. After sitting behind him for ten days in the comfort of the merchant's mercifully air-conditioned Mercedes, I found myself one evening mounting behind Souphon on his own vehicle, a modest moped. My comedown gave infinite amusement to the band of pedicab drivers whose hack stand was the sidewalk in front of the Royal Hotel and earned us their mocking applause.

The soccer game was a marvelous occasion for engaging Cambodians in relaxed conversation. I profited from their amused surprise at seeing a Westerner among them in the stands and from their eagerness to chat. The small resident foreign community, mainly French, tended not to mix with Cambodians who didn't belong to the limited French-educated elite, except on a quite colonial master-servant level.

The game pitted the amateur eleven of the Police Royale Khmère against a rare visitor, the high-powered East German major-leaguers of F.C. Magdeburg. It was the period during which the German Democratic Republic spared no expense to send its artistic ensembles and sporting teams across the world. The goodwill journeys were meant to gain favor among neutrals and votes in the United Nations for the poorer Germany, the one that did not produce the Mercedes that in countries like Cambodia had made an exalted reputation for the Federal Republic. The Communist East presented itself as not the rich but the "good" Germany. By its own definition it was "anti-Fascist" and therefore, somewhat anachronistically, always opposed to Hitler. Its propaganda pitched at the newly decolonized nations declared that West Germany was imperialist and the successor of Hitler's Reich. It was the "bad" Germany. That was the message that the athletes from Magdeburg had come to deliver to Phnom Penh. It failed to register.

To win the hearts and minds of Cambodians for the cause, the Magdeburg bruisers were clearly under orders not to embarrass the host team by scoring as often as they might have. This required some effort, and when the teams took the field after the halftime break, the strain of holding back and the tropical sun had clearly taken their toll on the northern visitors. Magdeburg was visibly fading, and the valiant royal cops looked as though they might even score. The large crowd, which had seen through the political maneuver on the field and laughed at it through the first half, began to follow the action with enthusiasm. A Cambodian behind us, who had befriended Souphon and me and had shared his ample supplies of local snacks with us, tapped me on the shoulder. "*Il est fatigué, Itlaire,*" he said, smiling over the full width of his broad, brown face. Clearly any Germany, East or

West, was inseparable from the memory of Hitler for ordinary Cambodians. And almost two decades before the fall of the Berlin Wall, I had in Phnom Penh's Olympic Stadium a first sense that the German Democratic Republic might be a lost cause. (Magdeburg, its sporting pride greater than its sense of official mission, soon got its second wind and won easily, 3–0.)

Souphon, with a driver's view of the police, cheered the result. Over dinner he made clear his dim view of the police and all other authority in his country — except Prince Sihanouk. The only thing that he found wrong with the prince was that he was too good to his wife, Princess Monique, and her mother, Madame Pomme Peang. Sihanouk let his consort and the rest of her family get rich with money that should go to the people, Souphon said. "You saw how poor they are when we were traveling."

My first meeting with the prince occurred during a state visit to France in 1964, an event that rated hardly a line in my newspaper. The American involvement in Indochina was still in the "military adviser" state and had not yet become the issue that for so many years to come was to dominate the American news media, until Watergate took its place. During a press luncheon, Sihanouk invited questions. I asked one or two, not because of a deep interest in Cambodia, terra incognita to me, but because I had found its chief of state a national leader unlike any I had ever met. During an informal speech that he gave between dessert and coffee, he blurted out with disregard for conventional hypocrisy truths that statesmen are supposed to keep to themselves, including delicate details of his conversation with President de Gaulle. Moreover, he dwelt on his country's weakness rather than praising pretended strength. He laughed at his own remarks more uproariously than his audience.

The prince had noticed the depth of ignorance of his country that my questions had betrayed, and as the gathering was breaking up he sent one of his aides to bring me to him. He promptly began a lucid exposé of the enduring Indochina crisis as viewed from Cambodia. "My dear friend," he said, "to understand what I am trying to achieve, just remember this: all of Southeast Asia is destined to become Communist. What I am trying to do is this — when it happens in Cambodia, I want it to happen without breakage."

"In a world without pity, the survival of a country as small as Cambodia depends on your god and my Buddha," he went on. Neutrality is Cambodia's only hope, he said, "no matter how much the United States dislikes it." In Sihanouk's memory there rankled condescending lectures that he had been treated to, in Washington and Phnom Penh, by Secretary of State Dulles. In 1953, while still king of a nation under French colonial rule, Sihanouk called on Dulles expecting support for Cambodia's demands for sovereignty. He counted on what he had believed to be American anticolonialism. Instead, Dulles hectored him on Cambodia's moral duty to take the Western side in the struggle against communism. Cambodia needs France as her strongest protector against the Communists, Dulles told him. Five years later Dulles visited Cambodia, by then independent and neutral, to urge Sihanouk, unsuccessfully, to join the SEATO. "You cannot be a Switzerland in Asia," Dulles admonished Sihanouk, according to the prince, who recalled his always edgy relations with the United States in *My War with the C.I.A.* The book was ghostwritten for him during the 1970–75 war by Wilfred Burchett, a Communist propagandist from Australia. "You cannot be neutral," Dulles said. "You have to choose between the free world and the Communist camp." With tartness of his own, Sihanouk remembered Dulles as "an acidy, arrogant man."

Sihanouk told me with astonishing, undiplomatic candor that although the Vietnamese Communists praised him for his refusal to be enlisted in America's cause, he had no illusions about Vietnamese goals. His eastern neighbor was bound to become Communist, despite America's support for South Vietnam. A "hopeless policy," he said. "I have had too many contacts with the Americans to have too much hope that they will change their policy in South Vietnam." He made this prescient forecast a year before the first marines landed in Vietnam, the vanguard of what was to become a military presence of a half-million Americans. When Vietnam is reunited under the Communists, Sihanouk continued, it will forget how much it had praised his neutrality and will turn against Cambodia. "They will seek to swallow us up, as they have been swallowing our lands for centuries." The same "expansionist dream" is harbored by Cambodia's western neighbor, Thailand, America's ally, the prince continued. Vietnam divided, as it was in 1964, was good for Cambodia, he said. "I am not suggesting a permanent division, but it helps the cause of Cambodia, and I hope it will last for some time."

This was my first lesson in two of the basic tenets that shape Cambodians' sense of their nation. They are in great numbers possessed by fear that not only their country but also the very existence of the Khmer people are in mortal danger, and they are convinced that the Vietnamese are their hereditary, implacable enemies, who hypocritically hide their true, rapacious intentions with words of false friendship.

Cambodia can count on only one Asian protector, Sihanouk continued in his lecture. China had never been a threat to his country, nor ever a friend to Vietnam. He relied on its might to restrain Vietnamese expansionism even after the whole country had become Communist like China. And he hoped that the United States would retain a strong presence in Southeast Asia, not only to curb Thailand's lust for Cambodian land but also to balance China's preponderant weight.

Sihanouk has often been depicted as a man whose changing moods provoke him to change his views with equal frequency. I do not agree. He has often changed alliances, and committed many an error, and his moods have certainly been aflutter. His foes have become allies and allies foes. But I believe he has been driven by a consistent view; a result largely of his leading a desperately weak country tossed about by upheavals caused by more powerful neighbors and by great outside forces pursuing their own interests. Sihanouk has been consistent in struggling to realize the goal on which he lectured me in 1964. Sadly, he has failed. Nowhere in Indochina has the "breakage" been more devastating. And as he lives out the drag ends of an extraordinary life, king once more but shorn of most power and self-exiled most of the time, incurably ill with cancer in Beijing, the breakage of his doomed country goes on, irreversibly.

And Souphon, my second mentor? We had an uproarious reunion a month after we took leave, I had thought for good. When I showed up at the Hotel Royal five days after the coup, there was Souphon, at the entrance, scouting for clients. He let out a delighted yell and pointed at the typewriter I carried. "You're a journalist!" he cried. "And I thought you were an American spy. All the questions you asked, and always wanting to go to the Vietnamese border! I knew you were not a tourist." We worked together for a day or two, until I decided to rent a car and be my own driver.

I was able to find Souphon employment, which turned out to be permanent until the war ended five years later, with one of the American television networks. But his sense of friendship prompted him to acts of disloyalty to his steady employers. He insisted on keeping me informed whenever my network colleagues covered something unusual. It was never information that was of competitive use to me, because in the days of film that needed to be shipped for processing and transmission to the United States, television suffered from a constant time lag behind the written press. But Souphon believed his information gave me a competitive advantage and felt he owed it to me as a friend. As a friend he also shared with me his feelings, and those of his family, neighbors, and friends, about Cambodia's decline into fratricidal war and growing chaos, about the failings of its new leaders and the hollow American pillar on which they rested, and about ordinary Cambodians' steadily mounting fears about the future. Those conversations greatly enhanced my understanding. The Olympic Stadium soon became a military camp and there were no more soccer games.

With his network earnings, Souphon became a man of means. He grew in assurance and social stature, and his slim frame filled out visibly. He was still in Phnom Penh when the Khmers Rouges conquered the city. I hoped to hear that he had escaped in time, but no word came. In one of the vast, squalid encampments of refugees that formed on the Thai border after Vietnam's invasion overthrew Pol Pot's regime in 1979, I met one of Souphon's friends. No, he said, no one had seen Souphon since Pol Pot. In the first months after Vietnam's liberating invasion, those who had made the Hotel Royal their working station before made their way there again from the four corners of Cambodia to which the city's population had been deported. They thought they would meet their family members, from whom many had been forcibly separated, and they hoped to find work and food there. Few came back, because few had survived. Souphon was not among them.

5

Dressing up for War: 1970

THE TEENAGERS CAVORTING in front of the Lycée Descartes, the French-language high school for the children of Phnom Penh's elite, couldn't have been more cheerful on a steamy morning in April 1970, a couple of weeks after Prince Sihanouk's overthrow. A surprising sight, because it was Sunday in the hottest time of the year, and they were not at a beach or the swimming pools of the Cercle Sportif or the Hotel Royal, their customary weekend meeting places. And what they had been called out to do was meant to be deadly serious. They were there to demonstrate their readiness to defend their country against the Communist Vietnamese invaders, to show their enthusiasm for the new leaders, and their rejection of the deposed prince. Their teachers were with them to organize the outburst of militant patriotism.

Only, how do you demonstrate a newfound martial spirit and hatred for a fallen leader when you are fifteen years old and used to living on what you had always been told was a happy island of peace, thanks to a godlike prince? The ways the boys and girls from Descartes chose, or had chosen for them by their teachers, was martial dress, or what they thought resembled it. They carried posters bearing ferocious slogans and vile caricatures and sang newly composed anthems in favor of unity, liberty, and Cambodia's sacred soil. So new were the compositions that most of the students merely hummed along or sang from texts that they had copied from their classroom blackboards. American fatigues, a long-standing fashion favorite from the smugglers' market on the South Vietnamese border, were fancied by the boys, tight khaki pants by the girls. White tennis shoes took the place of combat boots. There were also bits of French gear, perhaps from fathers who had worn it in the colonial army in an earlier war against Vietnamese Communists. American cartridge belts, empty of ammunition, completed many an ensemble; worn low, they produced something reflective of carefully negligent Saint-Tropez chic, the ideal of Phnom Penh's gilded youth of those days. Some of the boys felt that attaching a bush knife to the belts emphasized their preparedness.

To demonstrate the bellicose purpose of the gathering, the teachers now and again assembled their giggling charges into ranks and attempted to conduct them through the standard maneuvers of close-order military drill. But as they barked out their orders, which were haphazardly followed amid much laughter, they found it difficult to squelch their own giggles. It was left to the posters and banners that the students brandished to furnish a belligerent air. "Get out, dirty, aggressive Vietcong, eaters of Cambodian territory," trumpeted a homemade sign in English, for the benefit of tourists and the foreign press. "Let us chase, let us kill the Vietcong from our territory," pronounced a French version, and another, from the University School of Commerce, "Let us beat this evildoing beast, the Vietcong." Their Vietnamese classmates — they were usually the star pupils, their French teachers used to say — had not been invited, the demonstrators said, with more than a touch of self-righteousness. Vietnamese made up perhaps one-third of the capital's population of 600,000 and a good share of the Descartes student body.

Two sweetly smiling girls told me they hated Sihanouk. But a couple of weeks ago you loved him, didn't you? They agreed, and one added quickly, "But now I don't dare." "I waver between the two," said her friend. The first giggled. "But if Sihanouk comes back, I'll shout 'Bravo, Sihanouk!'"

It would have been easy to write off the performance as a charmingly innocent frolic by teenagers excited at something new and understandably unaware of the seriousness of the new reality. It was that, but it also resembled in every important aspect the reaction of most of their elders, including the leaders of the nation. The beguiling Khmer smile had not lost its charm on the face of the young innocents, but it was at the very least perplexing when it appeared as the response of adults, men in responsible positions, to a calamitous change of course for Cambodia made by its leaders. After all, the issue was, war or peace? Cambodia had brought down Sihanouk, the man who, not without paying a heavy price, had preserved for them a maximum of peace, and its new leaders had announced the reversal of the policies through which he had kept the war from touching the lives of most Cambodians.

Through its challenge to the Vietnamese Communists to withdraw their troops, a challenge that was recognized by all but Cambodia's new leaders as certain to be rejected, the nation had stumbled totally unprepared into war against the Vietnamese Communists, a most formidable foe. The Vietnamese already occupied large stretches of Cambodian territory with combat-hardened troops. These hostile forces greatly outnumbered Cambodia's military. The government of Lon Nol and Sirik Matak had flung at Hanoi the equivalent of a declaration of war while in a state of grievous unreadiness and without having obtained, it quickly became clear, any commitment of foreign assistance. Worse, there were few powers of any consequence that could be expected to provide effective aid.

The United States, of course, was the most likely and the most powerful ally. But by March 1970 it had amply proved the wavering of its commitment to an unpopular war in Indochina, as well as the destructive nature of its massive and bumbling attempts to defend South Vietnam and Laos against the same foe. The other main candidate was South Vietnam, entirely dependent itself on the United States, with half a million American troops on its soil and yet far from successful in its struggle for independent survival. Thailand was a remote possibility, but its record of hesitant participation in the war in Vietnam and Laos, despite rich financial compensation from the United States, should not have encouraged high Cambodian hopes. Besides, Cambodians were painfully aware that both Vietnam and Thailand had through the centuries been loath to withdraw from Khmer soil once they had placed armed men on it.

Men and women of the educated classes, a sparse minority in a population of perhaps 85 percent peasant farmers, but one that dominated the lives of all Cambodians, seemed to pay little heed to the risk of war. They rejoiced in great numbers at Sihanouk's fall and seemed oblivious to its consequences. Most had played their roles in Sihanouk's willful system, although muted discontent had greatly grown. The handful of resolute oppositionists, Communists like Pol Pot, or antiroyalist nationalists, had long ago gone underground in the jungle or into exile. The prince's conniving at corruption, the authoritarian arbitrariness and economic incompetence of his rule, his spiteful intolerance of those who would not be sycophants outweighed in the minds of educated Cambodians his principal achievement — warding off the ever-present menace of being drawn fully into the war of Indochina.

Among the educated, Sihanouk had clearly suffered an ever-spreading erosion of support that was inevitable after he had run the nation like a one-man show for a quarter century. That he had led Cambodia imaginatively and peacefully to the restoration of its independence in 1953 lay too far in the past to matter much in 1970. Like the giggling schoolgirls, the vast majority of Cambodians, either illiterate or equipped with only a smattering of education, cheered whatever their leaders told them to cheer and hoped their lives, lived from hand to mouth, would not suffer from whatever happened at the top. And they kept smiling.

Phnom Penh busied itself from the day of the prince's downfall with petty signs of change and gave little show of evidence that the big issue — war or peace — was being purposefully faced. Lon Nol governed, inasmuch as he did, mainly from his villa at the edge of the city. At the central seat of government, the building of the Council of Ministers, cabinet members chatted amiably among themselves or with visitors while servants passed through the corridors bearing trays of French pastries. Sihanouk's photos, as ubiquitous as those of Communist chiefs of state, were hastily taken down in public and private places. (In the first few days after the coup, it was still possible for a foreigner to persuade with a wink petty stationery sellers in Phnom Penh's main markets to dig into the bottom of boxes under their display tables and hand over facedown, with a conspiratorial smile, a portrait of the prince or a calendar bearing his image and that of his mother, Queen Kossamak. Prices were reduced. Then the images vanished, and visual de-Sihanoukizing was complete.) His portraits were often replaced in public places by those of Cheng Heng, a wealthy landowner and forgettable politician, who was given the title of chief of state by Lon Nol but none of Sihanouk's powers. His portraits went largely unrecognized.

Street signs were changed to remove any recollection of the monarchic past. The republic was not declared until October. The word "royal" was carefully painted out on signs at government and military installations. Monsieur Lou, the manager of the government-owned Hotel Royal, the Ritz of Cambodia, was put under heavy pressure by uniformed men to change the name of the establishment. It became Le Phnom. The Cinéma d'Etat (State Cinema), built especially to show Sihanouk's productions, took his last work, *Joie de Vivre*, off the program and replaced it with a Hong Kong kung fu thriller.

A few hundred of Sihanouk's political prisoners, mainly

conservative nationalists who had opposed his compromises with the Vietnamese Communists, were released. Newspapers that had until the day of the coup outdone one another in fulsome praise of the prince, outdid themselves again under unchanged editorship for the subsequent five years in reviling him. *Le Courrier Phnompenhois*, a French-language daily, had featured on top of every edition's front page a "Thought of the Day," signed by Norodom Sihanouk. Here, for example, from an issue three weeks before the prince's overthrow, is how a front-page editorial pleaded for his speedy return to a country that longed for him. Under the heading "A Proof of a Great Veneration," the newspaper commented on meetings across the land to wish the chief of state a full recovery in his antiobesity cure in France:

"Everywhere in the Kingdom the absence of Samdech Euv [Mylord Daddy] is regretted by all His children. . . . [The meeting of members of Parliament] was the occasion for them to reaffirm their sentiments of fidelity, loyalty and unfailing attachment to the August Person of our venerated Leader, as well as to the Throne. . . . It is testimony that the entire Khmer people profoundly venerates Mylord Norodom Sihanouk, Father of Independence. . . to whom Cambodia owes that it did not founder after the rejection of U.S. assistance in 1963. . . .

"In a region of the world in the grip of war and the struggle between two ideological blocs, we need at the head of our country a chief of State of the stature of Mylord Norodom Sihanouk, Who brings wisdom, foresight and firmness to high policy. The entire Khmer nation knows that with Mylord Daddy at the helm the vessel Cambodia will not founder in the tumultuous waters of Southeast Asia.

"The votive ceremonies organized throughout the Kingdom testify to the great veneration, the limitless confidence and the profound gratitude of the Khmer people toward the Father of the Nation."

Three weeks later, without missing a beat, and over the same editor's byline, *Le Courrier Phnompenhois* was pouring venom and often salacious scorn on the prince, demanding the abolition of the throne, from which Sihanouk had stepped down in 1955 to free himself from court ritual for more active political leadership, and calling for large-scale American assistance. It was no different in all other publications, except that the Cambodian-language press struck even more viciously below the belt, in words and cartoons, in vilifying the prince and his Eurasian consort, Princess Monique.

While the coup leaders in Phnom Penh seemed to wait inactively in March and April of 1970 for help to arrive from somewhere to give force to their defiant ultimatum, the resistance wasted no time in going to war. In Beijing, Sihanouk was quickly persuaded by Prime Ministers Zhou Enlai of China and Pham Van Dong of North Vietnam to join in a Chinese-sponsored fighting alliance with the Vietnamese Communists. He was placed at the head of the Khmer National United Front, whose initial fighting forces within Cambodia were Vietnamese regulars. But quickly, with the tempo mounting as war installed itself for the long haul, the Vietnamese Communists recruited Cambodians under the banner not of communism but of the struggle for the restoration of Sihanouk. They distributed badges bearing photos of the prince to their recruits. In the third of the country from the Vietnamese border westward to the Mekong River, Cambodian Communists who had made common cause with the revolutionary Vietminh during the Indochinese anticolonial struggle against France and had settled in North Vietnam and been trained and indoctrinated there, served as effective organizers of Cambodian guerrillas.

The front was soon joined, ironically, by those who had been Sihanouk's most determined foes, a largely younger, better educated generation of Communists, whom the prince while in power had persecuted mercilessly and derisively termed "Khmers rouges," or "red Cambodians." Their leaders were men and women who during their scholarship studies in France in the 1950s had turned to communism. One by one, they had fled into

Cambodia's deep forests during the early 1960s, usually one step ahead of Sihanouk's cruel security apparatus, and begun the patient creation of an armed resistance movement to the royal regime. They included Pol Pot, then still known as Saloth Sar, Ieng Sary, Son Sen, and Khieu Samphan — the intellectual elite of the Khmers Rouges.

Open pro-Sihanouk risings in several major provincial towns were harshly put down. They included one centered on Kompong Cham, a Mekong River town north of Phnom Penh, in which Lon Nol's brother, Lon Nil, was literally butchered and, a persistent rumor had it, cannibalized. But simultaneously, Vietnamese Communist troops, thumbing their noses at Phnom Penh's ultimatum, picked off one small government garrison after another in extending their hold over Cambodian territory all along the nearly six hundred miles of border. The thinly populated northeastern provinces of Rattanakiri, Mondulkiri, and Stung Treng quickly fell in their entirety, virtually without resistance. So feeble were the communication links and administrative and military structures that Phnom Penh was mostly unaware how much of its country it was losing day by day. Perhaps that is why it took so long for most Cambodians, including the country's leaders, to accept the reality that they were at war. And yet the sad, handwritten list at the main post office of provinces and towns for which mail was no longer accepted lengthened day by day.

For a short while I suspected that the Lon Nol government was simply hiding truths of which it was but too painfully aware. But then I made a stark discovery: the leaders really didn't know much of what was happening outside the capital. I learned this from the man who was no doubt closer to Lon Nol than any other, his youngest brother, Lon Non. The prime minister, who had no children with his wife (but four from other women), treated Lon Non like a son. Lon Non was a thoroughly unimpressive major of military police, appropriately placed, I thought, in a tiny office off a rear corridor in the Defense Ministry. Nothing in his personality led me to foresee the immense and grossly misused powers that Lon Nol, with whom he lived, would confer on him.

In 1970 I was the first foreign journalist whom Lon Non met, and no doubt the confidences of which I became a virtually daily beneficiary in the first months of his brother's leadership were due to his inexperience with the press and his eagerness to speak with an American. He was handicapped in this by knowing no English, and few of the Americans who had rushed to the latest theater of war spoke any other language but their own. I learned a great deal about his brother's plans, actions, and state of mind from Lon Non, and that included the distressing fact that even Prime Minister Lon Nol, who was also defense minister, was at that critical time remarkably ignorant of the state of military action in his country.

It became quickly evident that the principal providers of military information to everybody in Phnom Penh, including high military and government officials, in those early weeks of the war were the foreign correspondents. Like many of my colleagues, I set out early almost every morning in my rented car on one or the other of the roads linking the capital to the Vietnamese border, eastward or southward, to see how far it was still possible to go until the villages became ominously still and the paddy fields on either side of the road suspiciously empty of toiling men and women. Then I would backtrack to the first populated place or military compound and would learn that since the night before it had become no longer safe, that a small garrison had been attacked or had chosen to withdraw in the face of what was always called "Vietcong," who had established a roadblock a bit further ahead.

The price the press paid for serving as reconnaissance scouts for the sake of accurate reporting on the state of Cambodia was cruelly high. About a month after the opening of the new arena of the Indochina wars, twenty-three journalists — all but a few of them photographers or television crews in search of pictures — had gone missing on the roads of Cambodia. Twenty of them never came back. Covering the war in Vietnam, with air transport provided by the American military and the reporters always in the company of troops, was a joyride compared to Cambodia, where solitary journalists drove on their own to places where troops feared to tread. April 5–6, 1970, should figure as a black day in journalism history, illustrating painfully the fearful innocence and absence of foresight with which Cambodia slid into the grim adventure of war.

Journalists were advised by the Foreign Ministry before dawn on the sixth to gather in their cars and follow a military convoy that would take them to the small market town of Chiphou, near the Vietnamese border on the Saigon road. Chiphou, an official said, had just been liberated after having been captured by the Vietcong. The convoy traveled at the speed of its slowest vehicles, French armored cars of pre–World War II vintage, so my two British traveling companions and I pulled ahead and reached Chiphou early. Townspeople told us that they had not yet seen "liberating" Cambodian troops; the Vietnamese had withdrawn on their own during the night after setting fire to the military post, a small fort in the center of town, built by the French.

We stopped for a drink in a shop on the market square, where we were joined by two colleagues, who arrived on rented motorcycles. They were Sean Flynn, a photographer and son of the actor Errol Flynn, and his friend Dana Stone, a television soundman. Both wore items of American military camouflage uniforms. They told us that about two miles beyond Chiphou they had seen and twice approached a Vietcong roadblock, and intended to make another try at photographing it and perhaps talking with the guerrillas. We warned them not to get too close, particularly in their soldierlike costumes. They laughed.

My friends and I drove on a mile or so beyond town. The two motorcycles roared up behind us, swerving wide, one passing on each side of the car. Flynn and Stone waved back at us cheerfully; they were never seen again. The fields around us were deserted, the atmosphere even heavier than the torrid April heat; we turned back to Chiphou. The convoy arrived, and two Japanese television newsmen, after a brief stop in the town, set out on their own in their car and headed toward the border. A short while later, a pair of peasants excitedly reported to the military escort that they had just witnessed the Japanese and their Cambodian driver and interpreter being taken prisoner at the roadblock, which they said consisted of a communal taxi parked across the road and a handful of armed men. The peasants had been allowed to go on.

Would our escort, consisting of the Cambodian Army's eight armored cars and several hundred heavily armed troops, advance to eliminate the roadblock and free the journalists, who were certain by then also to include the two Americans on motorcycles? I asked their commander, a Cambodian colonel in charge of the entire military region. Oh no, he said, the press and their escorts were expected for lunch in the provincial capital of Svay Rieng. He ordered two jeeploads of soldiers and an armored car to do a reconnaissance in the direction of the roadblock, executed a U-turn, and led his troops toward lunch. The patrol returned a little later, having probably advanced only a short distance into the no-man's-land. What the regional commander ordered his troops to abandon, in full view of the world's press, was not only the kidnapped journalists. It was learned later they also included three French photographers seized at the same spot the day before. The troops also abandoned control of a vital highway, the border town of Bavet, and its isolated garrison of about thirty soldiers.

Since Cambodia still insisted on its neutrality for a few weeks after the coup that had brought down Sihanouk, despite the war that was eroding its hold over the country, Communist embassies and press representatives were still based in Phnom Penh. Two Soviet reporters and an East German were part of the press convoy. I asked them to come with me and my British colleagues to the roadblock and assure their Vietnamese or Cambodian comrades that the men they had seized were reporters, not soldiers or spies. Embarrassed, they declined. The East German, a friend, took me aside. "You understand, Henry," he said. "Like you, I also have a wife and children. You know them."

I did not see Chiphou again for twenty-two years. The village had been rebuilt after the war's destruction and its decay in the four years of Pol Pot's rule, when as in most of Cambodia's towns and villages its population had been forced into large labor communes in the countryside. But one elderly man, with whom I drank tea sitting on low stools in a primitive coffee shop — roughly on the site of the grocery in which I had shared a last drink with Flynn and Stone — remembered the morning the military and the Westerners arrived from Phnom Penh. He recalled with a shudder that the Vietcong were all around the village that day, hiding in the houses and watching the soldiers and the journalists. They had not withdrawn, but the villagers had been understandably afraid to tell us or our military escort. They were scared to death that a firefight might break out, with them in the midst of a cross fire, and their village destroyed. But the Vietcong held their fire, the man said, and didn't openly take possession of Chiphou until a day or two later.

Soon Svay Rieng, the border province traversed by the Phnom Penh–Saigon highway, one of the main routes of French colonialism, belonged to the Vietnamese invader. The large French-owned rubber plantations to its north were next to fall. Kratie, a provincial capital farther north, was soon lost, and the South Vietnamese National Liberation Front, the official title of the Vietcong, established its headquarters in the area, farther from the border sanctuaries and safer from ground attack by American or South Vietnamese forces.

While the government floundered between appeals for respect for its neutrality and pleas to all countries represented in Phnom Penh — including such unlikely sources as China and the Soviet Union — for military assistance, Phnom Penh improvised the incidental features of a capital at war. Almost overnight, the peaceful city took on the air of a besieged bastion. Barbed-wire barricades went up around all government buildings. They were deployed in such profusion that the city's center soon became a labyrinth, and access to some ministries or the post office became frustrating trial-and-error searches for the one opening among the many dead ends. But the guards at the sandbagged entrances were more somnolent than vigilant, and their rifles more often than not leaned unattended and probably unloaded in the doorways. Khaki or olive drab shirts and trousers became the prescribed working apparel for civil servants, and Prince Sirik Matak, a modest and peaceable man but the most active organizer of the coup that had plunged Cambodia into war, took to wearing his major general's uniform and carrying a black, silver-encrusted swagger stick to the office. (He owed his military rank to the fact that Cambodia had no officer corps when it became independent. When the small army was created as a necessary attribute of independent statehood, senior civil servants were given commissions, often despite their lack of military experience.)

One evening in early April, Lon Non asked me how I thought the Defense Ministry should cope with the many requests for information from foreign journalists. (Cambodian officials had a tendency to ask advice from any foreign visitor, including journalists. My defense against being drawn into such minefields usually was to pretend not to hear the requests.) I told the prime minister's brother that in Vietnam and Laos there were military spokesmen to answer questions and provide regular situation briefings. A day or two later, the press was invited to the upstairs tea room of the Magasin d'Etat, a small nonfunctioning government-owned department store, to be briefed by the latest wartime improvisation, the military spokesman.

He turned out to be an affable and intelligent major, who had returned a year or so before from France, where he had obtained a degree from the highly regarded state film school. But once back home, it was made clear to him that there was room for only one serious filmmaker in Cambodia: Sihanouk. (The prince made it a custom to humiliate young people of higher education by denying them the employment for which their often state-financed studies had prepared them.) He was commissioned a major, and the army created a film unit consisting of one lonely major, who had little to do. He was free to serve as spokesman.

He began the briefing by introducing himself as "Major Am Rong." He didn't understand why this should have occasioned disbelief and laughter among his largely English-language audience. He looked anxiously at me, the only one among the journalists whom he had met before. Clearly the spokesman knew no English. In perfect French, he began a summary of war news, much behind the state of information of the press, and was instantly interrupted by catcalls of "English! English!" He looked toward me again. I avoided his regard. Then he asked me directly, would I translate? I did, for the first military briefing of the Cambodian war. I told Am Rong, who became a friend, that as a journalist I could only be his interlocutor, not his assistant. "But where can I find an interpreter?" I suggested the English- and French-language glossy propaganda magazines that were among Sihanouk's favorite preoccupations. The next day, Am Rong was accompanied by a young contributor of poems to the magazines, who had studied in the United States and, like Am Rong, been relegated to a humble job on his return with a degree from Louisiana State University. Before the war was over, the poetic interpreter had risen to become the Lon Nol regime's last information minister. Am Rong was promoted to general.

Cambodia was at war, but only its enemy was fighting. The Cambodian Army retreated wherever it was challenged.

6

Cannon Fodder: 1970

_E_ARLY ON A SUNDAY AFTERNOON in mid-April of 1970, a month after the coup d'état, the Vietnamese enemy struck within fifteen miles of Phnom Penh. A force of about one hundred Communist troops seized the market town of Saang, on the Bassac River south of the capital. It met no resistance. A major in the village of Khau Khor, three miles nearer to Phnom Penh, which I happened to visit that afternoon, told me headquarters had ordered him to withdraw the infantry battalion of which he was the deputy commander.

What ensued in that small town of truck gardens that grew fruit and vegetables for Phnom Penh proved emblematic for the conduct of a war that was just beginning. It left no doubt that it could not but end in defeat for those who had taken it upon themselves to thrust Cambodia into war. That this would be disastrous for Cambodia's people was certain, although how dire the consequences of the Khmer Rouge victory five years hence would be for the survival of the nation could not be foretold.

That Sunday, no news of the sudden nearness of war to the capital was given to its people. Ignorance left Phnom Penh's life undisturbed. Even the following morning, when I took the road to Saang, I passed two roadblocks between the capital and my destination fifteen miles to the south and found them unmanned. I asked a Cambodian policeman at a third barrier, halfway to Saang, whether I was on the right road. He waved me on cheerfully, without a word of warning that I was a few miles from a war zone. Peasants still worked in the fields, although communal taxis could be seen going toward Phnom Penh, carrying on their roofs the belongings of families, probably from Saang, heading for the safety of the capital. The displaced masses of the Indochina War, sadly familiar for years in Vietnam and Laos, were making their appearance in the capital now. There were no troops along the road.

The combat zone began at Khau Khor, three miles from Saang. It was marked by lines of antiquated buses and trucks, their panels and hoods garishly decorated in the custom of Southeast Asia. They were parked on both sides of the road that follows the bends of the Bassac. Pepsi-Cola signs shone luridly on the flanks of the trucks. The motley motor pool was the dirt-poor Cambodian Army's hastily commandeered troop transport, an equivalent of the taxis that rushed the defenders of Paris to the Marne in World War I. Cautiously, their drivers had parked them pointing back toward Phnom Penh, hardly a sign of confidence. The troops, about one thousand men, had been moved up during the evening, and Colonel Dien Del, their commander, told me that their mission was to liberate Saang that day. He had set up his command post at the edge of the town at a farmhouse. The owner and his wife puttered about the yard, as though gunfire and troops in combat had already become an unremarkable part of daily life. Their two little girls were happy to have me push them to and fro on a makeshift swing.

The attack would be mounted after some preparation, said Colonel Dien Del. In midmorning two American-built light T-28 trainer planes armed with machine guns swooped three times over the center of town about five hundred yards ahead, guns blazing. The Vietnamese on the ground responded with automatic weapons.

Meanwhile, Dien Del had difficulty communicating with the pilots to direct their action, because his radio and theirs were old and faulty. He also lacked a map of the region. But after sending a message to the Geographic Service in Phnom Penh requesting a set of detailed maps of the area, they arrived in short order — all but the needed one. A second messenger was dispatched but didn't return. It was time for Colonel Dien Del and his men to lunch. The farmer and his wife retired to the shade beneath their house on stilts for a nap. April is Cambodia's hottest month.

Lunch was interrupted as the Vietnamese opened up on the command post with rockets, mortars, and automatic rifles. The guerrillas also directed their fire at the lines of trucks and buses. Then the shooting stopped as suddenly as it had begun. No damage was done, but the Cambodian counterattack was put off for a day.

On Tuesday, Cambodian officers told journalists that instead of a military operation to free the town, "psychological warfare" would be employed. Dozens of Vietnamese men, women, and young girls were lined up across the road and made to walk between the opposing forces into the no-man's-land. They were residents of the Phnom Penh region who had been interned by the thousands in a xenophobic campaign against the Vietnamese minority of about 400,000 throughout the country. They carried white flags and bullhorns, through which they called on the Communist troops to stop their unjustified aggression and withdraw. A handful of Cambodian soldiers were deployed behind them. When a single Communist soldier rose from cover at their approach and waved them away, a Cambodian fired his rifle at him. This drew a Vietnamese barrage in return. The captive psychological warriors were caught in the cross fire. About ten were dragged away wounded; it isn't known how many lost their lives in this cruelly harebrained sacrifice of the innocent. On that Tuesday, the liberation of Saang was postponed once more; psychological warfare had failed.

On Wednesday, Major Am Rong announced that fifty

Cambodian soldiers had been killed in combat around Saang, but he had no news of the casualties among Vietnamese civilians the day before. Finally, on Thursday afternoon Cambodian forces, preceded by an artillery and mortar barrage of the town, advanced into the center their guns had destroyed, only to learn that the invaders had withdrawn before dawn. While for five days an enemy force had been within easy striking distance of Phnom Penh, for the great majority of the 600,000 people of the capital the days passed as if nothing had happened. The Khmer smile continued as serene as ever.

The Vietnamese Communist forces had shown by this brief raid that their small, highly mobile units could strike at any place of their choosing between the border and the Mekong, including Phnom Penh. Seizing the initiative, they imposed upon an unprepared Cambodian army the kind of warfare in which they had acquired years of experience. They made all roads out of the capital unsafe by mounting roadblocks and ambushing vehicles at times and places of their choosing. The Cambodian military, far from being able to deliver on its leaders' foolish ultimatum, was on the defensive everywhere and was abandoning small military posts in order to consolidate its thin manpower. In fact, withdrawals of unprepared and untrained troops that would otherwise have been overrun were the high marks of Cambodia's military successes in the early stages of the war. The army was recruiting soldiers, but who was to arm and train them?

In the first days of May I made the acquaintance of what was proudly called the "First Battalion of Commandos of the Teaching Profession." Never have I seen so sad a spectacle of docile and cheerful cannon fodder.

The "commandos" consisted of schoolteachers who had been recruited after their schools, mainly south of Phnom Penh nearer the Vietnamese border, had fallen into the hands of the Vietnamese invaders. There were 474 of them, young men all with hardly more education than their pupils. All loyally said what they were supposed to say: that they had volunteered at the

Education Ministry to join the army to reconquer their schools, their villages, and their provinces. With an allowance of about nine dollars, their only pay, they were told to buy uniforms. The black market was their supplier, and the result was a potpourri of khaki and olive green American fatigues, varied headgear, and sneakers or plastic sandals.

With their British World War I Lee Enfield rifles, they presented arms with enthusiasm for a couple of visiting reporters, and confessed that no one had yet shown them what else to do with their rifles. They had never fired them and had no ammunition. But later in the week, they had been told, they would receive eight rounds each. They would learn what rifles are for and find out whether their British antiques had survived World War I in working order. That would be all the training they would receive, said the principal of the elementary school. The "commandos" would immediately be assigned to combat units.

Pointing at a rusty bush knife hanging from his belt, with a buckle marked "007," a teacher-soldier said it was their only reliable weapon. "I'll throw it at the Vietcong," he said. Laughter went all around, as almost everything said about their going into combat caused mirth. But those who had seen the guerrillas warned that they looked very tough. A week or so later I checked on the unit's whereabouts. "At the front," said the principal.

Recruiting went on indiscriminately, particularly among the very young. In mid-July, when the American-equipped South Vietnamese military were already taking an active part in the fighting on the Cambodian side of the border, I flew to the beleaguered and largely destroyed provincial capital of Kompong Thom, north of Phnom Penh, with a fleet of South Vietnamese combat helicopters. About five hundred fresh troops were airlifted to help the town ward off an expected all-out Communist attack. It was the first time the new soldiers, mostly farm boys, had flown. Afraid of falling out the open sides, they huddled close together in the middle of the aircraft, making the South Vietnamese crew laugh.

Many of the recruits were young enough to have sat in the classes of the teacher-"commandos"; sixteen seemed the average age. But Sok Khieu, who was on my helicopter, manfully said he was fourteen. He looked younger. He wore a khaki shirt that hung to his knees; the pants beneath were split from top to bottom. He carried his belongings tied into a red and white checkered cloth, the Cambodian multipurpose *khrama*, which serves as a scarf, head covering, or carry-all. He opened it to let me see all that he owned: two plastic bags of cooked rice, a tin plate and spoon, and a handful or two of loose rifle bullets. A straw mat to sleep on and a rusty and dirty old single-shot rifle of Soviet manufacture completed his gear. He hadn't fired the rifle yet, the boy told me, and I thought that was good. In its neglected condition, the rifle was just as likely to blow up in Khieu's face as to send a bullet toward an enemy.

The fighting around Kompong Thom grew very heavy and no doubt killed or maimed many of the boy soldiers. And being seriously wounded more often than not meant a sentence of death; medical services for soldiers or ordinary Cambodians in general were minimal in Phnom Penh and almost nonexistent in the field.

In fact, the Cambodian military lacked almost everything to make war except men. As the army grew in numbers, the deficit in weapons for them to bear grew steadily. This was so even after limited American arms shipments began to arrive and would grow gradually to massive proportions, as step by step President Nixon adopted Lon Nol as a full-fledged client. While the United States mounted its two-month incursion into Cambodia in May and June, there were still Cambodian infantrymen going into battle bearing no arms but two or three hand grenades. After they had thrown them, the Cambodians would stand defenseless before the enemy. While American troops in Vietnam's Mekong Delta were driving battle-hardened North Vietnamese regulars across the Cambodian border, I talked with a Cambodian brigade commander. His unit was meeting the onslaught of the Vietnamese, who were retreating in good order toward the Cambodians to avoid clashing with the heavily equipped Americans. "Of forty-seven hundred men in the brigade, three thousand are armed only with grenades," Major Thach Poch told me.

In those early months of the war in 1970, the Cambodian leaders' minds were focused on one big question: when will the Americans come to our aid without limits? I don't believe that there was a prior American commitment to do so and have seen no evidence that the overthrow of Sihanouk was engineered by the Central Intelligence Agency. On the contrary, since 1969 Washington had reason to be pleased with Sihanouk's hardening attitude toward the Vietnamese Communists, who were extending their border sanctuaries and flexing their muscles toward Cambodians, by his acceptance of some American military action on his side of the border and his agreement to the resumption of diplomatic relations.

This does not preclude a possibility that ground-level American agents, who had close connections with the large ethnic Cambodian minority in South Vietnam and recruited thousands of them as mercenaries for the American Special Forces, had on their own assured some of their Cambodian contacts of certain support if they got rid of the prince, whom they considered a Communist stooge. The political unsophistication of some American intelligence operatives and "psychological warfare experts" in Indochina was on a par with the naïveté of Cambodian military men and politicians.

In the Lon Nol leadership's befuddlement in the face of the consequences of the overthrow of Sihanouk, I could observe almost daily change in its expectations. It began with vague optimism that the Vietnamese Communists could be persuaded to modify their involvement in Cambodia and culminated in a fervent desire for American intervention as the only way out of the mess into which it had plunged its country.

On March 25, 1970, a week after the coup against Sihanouk, Prince Sirik Matak in our first meeting placed all his hopes in international support to obtain the withdrawal of the Vietnamese Communists and the preservation of Cambodian neutrality. Five days later, in his first news conference, Lon Nol first replied "Certainly not!" in response to the question of whether he would accept American military aid. When asked the same question moments later, he amended his answer: he would accept aid from any friendly country, and he regarded all countries with which Cambodia maintained diplomatic relations as friends. In any event, Cambodia would never request military intervention from anyone. Four days after the conference, an official acting as an anonymous but authorized contact between the government and some foreign correspondents sought me out to show me an official transcript of the prime minister's press conference just published by the government's press agency. It contained a question that had never been asked and an answer that Lon Nol had never given. The question was, would Cambodia call for American troops? And the answer put in the prime minister's mouth was, a friendly country might be allowed to intervene, but only if Cambodia requested it.

By April 14, 1970, Lon Nol, casting aside all hope for neutrality, made a surprise, desperate public appeal in a radio address in Cambodian and French for "all unconditional foreign aid, from wherever it may come, for the salvation of the nation." A week later he followed it up with an urgent personal letter to Nixon requesting arms aid and the dispatch of America's Cambodian mercenaries in Vietnam to fight in Cambodia. The military situation was "critical," said Lon Non, the prime minister's brother, who disclosed the letter to me. Two days later the first weapons from America arrived before dawn — three planeloads of Chinese-made small arms, captured in Vietnam. Before a week had passed, I saw on the streets of Phnom Penh smartly uniformed soldiers whose officers spoke English, not French like Cambodian regulars, and who punctuated their replies to questions as American troops did, with many a "Sir," and said "Say again" when they hadn't understood. The Cambodian mercenaries from Vietnam had arrived, to be put under the command of the Cambodian Army. Lon Non, the deskbound major of military police, was named commander of this elite combat force. Before too many months had passed his brother promoted him to colonel, as a brief way station in his rise to general.

I saw Lon Non on the evening of April 30, 1970, and mentioned in passing that the American radio in Saigon had announced it would be transmitting live an important speech on Indochina by President Nixon in Washington that evening, which would with the twelve-hour time change be early morning of May 1 in Phnom Penh. Lon Non asked eagerly if I would please listen and tell him what Nixon had said. Didn't the prime minister have speakers of English on his staff who could listen and report? I asked. No, said his brother, he didn't. I agreed to drop by the following morning, requesting in exchange to be taken afterward to his brother. I wanted to ask the prime minister to comment on Nixon's speech. I was still listening to Nixon in the hotel garden when a Lon Non aide tapped me on the shoulder to tell me that he was waiting to rush me to his boss. Nixon had just announced that at that very moment American troops were fighting on Cambodian soil and would continue their incursion, to a depth of thirty kilometers, until June 30, 1970. Their objective was, Nixon said, to "attack the headquarters for the entire Communist military operation in South Vietnam" and forestall "massive attacks" from Cambodian bases on American troops in Vietnam.

At Lon Non's office, no longer a back room of the Defense Ministry but an ample villa on one of the capital's main avenues, I found not only the major but a group of about a dozen men, whom he described as a "committee of intellectuals," and who were waiting to be briefed by me. They broke into cheers at the news. "I approve with applause," said Lon Non, doing just that. The others joined in the clapping. Lon Non rose to go to inform his brother. He asked me to wait outside the prime minister's villa; he would call me when his brother was ready to see me.

Just at that moment, an American embassy car delivered the chargé d'affaires, Lloyd M. Rives. Sheaves of paper trailed from the jacket pockets of his white suit. They were an advance summary of Nixon's text, cabled to the embassy from Washington. This important document was delivered to the embassy hours after it arrived. In fact, the mailman brought it while the chargé was listening to the speech at his residence. Even in times of emergency, no one manned Cambodia's central post office between two o'clock and seven o'clock in the morning. The small, intentionally low-profile embassy, reopened less than a year earlier by Rives, did not have its own communications channels. Its coded messages were handled by the Australian embassy; other traffic, like the Nixon text, was sent on the ordinary commercial channel received by the post office and delivered after the post office opened for business. I don't know whether Lon Nol received the first news of his country's invasion by the United States from his brother, who had learned it from me, or from the American chargé.

Unless the prime minister and his brother were better liars than I think they were, their surprise at the American intervention was genuine. Lon Nol affirmed emphatically that he had not been consulted in advance, and with clearly less sincerity said he was considering lodging a protest with Washington. This was a violation of Cambodia's territorial integrity, said Lon Nol, comparing it to what the Vietnamese Communists, South Vietnam, and the United States had been doing for years. But the "Vietcong are the first cause," he said, and then, with a laugh, the Americans are now acting "a little like the Vietcong." It was clear that the prime minister was glad that the United States had taken a major action in his regime's defense, but he repeated his request for arms instead of men. "We would like our friends to give us the arms to do the operation ourselves," he said. Nixon had made it clear in his speech that he judged the Cambodian military incapable of effectively using the extensive armaments necessary to perform the mission that he had assigned to the American forces.

Whatever Lon Nol's reaction, he and his entourage had once again proved how remote they were from the harsh world in which they lived. However dire the emergency, and however high their hopes for American support, no one had bothered to listen to a Nixon speech, a declaration of crucial national interest, announced well in advance, that they could have tuned into on any ordinary radio. And to add another note of unreality, the prime minister repeated that he was still ready to negotiate with the Communists for withdrawal of their troops, but his demands would now also include compensation for the destruction of property such as "houses and bridges" that their aggression was causing.

Lon Nol wasted little time in openly embracing the American invasion. On its second day I received a surprise visit from a friend, Senator Benigno Aquino Jr., the Philippine opposition leader, whom the regime of President Marcos murdered in 1983. He had been sent on a fact-finding mission by a Senate committee and had just seen Lon Nol. The prime minister had told him that the American action was a positive response to Cambodia's appeal for help to restore its neutrality. Aquino was shocked by Lon Nol's naïveté. The prime minister had insisted that there was no coordination even now with the American military and said that he was unperturbed by not being informed by the Americans of the progress of the fighting. "What world are they living in?" Aquino later asked of me. And two days later the Cambodian government publicly expressed its thanks to the United States, calling the invasion an act of assistance "in the defense of the neutrality of Cambodia, violated by the North Vietnamese."

Cambodia had now become, like Laos, fully part of the Indochinese theater of the war that pitted the United States against North Vietnam and relegated those on whose soil the war was fought, in greater or lesser degree, to function as minor actors and inexhaustible cannon fodder. No people seemed more minor or more expendable than the Cambodians.

7

Murder of the Scapegoats: 1970

*I*N THEIR FRUSTRATION at their inability to repel the Communist attacks, Cambodians took refuge in one of the oldest and ugliest ways of venting their impotent fury — murderous ethnic hatred. The target was in their midst, the Vietnamese minority of about 400,000 living in Cambodia. The pogroms and other abominations of which this minority was victim in full view of the international public contributed greatly to the scantness of sympathy and humanitarian assistance for Cambodia and its suffering population during the five years of the war that began in 1970.

Many of the Vietnamese families under attack had been established in Cambodia for generations; Cambodia is thinly populated, while the Vietnamese have always been pushing at the edges of their habitat under the pressures of an ever-growing population. They found an outlet on the soil of their western neighbor. The Vietnamese people's demographic history is the unending drive southward of a rapidly increasing population, from their ancestors' origins in China's mountainous southern provinces of Yunnan and Guangxi to the shores of the South

China Sea. In the seventeenth century, having defeated and made extinct the Kingdom of Champa in what is now central Vietnam, the Vietnamese pursued their advance at the expense of the weakened Khmer kingdom. They wrested land from feeble and internally divided Cambodian dynasties and colonized it. Saigon fell under Vietnamese suzerainty. By the middle of the eighteenth century the Vietnamese had reached the tip of the Indochinese Peninsula, the end of their long march from China, and seized from Cambodia most of the Mekong Delta, roughly along the lines of today's borders. To this day the border remains disputed.

Under French rule, large numbers of Vietnamese were settled in Cambodia by the colonial power. They worked as petty civil servants, teachers, and artisans, and later also as plantation laborers. The French administrators had a higher regard for the Vietnamese's aptitude for modern skills than they did for that of the Cambodians and Laotians.

Bad blood has always existed among Cambodians toward the Vietnamese. The Vietnamese became the Cambodians' neighbors only when, coming from the north, they descended upon their lands. Cultural and linguistic differences between the cultures are great. Cambodians represent the "Indo" part of Indochina, a region subject to the cross-currents of the great Indian and Chinese civilizations, and the Vietnamese the "China." The Vietnamese responded to understandable Cambodian resentment of their presence with thinly disguised disdain. Unlike the large Chinese minority, which was by and large successful in integrating with the Khmers, the Vietnamese made no effort to do so, and it is unlikely that such efforts would have been welcomed.

Official Cambodian discrimination against the Vietnamese, who were largely craftsmen, petty traders, and office and domestic workers in Phnom Penh, and fishermen and truck farmers in the countryside, existed already under Sihanouk's rule. Worried over the virtual Vietnamese monopoly in the skilled trades, the prince enacted a list of eighteen occupations that were barred to them. The list included mechanic, barber, driver, and fisherman. But even government ministers, respecting the tried-and-true skills of the minority, continued to confide their cars or refrigerators to the experienced Vietnamese mechanics whom they trusted and had their hair cut by Vietnamese barbers, who brought their scissors to their homes in plain, unmarked bags. Despite the "eighteen métiers," the Vietnamese of Cambodia saw in Sihanouk's rule a measure of protection against what they feared might become the unrestrained envy and hatred of the majority around them.

Trouble began even before the prince's overthrow. The rioters who sacked the two Vietnamese Communist embassies — those of North Vietnam and the Provisional Revolution Government of the South — a week before the coup had certainly not acted spontaneously but were organized, possibly even with the consent of Sihanouk. He was growing impatient with the Communist troops' growing numbers along his borders and wanted to heighten dramatically the pressure on the Vietnamese to soften their militancy in Cambodia. But what followed later that day and evening in Russey Keo, a Phnom Penh neighborhood of Vietnamese character on the banks of the Tonle Sap River, had all the earmarks of a rabble running riot. The outrages were directed against an almost exclusively Roman Catholic community, which should have been immune from suspicion of Communist sympathies. The parish church and its annex a few hundred yards farther down the river were invaded by mobs, and many of their stained-glass windows and statuary were clubbed into shards. After the churches, the rioters ransacked and vandalized many of the family homes around them, carrying away whatever possessions seemed worth the effort. The police arrived late and did nothing.

From that day on, the fear among the Vietnamese of Phnom Penh, thought to number about 200,000, was such as to remind me viscerally of the mood of Jews in my boyhood in Germany from the day that Hitler came to power. Fear mounted steadily following the coup, as the new regime's propaganda quickly blurred any distinction between the Communist invaders and Vietnamese in general. Within a week of the coup, the "Thought of the Day" of Norodom Sihanouk at the top of the front page of *Le Courrier Phnompenhois* had been replaced by "Viet Cong, Sworn Enemies; Vietnamese, Hereditary Enemies of the Cambodians." The government radio in Khmer vituperated shrilly on the "hereditary enemy" theme. Many who could afford the necessary bribes bought their way out to South Vietnam, where neither home nor job awaited them.

On April 10, 1970, three weeks after the coup that overthrew Sihanouk, the first news of a massacre of Vietnamese residents by Lon Nol's army became public, although there is reason to suspect that it wasn't the first to take place. More than one hundred children, women, and men, who had been driven from their homes and detained in the yard of a farming cooperative in the village of Prasot near the Vietnamese border, were gunned down. Many more were wounded. Like most Vietnamese in the regions most immediately threatened by the invaders, they had been rounded up in an atmosphere of hysteria and placed under detention in any available locality or open space. Their homes became the prey of looters, and military and police were prominent among the pillagers. When Western reporters came upon the scene of the slaughter, the unapologetic government felt obliged to offer an explanation. The victims had been caught in a cross fire during a Vietcong attack, it announced in a threadbare lie. Prasot rests astride on the Phnom Penh–Saigon highway, which made the massacre impossible to hide from the press; what went on in the many villages off the main roads can only be imagined.

Terror among Phnom Penh's Vietnamese rose to a fever pitch when on the day after the Prasot massacre the Lon Nol regime staged a meticulously organized patriotic mass rally in the Olympic Stadium, in the presence of Lon Nol, Sirik Matak, and most of their government. For four hours, marching contingents from schools, ministries, and state enterprises trooped into the arena to a steady beat of martial music. Instead of weapons, many of the marchers carried clubs, with which, they told me, they wanted to beat the Vietnamese. They said that most of the Vietnamese living in Cambodia favored the Vietcong and were enemies of Cambodia. In fact, the great majority of the Vietnamese of the cities and towns were happy not to have to choose sides in Vietnam's war but tended to favor, without enthusiasm, Saigon. However, among the workers on the French-owned rubber plantations along the border, Communist recruiters had been active; how voluntary was the support of many workers for the Vietcong was is an open question. The conclusion of what Lon Nol described as the "March of National Concord" was a noisy pageant that depicted the history of Cambodia as a constant struggle against Vietnamese aggression and the greed and mendacity of the monarchy. In its strident chauvinism and xenophobia, the rally stirred in me unpleasant reminiscences from my childhood among the Nazis.

Few in the Vietnamese community went to work that day, fearing that the rally might set off new incidents of violence. As of the night before, the government had put the Vietnamese under a 6:00 P.M. to 6:00 A.M. curfew, asserting that Vietcong sympathizers were stepping up "subversive" activities among them. A state of paranoia about such imagined activities had been attained. The day before, Lon Non had told me that he had placed a Vietnamese businessman under arrest because he was receiving "coded telegrams" from abroad. He showed me an example. It carried, after the sender's signature, a string of numbers. So did most of the telegrams I received from my newspaper. They were repeats of all the numbers that appeared in the text, as a kind of insurance against errors. Lon Non seemed unconvinced, until I brought him examples of similar "coded" telegrams from the *New York Times*. He would have the businessman released, he said, unless there was other evidence against him. I doubt he did. It became plain later that Lon Non was playing a leading role in organizing the atrocities that followed. Mass detentions of Vietnamese, including women and children, began immediately after the rally. At a Catholic school, La Providence, frightened prisoners told me that men were being taken away, perhaps for questioning, but were not coming back.

Two days after the rally, grisly evidence of the fate of some Vietnamese men began to appear about forty miles from the capital, where the Phnom Penh–Saigon road reaches the Mekong, and travelers cross on ferries. For about a week, the broad, surging river carried a flotsam of bodies of Vietnamese men in civilian clothes. I took the ferry five days after the ghastly flow began and saw a group of five bodies tied together by their feet with rattan cord, as well as four bodies, their hands tied, floating singly toward Vietnam, about thirty miles downstream. A French missionary priest stood on the riverbank counting, as he said he had done since the beginning. He had counted about one thousand bodies, he said. One day he saw about a hundred during a single crossing on the ferry. "We don't know their names; let us at least know their number," he said, his tears flowing. (One of the cruelest ironies of the war was that a little later this man of infinite compassion was found dead, his throat slashed, after the South Vietnamese Army drove out the Vietnamese Communist forces from the crossing town of Neak Luong, which they had seized from its small Cambodian garrison.) The Vietnamese war had annexed Cambodia, after Laos, to its battlefield.

The village madman entertained passengers waiting at the crossing by imitating the grotesque postures of the dead. He mimed their killing by shooting, and concluded by playing a lilting tune on a bamboo pipe.

The fool's crude pantomime was accurate: the Mekong's grim burden was virtually all the men from a large Vietnamese settlement on the small island of Chrui Changwar, across the river from Phnom Penh. They had been rounded up one night over the tears and pleading of their wives and mothers, sisters and children, and handed over to the Cambodian Navy. An aged invalid and a man whose daughter was married to a Cambodian were the only men left. Navy craft transported the prisoners down the river to one of the many small islands between the capital and the ferry crossing. There they were mowed down by machine guns and dumped into the Mekong. The first bodies were sighted at Neak Luong the following day. On Sunday I went to attend mass at the Carmelite chapel near the Church of the Apostles Peter and Paul on Chrui Changwar. Mass could not be celebrated in the church; the authorities had seized it to serve as a detention center for "Vietcong suspects" from the capital. Fourteen women and four boys formed the congregation. Grief stained the women's faces, and the mass seemed more a threnody than a celebration. A French Benedictine monk looked pityingly at the women when the French priest chanted of those who had left this world. An overwhelming majority of Cambodia's Catholics were Vietnamese; Buddhism is too firmly rooted among the Khmers to have made Cambodia a fertile field for proselytism.

In April and May 1970, atrocity reports continued to reach Phnom Penh and were met with painful indifference by officials and ordinary Cambodians. Late one afternoon, a tale of tragedy reached me from the provincial capital of Takeo, about fifty miles south of Phnom Penh. Time was short, because after dark the road was thoroughly insecure. What I found was worse than what I had expected. Moans were the only sounds I heard as I approached. A sickly smell hung over the scene, a freestanding building with a large open space at its center. It was a school; the open area had served as an outdoor classroom. On its raised floor there sat or lay about forty or fifty Vietnamese men of all ages and teenage boys. Three bodies — a woman, a boy, a man — lay partly covered by straw mats. Four men, clearly at death's door, agonized unattended, eyes vacant, flies feeding on their wounds.

About half of the men were wounded; no one tended them. No bandages or medicines were in view. The clothes of the living and the dead were spattered with blood. There were pools on the floor and stains on the low walls. Mounds of soiled clothing and sandals were scattered about. Hundreds of bullet holes scarred the walls and posts sustaining the roof. The Cambodian soldiers milling about the grounds made no attempt to bar me.

"Take us away or we will all die tonight," an elderly man whispered hoarsely as I mounted the few steps, fighting against nausea. A massacre had taken place the preceding night, the survivors told me. Many spoke fluent French, a mark of their middle-class background. Takeo's commercial life had been active, and the Vietnamese played a vital part. About 150 of them had been rounded up and dumped into the school building four days earlier. Each evening, their wives and children were allowed to bring them food. It was at that time the day before that a group of soldiers approached and without warning raised their automatic rifles and fired point-blank into the cluster of men and their relatives. Three times after that first salvo they came back, and three times they fired again into the living, the wounded, and the dead. Then a truck came and took away the dead. Perhaps not all those carried away were already dead, a survivor said, emphasizing "already." The survivors said they had numbered 150 before the massacre and estimated the victims at 100. A fellow reporter who had been there two days earlier confirmed that there had been about 150 detainees.

The Vietnamese survivors were terrorized about what lay ahead, and with good reason. The soldiers in the school grounds, which were still littered with the cartridge cases of the previous evening, looked on with indifference. "The others did it," a young soldier told me, unasked. "They're back in town." He smiled the Khmer smile. By way of explanation, some soldiers said that the Vietcong had raided Takeo two nights earlier and wounded a number of civilians. The survivors made pleading gestures, raising their hands, palms joined in Buddhist prayer.

"Get a truck to take us to Phnom Penh," one pleaded. Others echoed the request silently, pleading with their eyes.

I rushed back to Phnom Penh and into Lon Non's office. I pleaded with him to protect the survivors. I threatened him: now that he knew what had happened, I would hold him responsible in print for what might still occur in Takeo. I urged him to send a truck and bring the survivors to be cared for by the Vietnamese community in Phnom Penh, most of whom were also in detention. He promised he would do what he could, but the road was unsafe now and the telephone link had been cut during the Vietcong raid. No further violence was done to the survivors, the Vietnamese informed me over the next few days, and eventually the prisoners were evacuated to South Vietnam.

Like other foreigners, I used every possible contact with important officials, including Sirik Matak and Lon Non, to urge them to tell Cambodians not to interpret the public condemnations of the Vietnamese aggressors as declarations of an open season on the peaceful Vietnamese living among them. No such appeal was ever made. As the certainty of widespread atrocities grew, so did the silence of the regime and the ostentatious indifference of private Cambodians, even open-minded, French-educated members of the elite. The responses of friends and acquaintances were little different from those of officials: You foreigners don't understand the historical context. The Vietnamese have for centuries done unspeakable things to Cambodians and would do worse if today they were in the Cambodians' position. Believe us, we know that the Vietnamese here have long been thoroughly infiltrated by Vietcong agents. We have to defend ourselves.

Despite a strong international backlash in public opinion as the massacre reports multiplied, the Lon Nol regime never hesitated to give itself a black eye in full view of the world. On an early April morning in 1970, soldiers descended the bank of the Tonle Sap River in Phnom Penh and cut loose dozens of floating houses, a large waterborne village of Vietnamese who had lived there peacefully for decades. With most of the families still within, tugboats pulled and pushed the simple wooden homes down river, out of sight of the capital. We have to do it, said Lon Non, when I went to raise the issue. We no longer know how to assure the security of Phnom Penh with these potential enemies and subversives among us, he said. Even at that early stage, Lon Nol was in charge of everything that was considered a security issue in the capital. His authority later spanned all of Cambodia that remained under Phnom Penh's control.

Soldiers were deployed along the riverbank to keep the dwellers of the floating houses from slipping into the city. I made use of the somewhat colonial license still accorded people of European origin to drive a number of families from their boats to the houses of their French employers for safety. Most of the French-owned enterprises employed Vietnamese in their most responsible positions, and French families were usually served by Vietnamese women as cooks and nursemaids for their children.

As the roundups of Vietnamese men continued, business-men, including Cambodians, began to complain that their book-keepers, chief mechanics, or cooks and headwaiters were gone. Cars or air conditioners went unrepaired for long periods, and Vietnamese shopkeepers held bargain sales before lowering their shutters for good. The capital's life slowed considerably with the loss of Vietnamese skills.

As the military situation continued to worsen throughout 1970, Cambodia's dependence on South Vietnamese forces, who ran roughshod over Cambodians and often behaved like crude conquerors, finally gave the defenseless minority a strong advo-cate. In late April a senior Saigon diplomat came to Phnom Penh to lay the basis for a resumption of diplomatic relations, which Sihanouk had broken in 1963. The diplomat demanded publicly that Cambodia "preserve the lives and property" of the minority and received official assurances to that effect. The Saigon gov-ernment quickly began a major military-humanitarian operation to repatriate those who wanted to seek the relative safety that Vietnam at war would offer. Because of general road insecurity, the evacuation was mainly carried out by the South Vietnamese Navy. It transported tens of thousands of Vietnamese to South Vietnam, while at the same time conducting military operations to clear the Mekong's banks of guerrillas.

When in October 1970 Cambodia declared itself a republic, the houses of the Vietnamese village on Chrui Changwar were crumbling, and the rain-swollen river was carrying away their ruins, as it had borne toward Vietnam its murdered men. Sister Gertrude de Notre Dame, the aged Belgian mother superior of the Carmelite convent, said her seventeen nuns were the only Vietnamese who remained on Chrui Changwar. Phnom Penh had been ethnically purified.

But Saigon did not repatriate all of the minority. In provincial towns, particularly in the west of Cambodia, which remained largely untouched by the fighting, Vietnamese remained under detention, in cruel conditions and unseen by the outside world, from 1970 until the Khmer Rouge victory five years later. Then, as happened in France in 1939, when Jewish, Socialist, and Communist refugees from Germany and Austria were interned at the outbreak of war as "enemy aliens," the Khmers Rouges, like the Germans, found their victims already conveniently concentrated and ready to be exterminated. Few members of the Vietnamese minority survived in Cambodia.

8

A Republic Stitched Together: 1970

O N OCTOBER 8, 1970, Madame Sim Song Lung was awakened by the telephone at two o'clock in the morning. An official informed her that Parliament had just decided what the flag of the Khmer Republic, to be proclaimed the following day, was to look like. It must be consecrated by vestal virgins, the official said, hinting that Prime Minister Lon Nol himself had declared this to be an ancient Khmer tradition. The government must have thought that a girls' high school like the Lycée Neany, of which Madame Sim Song Lung was the principal, offered the appropriate assurances. So would she hasten to school and prepare for the fashioning of the republic's first flag, which the prime minister himself would hoist up the flagpole at the proclamation ceremony?

At dawn a group of students from the Fine Arts University, who had also been summoned, came to the school and translated the Parliament's description into a design. Madame Lung rushed to the Central Market and waited for the first shops to open. She quickly bought yards of red, blue, and white satin. Back in the school's large assembly hall, she gathered nine students who she presumed met the prime minister's moral qualifications and set them to work. With Madame Lung hovering mother hen–like over them, they stitched onto the huge blue flag a large red field in the upper left-hand corner. Then, using a cardboard template made by the art students, they cut an outline of the three main towers of Angkor Wat out of white satin and sewed it onto the red. The temple of Angkor Wat is the most salient symbol of the Khmer monarchy, which was to be abolished the following day, not for five thousand years, as Lon Nol had said he expected, but, as it turned out, for twenty-three. In October 1970 the emblem was also a wrenching reminder that for the last four months Angkor Wat, with all its splendid outlying monuments, had been in the hands of the conquering North Vietnamese Army.

Madame Lung measured out the spaces between three white stars at the top of the flag, and the vestals basted them on. I inquired in the course of the day from a number of officials what the stars represented. The surmises ranged from "Liberté, Egalité et Fraternité" to the three stars on Lieutenant General Lon Nol's uniform. No one, including members, knew what Parliament had had in mind. While the girls sewed, an aged and bent master of rites, a layman wearing horn-rimmed spectacles, an ankle-length black skirt, a white tunic, and a cigarette dangling from a corner of his mouth, supervised the installation of a Buddhist altar. Rugs were placed before it, and at its foot silver bowls of bananas, oranges, and grapes. Tall candles were lit. In a corner of the hall, two old women wrapped traditional white sarongs with lace sashes around twelve of the youngest students. The girls giggled and fidgeted; the women chided.

With only one side of the flag sewn, four monks in orange robes came to bless it. The master of rites improvised a ceremony, like a theatrical director at a first rehearsal. He told the monks to chant mantras and made the twelve girls kneel around the flag holding lotus blossoms. Then he ordered the girls to wrap the flag about a tall gold-and-silver candlestick, then to unfurl it again. The monks showered jasmine blossoms over the girls and the flag. The girls giggled. The master of rites pronounced the ceremony concluded and the flag ready to flutter on the tall flagpole that was being erected at that moment on the grassy square between the Royal Palace and the Tonle Sap River.

On the square, a large work crew, commanded by two lieutenant colonels, was putting up signs renaming it "Place de la République." A tall pedestal was being erected in the middle of the lawn for a republican symbol yet to be devised, one of the colonels said, and five principles were to be engraved onto the base. The principles were as yet unknown, and the pedestal remained blank the following morning when Lon Nol ran up the flag on its shaky pole. The republican national anthem was sounded for the first time in its new role; the snappy tune had been lifted from a French operetta of the nineteenth century. Lon Nol and Sirik Matak, who in July had assumed unlimited powers for the duration of the anti-Communist war, each received, served in a golden bowl, an additional general's star. The entire ceremony was to have been conducted to the booming of a 101-gun salute fired from a gunboat on the Tonle Sap. It ended after seven shots had been heard; the last misfired, injuring five sailors.

The way in which the Khmer Republic was born in 1970 — last-minute improvisations, borrowed forms devoid of meaningful content, and destructive blunders in the execution of plans — marked its life of four and a half years. At the time the republic was proclaimed, about half of its territory was already occupied by North Vietnamese troops, Cambodian guerrillas organized by the Vietnamese, and, gaining in strength rapidly, purely Cambodian units formed by the Khmer Rouge leadership. They were the nucleus of Pol Pot's forces, the army that conquered the country in 1975 and the "cadres" that tyrannized and decimated the Cambodian people.

As Cambodia's Communist-occupied territories grew larger, much of their populations fled to Phnom Penh in the hope of finding safety from the fighting, above all from the most destructive American bombing. The capital also offered a hope of shelter and the bare necessities of life. Quickly Phnom Penh, the once remarkably well-tended capital, became pockmarked by jerry-built slums. Entire families lived on sidewalks or public patches of grass. The outstretched hands of begging children tugged at one's trouser legs or pinched one's arms. Cambodian women and girls took over from the banished Vietnamese the sad métier of prostitution. Petty crime flourished.

Shortly before the Khmer Republic was proclaimed, I met a Cambodian army lieutenant who had just escaped from the Communist-occupied zone after six weeks as a prisoner of war. He reported that even in provinces close to Vietnam, 70 percent of the Vietnamese-commanded forces were freshly recruited Cambodians. Their motivation was simple, Lieutenant Nop Nem — who in his premilitary role had been the most popular star in the flood of cheap soap-opera movies — said: escape from the steady bombing, strafing, and napalming by American, South Vietnamese, and Cambodian planes, which was causing heavy civilian casualties. Yet the government steadfastly maintained that the Vietnamese met little success in recruiting Cambodians. It was not only the Vietnamese Communists' actions that were responsible for the mounting appeal of the revolutionary cause. The South Vietnamese military, who were campaigning in eastern Cambodia against their Communist foes, acted as though they were in their own country, and vitiated their frequent military successes by excessive violence, needless destruction of civilian property, and limitless looting.

The South Vietnamese soldiers rode roughshod over eastern and southeastern Cambodia until early 1972, when the North Vietnamese Army stepped up its offensive campaigns in Vietnam and drew them back home. Their attitude expressed frustration and anger. These sentiments had certainly been stored up through the years of French rule and American intervention on Vietnamese soil, when Vietnamese saw their country serve as another's "area of operations," as American military language called it. In Cambodia, the South Vietnamese Army felt it-self the older brother to the Cambodian army in its country. It was a feeling it knew but too well on the receiving end. And their looting? The South Vietnamese were grossly underpaid, and constant inflation was making life for their families back home an ever-growing hardship. They stole for the most part things of small value they couldn't afford back home. But they stole from people who were just as poor as themselves.

Underlying their lack of discipline in Cambodia was surely something much deeper. It was a clear disregard for Cambodi-ans. To the Vietnamese, their western neighbors are not an ob-session, as the Vietnamese clearly are to Cambodians. They responded to the Cambodians' open hatred, which found such violent expression in the pogroms still fresh in the minds of the South Vietnamese when they went to war in Cambodia, with condescending disregard or disdain. Their pejorative term for Cambodians, occasionally used, is *tho*; it conveys a meaning of "rude and rustic." Conversely, the Cambodian pejorative for Vietnamese, *yuon*, is constantly used in ordinary conversation and is much more hostile than condescending. A note of racism, based on skin color, is also not uncommon in Vietnamese atti-tudes toward their neighbors. Giving a Vietnamese naval lieu-tenant a lift in Phnom Penh one day, I pointed out, in passing, a street of many bars. "The girls here don't interest me," he scoffed dryly. "Too black."

Much of Cambodians' bad blood toward the Vietnamese military derived from the Vietnamese's lack of respect for their Cambodian counterparts, which resulted in a critical absence of coordination. The South Vietnamese forces were, by Asian stan-dards, superbly equipped by their American sponsors. Cambo-dia's troops, in the years in which the South Vietnamese fought in Cambodia, had very little, and what they had came from the dregs of the armories of many nations — China, the Soviet Union and its European dependencies, France, the United States. The Vietnamese uniforms were as truly uniform as the weapons they carried; Cambodian troops showed as confusing a variety in their clothes as in their arms and equipment. And the Vietnamese troops left Cambodians in no doubt over their sense of superiority. In addition, Vietnamese officers had a distinct advantage over Cambodians through their long experience in war and their higher level of tactical training with the help of their American "advisers."

The war in Cambodia was barely a month old in May 1970 when I was witness to a series of minor disasters that forecast clearly what the military relationship between the two ill-matched allies would turn out to be. A sequence of Cambodian military misjudgments left a handful of Vietnamese officers coolly polite to their counterparts but scathingly condescending in their asides to me. A Vietnamese flotilla had steamed up the Mekong to Kompong Cham, a provincial capital, to ferry to safety in Vietnam about 3,500 Vietnamese residents who had been rounded up during the days of anti-Vietnamese hysteria and jammed together in internment in the river town's stadium. The convoy of sleek American-provided river patrol craft escorting large troop carriers arrived from Phnom Penh in early afternoon.

Earlier in the day, Cambodian troops had been sporadically shelling the small town of Tonle Bet on the opposite bank. Their commander explained to me that it was occupied by the Vietcong, and his troops had been unable to drive them out. He feared the Communists would shell the boats when they had loaded the refugees and were heading downstream. The flotilla's commanders clambered up the steep riverbank to greet him. I was called on to interpret, as the young Vietnamese naval officers, American-trained, spoke no French. The Cambodian commander, Lieutenant Colonel Jean Littaye, decided to impress his South Vietnamese guests with a final effort to dislodge the Communist enemy from the town on the opposite bank. He sent two companies of infantry across the Mekong slightly upstream from Tonle Bet. Ashore, they moved toward the town under cover of mortar and rocket fire, but short of their objective they halted and gave up the attempt. The Vietnamese officers wondered why, as there seemed to be no enemy fire coming from the town.

Colonel Littaye told his South Vietnamese allies that he would have to sacrifice Tonle Bet for the safety of their convoy. The Vietnamese officers looked worriedly at the river, on which their ships were standing by. They were in the line of fire. The flotilla commander eagerly offered fire support from his escort craft, but the Cambodian colonel said it wasn't needed. He signaled the heavy mortars and recoilless rifles positioned near us to open fire on the town across the broad Mekong. The first mortar round fell drastically short. It struck into the river about fifty feet from an escort boat. The Vietnamese officer looked at his counterpart and then at me and bit his tongue. "Now the big ones will raise their voices," said Colonel Littaye. But the first round from the Chinese-made recoilless rifles also struck short, falling a little behind a group of Cambodian troops who had just disembarked from the river ferry that had served as their makeshift landing craft.

In pained embarrassment, Colonel Littaye ordered the barrage halted. There was no counterfire from Tonle Bet, leading the Vietnamese officers to surmise that the Vietcong had withdrawn hours ago, so as not to become targets of the flotilla's superior firepower. The South Vietnamese took leave, clearly in a hurry to get their ships into safer waters, where they needed to fear only the Communists' guns. They departed for Phnom Penh under clouds of black smoke billowing from Tonle Bet, a Cambodian town being destroyed by Cambodian fire by a colonel eager to impress his allies with the uncertain might of his arms — whether the enemy was in the town or not.

With the American army out at the end of June 1970, never to return, Cambodians felt they had been, as the catch phrase of the Nixon administration had it, "Vietnamized." They saw their country being turned into a battleground by Vietnamese foes and friends and hardly knew which to hate and fear more. With

Cambodia an annexed theater of Vietnam's civil war, the destructive power of the United States Air Force was the most effective weapon on Cambodia's behalf. Horrendously effective. The Lon Nol regime and its military commanders seemed not to worry about the appalling cost of American bombing, strafing, napalming, and defoliating to their country. But as those who fled to escape from it straggled in ever greater number into Phnom Penh, their presence and their tales weighed heavily on public morale.

The refugees brought with them reports, still strenuously denied by the government, that many villagers were joining the Communist guerrillas. It sank into many a Cambodian consciousness that what had begun as a foreign invasion, followed by the intervention of other foreigners, was rapidly turning into an all-out civil war. The patriotic fervor of a restricted circle of politically aware Cambodians that had followed the seizure of power by a new regime promising an end to Sihanouk's one-man rule and corruption, gave way to the awareness of a long and destructive conflict. The great majority of Cambodians seemed passive and resigned. Privileged Cambodians, particularly those with family abroad, mainly in France, began actively looking for a way out.

The government had hoped for aid from its regional neighbors, notably Thailand, which shares, albeit to a less morbid degree, Cambodia's distaste for Vietnam. But by the time the kingless kingdom became a republic, it had received from Thailand in military assistance only the loan of five light American T-28 trainer-bombers while the United States overhauled Cambodia's own, and the gift of ten thousand pairs of black socks, five thousand raincoats, and twenty thousand mosquito nets for the army.

9

The Mystical Marshal: 1970–1975

WHAT WERE THE PRINCIPAL CAUSES, in addition to the ruthless effectiveness of it enemies, of the Khmer Republic's brief and disastrous life and tragic end? Two seemed dominant to me, and grew more so as the war wore on. First was the unfathomable melange of mysticism and dictatorial nonleadership of Lon Nol, combined with the relentlessly ambitious and divisive machinations of Lon Non. And second was America's cruel exploitation of Cambodia's uncomprehending, blind confidence that the United States would protect it and never let it down.

Lon Nol was a Sihanouk loyalist until the night before the coup that overthrew Sihanouk, when Prince Sisowath Sirik Matak cajoled and threatened him into making common cause with the plotters. "When did you stop being a faithful servant of Sihanouk?" a reporter asked Lon Nol at his first press conference after the prince's overthrow. "On the eighteenth of March at one o'clock," the prime minister answered unhesitatingly. That was the hour of the parliament's vote to depose the chief of state. And Sihanouk had no argument with that. The quality that

Sihanouk most prized in Lon Nol, whom he had appointed prime minister and chief of staff and who had served him in a wide range of ministerial and military jobs, was his unquestioning loyalty. Sihanouk told me three years after his downfall, when I spent a day with him in the Carpathian Mountains while he paid a state visit to Romania on the invitation of Nicolae Ceausescu. (As nominal leader of the pro-Communist Cambodian Front, based in Beijing, the prince often toured the Communist and pro-Communist countries that recognized the front as Cambodia's government.) "He wasn't exactly intelligent, but I had known him since he was a young governor, and he seemed not bad in his youth," Sihanouk said.

The prince recalled also that the chief conspirator, Sirik Matak, came to take leave from him as he left for his obesity cure two months before the coup. He prostrated himself and kissed his foot, Sihanouk said, to assure him of his loyalty. Members of Lon Nol's entourage, among them Lon Non, told me that it was only when Lon Nol came reluctantly to believe, not long before the coup d'état, that Sihanouk had sold out to the Vietnamese that Lon Nol began to lend an ear to criticisms of the prince. He voiced none himself.

Two strands of deep sentiment shaped Lon Nol's character and intertwined to form his all-encompassing faith: a highly personalized, unorthodox Buddhist belief, marked by what more modern Cambodians called eccentric superstitions, and an equally individual, exorbitantly nationalist view of what he perceived as Cambodia's exalted destiny. Both these strands fixed his mind on one enemy: Vietnam. "He has never liked the Vietnamese," Lon Non told me, even though Lon Nol received an excellent French education at the Lycée Chasseloup-Laubat in Saigon, the elite school that shaped many Vietnamese, Cambodians, and Laotians who later became leaders of their nations. Prince Sirik Matak told me that his Saigon classmate greatly enjoyed life in what was then the capital of Cochin China.

But as wartime prime minister, and later, after massively

rigged elections, president, General Lon Nol, subsequently Marshal, spoke of the Vietnamese as the *thmil*. The word evokes religious anathema, combining the notions of "infidel" and "enemy." Khmer nationalism fed largely on the hatred of Cambodia's neighbors, Vietnam and Thailand.

Lon Non, who lived most of his life in his brother's house, said that being the leader of a nation at war had not greatly changed Lon Nol's way of living. He hardly ever used the telephone, received no regular briefings on the state of the world or the region, and did not listen to the radio, watch television, or read newspapers. Lon Non ventured sometimes to mention interesting world events when he took his morning coffee with the man who guided Cambodia's destiny. A shy man always — Sihanouk used to tease him publicly for being the only prominent Cambodian who would never accept a role in one of his films — Lon Nol allowed his timidity free rein when in 1970 he became the head of a nation at war. He was a dictator without being a leader, and in a nation docile and passive, that seemed enough.

During his reign, from 1941 until 1970, Sihanouk governed by public appearances throughout the country and loved to be surrounded by his ministers as supporting players and butts of his jests. As a result, Lon Nol was a well-known public figure. But paradoxically, Lon Nol took advantage of having become Number One in 1970 to make his appearances rare and public speeches rarer. When he felt it necessary to speak to the nation, he would record a radio message. Even when he presided over the proclamation of the republic, as its first prime minister, he did not address the people. He rarely left his villa, preferring to summon his ministers and military commander there. Such meetings did not happen regularly; some ministers rarely saw their chief. Written reports, mainly in French, were delivered to his house, and he communicated his orders in writing. This, of course, made for minimal exchanges of ideas. Cambodia's troops had been at war for five months before their commander in chief and defense minister paid his first visit to the troops in the field. Few such visits followed in the five years of war.

By all accounts, Lon Nol concentrated his governance principally on military matters. First he organized the expansion and arming of his small forces, later the conduct of the war. Trying to keep the roads, waterways, and airports open for the flow of American assistance and defending the towns, mainly Phnom Penh, that remained under the regime's control, were his main concerns. As prime minister and later as president, Lon Nol left the day-to-day administration of the country to others, leaning heavily on Prince Sirik Matak. "It happens that for the time being the principal task is to win the war," the prince explained to me. "The task of winning the war naturally belongs to His Excellency the President of the Council of Ministers [Lon Nol], who is also the Minister of National Defense. For my part, I take care of the civil half."

While Lon Nol took care of the military half in considerable detail, it was not always evident that he saw the forest for the trees. Nor was his stewardship enhanced by his blissful unawareness of international realities, which caused him no concern. Early on, when he realized that the ultimatum had left no way open to avoid full-scale war, he called each chief of the diplomatic missions in the capital to his villa for a private meeting. To each, including, absurdly, the ambassadors of Communist countries, he presented a specific request for military assistance — so many tanks, so many artillery pieces, planes, or rocket launchers.

The Laotian chargé d'affaires, a man with a wry sense of humor, told me that naturally, given the weakness of his small country, he was the last to be called. After opening amenities, Lon Nol took from his shirt pocket a slip of paper and handed it to the envoy. It was a request for arms for a battalion of light infantry. The Laotian told Lon Nol he appreciated the modesty of the order, but it outstripped his country's possibilities. After all, Laos was fighting against the same enemy and depended entirely on the United States, not only for military aid but also for the bulk of its budget. But, as a subtle diplomat, he told Lon Nol he could offer something that might be worth much more than the arms he asked. "Laos could advise you on how to proceed to get what you want from America," he told Cambodia's leader. "But Lon Nol never asked me."

Lon Nol was a nuts-and-bolts man. The American who got to know him better than any other member of the low-profile, ambassadorless embassy that Rives headed at the outbreak of war was Jonathan F. Ladd. Fred Ladd, as he was known, was a personable, independent-minded retired army colonel, a former commander of the Green Berets in Vietnam. Because of his reputation for opposing the substitution of the American military for that of the countries directly involved, Nixon and Henry Kissinger chose him to head the aid program when Nixon decided in June 1970 to provide Cambodia with modest military assistance. Ladd's instructions at that stage were to prevent the program from sprouting into another huge, highly visible American political and military establishment in Southeast Asia, comparable to those in Vietnam, Laos, Thailand, and the Philippines. This corresponded to Ladd's own thinking.

Ladd was made an instant diplomat and came to Phnom Penh as political-military counselor of embassy. True to his own beliefs, he made do with minimal staff and transacted most of his business personally with Lon Nol. (Unfortunately, he was outmaneuvered by the Pentagon and the American command in Saigon, who succeeded in placing Cambodia under their operational control of all the fighting in Indochina. Ladd left in 1972, bitterly disappointed over the flooding of Cambodia with more American assistance than it could digest.) He told me there was no one but Lon Nol in the Cambodian leadership authorized to work with him. When the American aid program was at the "modest" fifty-million-dollar-a-year level, Ladd told me he was sure "that Lon Nol knows where every nut and bolt has gone." Lon Nol's answers to questions on expanding the army were always detailed and precise, sustained by frequent reference to leather-bound notebooks filled in with the prime minister's own hand, Ladd reported.

But beyond military details there were fatal limits to Lon Nol's competence. I asked him whether he found the level of aid sufficient — a question that other statesmen who depended on American assistance would have snapped up as a chance to plead for more. He replied with the nebulous vagueness that characterized his pronouncements, "You know, with us, *n'est-ce pas*, in general all that is seen more in terms of goods. *Alors*, we receive like that, little by little, supplies, equipment, especially arms, ammunition, and all that. *Alors*, we, we look at the amount rather in material terms. Over there, *n'est-ce pas*, you speak in dollars. But for us, it is in supplies." Trying once more to make him say something concrete, I asked him whether he thought the amount of aid too low, a patsy question if ever there was one. He replied, "To speak frankly, *n'est-ce pas*, about these things, personally I have not kept track of the mathematics of this subject."

It happened to be a life-or-death subject for his Khmer Republic, and only he was in charge of keeping track. Lon Nol's estrangement from the world, the elliptical nature of his discourse, his fondness for employing to the full the riches of the French language in empty phrases, his softness of voice, and the long pauses in midphrase that marked his conversation were the despair of his foreign callers, especially Americans expecting direct answers to blunt questions. They were rarely sure whether they had understood or been understood, or whether the head of government had finished what he intended to say and their turn to speak had come. Lon Nol was a leader of a nation in permanent crisis, and therefore of high journalistic interest. I enjoyed the good fortune of easy access to him, and he seemed to speak openly. Yet more often than not interviews that he allowed to go on as long as I wished yielded nothing worth reporting.

Lon Nol established no meaningful communications with American leaders, on whom his country depended for the tools of war and increasingly the necessities of all basic sustenance. Despite this virtually exclusive reliance on the United States and his unceasing faith in American goodwill, Lon Nol never received the customary honor of an invitation to Washington to meet Nixon in the four years in which they were allies in war. The slight was symptomatic of the low value the United States attached to Cambodia, little more than a piece of conveniently situated real estate in its Vietnam fixation. Nonetheless, Lon Nol regarded Nixon as a close personal friend, on whom he and Cambodia could count in all its needs.

10

The Price of Trusting America: 1970–1975

WHATEVER PRESIDENT Nixon and Henry Kissinger thought about Cambodia until the overthrow of Sihanouk, the coming to power of Lon Nol and a regime fiercely hostile to the Vietnamese Communists clearly set them to thinking about how to exploit a new opportunity. I doubt that as late as the time of the 1970 coup Washington still harbored high hopes for saving its Indochinese "dominoes." Bringing American troops home as quickly as possible and with minimal losses was the order of the day. The way out was to negotiate in the Paris peace talks, which had begun in 1968, an agreement with Hanoi that would put the best possible face on America's embarrassment at being unable to win the war that it had recklessly entered and at leaving South Vietnam and Laos to their own devices.

The opportunity that Cambodia's lapse into war presented was a potentially major disruptive campaign against the Vietnamese Communist bases and supply routes on the Cambodian side of the frontier, a vital source of strength in North Vietnam's war against America and South Vietnam. The geographic and temporal limitation of the American invasion — thirty kilometers and two months — would disperse important North Vietnamese forces to a new, larger battlefield, so as to keep them out of the Americans' way for the limited period. The dispersal of its forces would prevent the Communist command from mounting a significant offensive in Vietnam for some time and would give the Saigon government a breathing spell. Apparent stability in South Vietnam would allow the United States to quicken the pace of withdrawal of its contingents in greater security, in time for the 1972 American election campaign.

The interests of Cambodia did not seriously enter into the Nixon-Kissinger strategy. This country of seven to eight million people became a lightly regarded pawn in a game whose objective was to put an end to the effects of an arrogant miscalculation and ease America's way out of a no-win war, cutting its losses in lives and prestige.

In its fatal innocence of American guile, the Cambodian government believed that Washington's insincerity was directed at deceiving not Cambodia but their common foe, North Vietnam. It did not for a moment take seriously Nixon's announcement that American troops would withdraw on the June 30 deadline. As early as May 25, Foreign Minister Yem Sambaur announced that Phnom Penh would ask Nixon to keep his troops in Cambodia until the end of the war. On the eve of the pull-out deadline, when Cambodia had been told that nothing would hold up the departure of the Americans, Lon Nol called a rare press conference to express his regret and to plead for American troops to return if the military situation required it. He requested that the United States Air Force continue to be active over Cambodia, both in strategic bombing and tactical support of Cambodian ground forces. That was pushing against an open door. Having bombed Cambodia secretly even before it had joined in war, the Pentagon was happy to enlarge in full view of the world its theater of Indochinese operations. After all, bombing cost only money; its casualties occurred with minimal exceptions on the ground, where there were no Americans.

As the American troops withdrew back into Vietnam, educated Cambodians who had welcomed the new regime awoke to a startled realization that they had greatly overestimated what America was willing to do to help Cambodia and had failed to recognize the divergence between their own war aims and America's. It dawned on them that they were, in fact, alone, except for the rampaging military intervention of the South Vietnamese, whom they feared little less than those of the North. They were alone and at war with the fiercest of adversaries. The realization plunged the modern, educated elite of Cambodia, a small but vital class indispensable to a singularly placid nation in time of crisis, into gloom and disaffection with the new leadership. It set off a brain drain that continued throughout the war, although restrictions on emigration grew ever tighter.

A great number of its best-trained people quit Cambodia, leaving it in the hands of an increasingly isolated leader, who abandoned himself to his visions and gradually allowed the running of the country to slip into the hands of his manipulative, scheming brother. The door of Lon Nol's villa, passed too infrequently by his ministers and generals, was always open, without appointment, to Buddhist monks of varied interests. He found time for all of them.

But more and more Lon Nol paid heed to monks who read a mystical meaning into the conflict, who saw it as a long-prophesied challenge to the survival of Buddhism. They elevated the Khmer nation to the station of the divinely chosen defender of the faith and found in Lon Nol a most ardent disciple. He formulated around this central creed a vast theory of what he called the "Khmer-Mon civilization," reversing the order of what historians and archeologists classify as the "Mon-Khmer civilization," a term that follows the chronological sequence of the entrance of the Mon and Khmer people onto the stage of recorded history.

From the intermingling of those ethnic groups emerged the high, Indianized culture in the region stretching from the delta of the Irrawaddy in today's Myanmar across Cambodia, Laos, and Thailand into the delta of the Mekong in southern Vietnam. But to Lon Nol it was the Khmer part of the equation that represented the highest in Buddhist culture, and before long he had derived from it a philosophy that he entitled "Neo-Khmerism." He published it, a mishmash of Khmer history as seen by its author and sweeping platitudes on the "brilliant future" of Cambodia, in booklet form in Cambodian and French, as a spiritual guide for civil servants on how to win the war and save Buddhism for five thousand years to come, "as foretold."

Lon Nol's ever-deepening belief in what monks told him of the future became the despair of those who had to deal with him about the present, both Cambodians and Americans. His principal spiritual adviser was a monk whom he had brought to Phnom Penh from the countryside because of his renown as a visionary. To his admirers the monk gave cloths to protect them from evil. The cloths bore his name, Mam Prum Moni, and the inscription, in Cambodian and French, "Great Intellectual of Pure Glory." I met the monk in the company of a prominent Lon Nol supporter, Madame Nou Neau, head of the Patriotic Women's Youth Commandos and a member of Parliament, a well-educated, elegant woman in her thirties.

"He is the most important man for General Lon Nol," she said. "He is the most important of the ten monks whom the general consults regularly. Monday they talked for four hours, just two of them. He comes from all the mountains of Cambodia. He says he is the reincarnation of Jayavarman VII." She appeared to take this claim at face value. That great king's reign, which began in 1181, marked the summit of the Angkor civilization. "Soldiers to whom he has granted his protection have stepped on mines and they have not exploded, and when they do explode they cause only black spots and no wounds," Madame Neau said, her eyes shining in admiring faith.

Repeatedly Lon Nol instructed his troops to make use of the magic that had served their ancestors so well through history. This would protect them from enemy bullets. Early in their relationship the commander in chief showed Fred Ladd a new manual of basic military doctrine that he had helped write for the thousands of new noncommissioned and junior officers joining the expanding army. The former American colonel was still shaking his head in wonderment as he told me it contained as many citations from Buddhist scriptures, a pacifist creed, as it did lessons lifted from French military manuals. Like most Cambodians of high military rank, Lon Nol was essentially a civil servant to whom Sihanouk had assigned military rank when newly independent Cambodia formed its army in 1953. The French in their day had trained few Cambodians to serve as officers.

What made Mam Prum Moni so valuable to Lon Nol was that "not only can he foretell the future, make soldiers invulnerable to the enemy and cannot be hurt himself, he is also the greatest scholar of the history of our country," a civil servant told me. The monk warned against the return of American troops to Cambodia; this would bring total destruction, an unexceptionable view. But if America helps in all other ways, Mam Prum Moni predicted, it would make for twenty-five hundred years of friendship and happiness for both countries.

But the present held no happiness in the relationship between the United States and the country that quickly became its latest and least self-reliant Southeast Asian client. "I can't help a sad feeling that Cambodia is a little country that we have used and for which we must now bear a moral responsibility," Ladd told me in 1973. We were sitting on his balcony at the Watergate in Washington after he had yielded his assignment in Phnom Penh to emissaries of the American command in Saigon, and Nixon, Kissinger, and the Pentagon had totally cast aside Ladd's concept of a military assistance program that even an incompetent government and military command such as Cambodia's might be able to handle. What followed in 1971–72 was akin to placing the latest Ferrari racing car into a child's hands and letting it loose among the best of the world's drivers.

The partial American involvement in 1970 — a brief invasion and a long-term commitment to bomb — served American and South Vietnamese interests, but it mired Cambodia deeply in a full-scale, countrywide war. At worst, Cambodians had believed that the war in the border sanctuaries might become more intense, but that American intervention would prevent the Communists from going beyond those limits. But early in June 1970, less than three months after the fighting began, with American troops still engaged on the Khmer side of the border, Cambodians awakened to learn that Angkor, the nation's emblematic shrine, deep in the northwest and far from Vietnam, was firmly in North Vietnamese hands.

In the hope of recouping it, Lon Nol launched the first of his few offensive operations in September. Its aim was to relieve the beleaguered town of Kompong Thom, about halfway on the road from the capital to Angkor and essential if any attempt was to be made to drive the enemy from the sacred site. The campaign ended inconclusively, although the Lon Nol government claimed a great victory. Heavy American bombing kept the Vietnamese at a distance from the Cambodians, who slowly advanced along the main road northward from Phnom Penh. The campaign accomplished little, the Cambodian troops did not stay to protect the town and keep the road open, and before the year was out the Communist forces had cut off Kompong Thom once again.

The beginning of 1971 brought to the people of Phnom Penh the first terrifying realization that no place in Cambodia remained safe. A Vietnamese Communist hit squad raided Phnom Penh's airport, destroying all the airworthy military planes and helicopters, as well as others that were undergoing refitting. Casualties among the totally unprepared troops stationed at the field were heavy. The blow to morale was such that from that event onward I never again heard an expression of confidence over the war's outcome from Cambodians speaking their minds. Even high officials, required to reflect optimism when speaking for publication, often shared with me their much less hopeful thoughts in private conversation. A month later, in March 1971, Lon Nol suffered a stroke and was evacuated to Hawaii for hospitalization. A sense of doom became palpable, as many Cambodians saw their leader's affliction as an evil omen. The following month, guerrillas destroyed the country's only petroleum refinery in the port of Sihanoukville, which had resumed its old name, Kompong Som.

The first anniversary of Lon Nol's 1970 coup d'état was little noted in what had become a fear-ridden capital. Soldiers, who were paid only irregularly, terrorized shopkeepers and restaurant owners by buying or eating and drinking without paying, or simply demanding money while putting their hands on their weapons. "When I see soldiers in a restaurant I go to another," a minister told me. Officers would put "phantom soldiers" on the payrolls that they submitted and pocket the money. This became a particularly widespread form of corruption. American diplomats, after demanding a head count of the army that the United States was subsidizing, reduced the Cambodian claim of 200,000 troops to a maximum of 150,000. Ministers admitted that corruption, now fueled by a steadily rising flow of American money, exceeded by far the degree of corruption that had helped to bring down Sihanouk.

Unsurprisingly, Lon Nol's two-month absence in Hawaii brought the first perceptible rumblings of political intrigue, as potential successors raised their heads. Sirik Matak, who had acted as prime minister during Lon Nol's convalescence, was the subject of much speculation, largely because of his long-standing prominence, recognized position as Number Two, and the known American preference for him. But he did nothing publicly to promote a candidacy. He missed no opportunity to affirm his loyalty to Lon Nol — sincerely, I believe — and his impatience to see him return to his post. The president of the National Assembly, In Tam, a populist politician with a considerable following, was a more open contender.

But most active in the political jockeying was a man whose future depended on the survival in power of Lon Nol, no matter how incapacitated. Lon Non made it clear that he would accept nothing short of his brother's return to the prime ministership, even if, on his doctors' orders, he could devote no more than thirty minutes a day to the job. To add weight to his demand, the deskbound major of the military police, whom his brother had promoted to lieutenant colonel and placed in command of an oversized infantry brigade of more than ten thousand elite troops stationed largely in Phnom Penh, had drawn to himself a number of colonels who commanded almost all the troops surrounding the capital.

"Little Brother," as he was called by the Phnom Penh elite, including ministers of government, had become a feared man, whose troops were stationed in perfect coup position. He had also formed under his leadership a sinister political cabal, the National Committee of Special Coordination, which he claimed represented "youth" and "intellectuals." I saw Lon Non daily, often together with his colonels, his "youth" representatives (rather on in years), and his "intellectuals." He commissioned some of the civilian committee members as "political counselors" in his infantry brigade. They numbered among them the most notorious profiteers and peddlers of political influence, freely using the names of the prime minister and his brother for their personal advantage. I doubt Lon Nol was aware of his brother's activities and reputation before his stroke or cared much afterward.

In April 1971 the prime minister provoked more than two weeks of crisis by resigning on his return to Phnom Penh, citing the lasting impairment of his health, a partial paralysis. In an elaborate ritual of Asian courtesy, Cheng Heng, the head of state, accepted the resignation and immediately asked Lon Nol to form a new government. It never became apparent whether this was a ceremonial invitation, which the invalid leader was expected to refuse, or whether Lon Non had already made clear that he and his colonels would accept no other head of government. When Lon Non finally persuaded his brother to resume his post, at least in name, the prime minister imposed the condition that Sirik Matak, who continued to enjoy Lon Nol's confidence, would at least temporarily run the day-by-day affairs of government, with the odd title of prime minister–delegate. Lon Non accepted reluctantly. As a sign that Lon Nol would continue to run the war, he received the rank of marshal, unique in Cambodian history. Lon Non in our conversations frequently insisted that Sirik Matak's special position was temporary, and that his brother would resume full authority before long. At the American embassy, the opposite was the hope.

In an effort to assure that Little Brother would not undercut his "delegate," a condition that Sirik Matak had specified, Lon Nol made his brother appear before the foreign press at Major Am Rong's military briefing in the department store tearoom to pledge publicly his allegiance to Sirik Matak. He wasted no time in demonstrating the hollowness of his promise with a campaign of vicious rumor against Sirik Matak. He made of his first appearance before an international public a stage-managed show of muscle. Wearing a dashing, one-of-a-kind camouflage uniform, he drove up to the Magasin d'Etat at the wheel of a long maroon Mercedes, a rarity in Phnom Penh, preceded by a radio jeep and followed by two truckloads of gun-toting bodyguards. It was a sight of personal power never before seen in Phnom Penh. Little Brother delivered his brief declaration in French, did not wait for its translation into a language that most of the press understood, allowed no questions, marched out, and drove off.

A few months later, in a scene of consummate mutual hypocrisy, I watched the prime minister–delegate pin a military medal on Lon Non on the battlefield of a renewed campaign to free the road to Kompong Thom. He kissed him on both cheeks and smiled sourly at me as we walked back to his helicopter. Lon Non had by then been elevated to the command of five brigades.

The second Kompong Thom campaign ended in disaster. Lon Nol finally ordered his battered troops to retreat toward Phnom Penh at the end of 1971. Casualties were the heaviest the Cambodian army had suffered, and soldiers deserted in all directions. They left their American-supplied gear along the main road, either to be captured or to be bombed by the United States Air Force to keep it out of enemy hands. It was the last major government offensive of the war.

The prolonged first government crisis of the Khmer Republic in 1971 brought into clear view many symptoms of its fatal illness. Most important, perhaps, was how the United States, the godfather of post-Sihanouk Cambodia, reacted. In private conversations, the diplomats of the American embassy, headed by Ambassador Emory C. Swank, a suave and accomplished diplomat clearly out of step with Washington's entirely self-interested view of Cambodia, did not hide their conviction that Lon Nol was unsuited to his job. They would have preferred Sirik Matak, a rational, even if uncharismatic, nonmystic, and efficient administrator, or In Tam, an energetic man with a popular touch and a reputation for honesty. Yet despite America's make-or-break influence, it refused to use it to intervene as king-maker, as it had done many times in settling South Vietnamese or Laotian government crises.

By failing to show its preference for Sirik Matak and lack of confidence in Lon Nol, America left Sirik Matak in his ambiguous position as acting head of the government subject to recall at any moment and exposed to the intrigues of Lon Non, his colonels, and his cabal. Nor did the United States put its weight on the scales when Lon Nol suddenly dismissed In Tam, whose popularity worried him and his brother, and probably Sirik Matak, as deputy prime minister. America's inaction was another sign that Cambodia had jumped headlong onto the American bandwagon at a time when the bandwagon's gear had shifted into reverse. Washington was loosening its engagements in Indochina and didn't care how badly its latest client ran its affairs. What mattered was a smooth American exit from Vietnam, not the fate of the new pawn.

The crisis also pointed up how unready Cambodia was, as it remains to this day, to make even a nominally democratic system function. Except for the small number of the politically aware or ambitious, Cambodians tolerated inertly, and without any noticeable show of public interest, the fact that, in the midst of war, their country was for so long leaderless and as paralyzed in decision-making as was its afflicted leader. And Lon Nol, the man who proved so indispensable as to be finally returned to power that he had rightly resigned, was clearly physically and mentally unfit. Son Ngoc Thanh, the old nationalist leader and a former and subsequent prime minister then serving as a counselor to Lon Nol, met me for an interview. He had been briefed by the health minister, Lon Nol's personal doctor and friend, on the diagnosis of the American and Cambodian physicians treating him. The doctors' verdict was clear: Lon Nol was too ill to make important decisions or to be told bad news, Thanh said.

In October 1971 a large part of the semblance of democracy was dropped. Lon Nol turned Parliament into a constituent assembly to draft a new, presidential constitution. He took power to rule by decree. In words written for him in ringing French by his *chef de cabinet*, he declared that the time had come to end "the sterile game of outmoded liberal democracy," a phrase that Marshal Pétain might have uttered in 1940 about his Vichy regime under German occupation. In fact, the Parliament had consistently, out of servile habit, approved all measures put before it by the government. In March 1972 Lon Nol disbanded the constituent assembly he had created and named himself chief of state as well as prime minister. His ill-health was clearly no brake on his lust for power. His brother used his "intellectuals" and "students" to stage a wave of demonstrations against Sirik Matak. The prince, bitterly disappointed by the American silence that contradicted the support that he had received on a visit to Washington, resigned.

Lon Nol used the second anniversary of the coup against Sihanouk in 1972 to declare himself president, as well as prime minister, defense minister, and marshal of the armed forces. Three farcically corrupt votes to create an aura of legitimacy — a referendum on the constitution the regime had decreed and presidential and parliamentary elections — held in the limited territories remaining under Phnom Penh's management gave Lon Nol his constitution, the presidency (which he had already conferred upon himself), and a one-party parliament. Lon Non, leader of the tiny ruling party, deployed all the force and chicanery necessary to make those tallying the votes deliver the desired results. He had at his command not only all the uniformed and plainclothes strongmen necessary but also unlimited funds derived from "phantom soldiers" in his brigades — American money.

The American embassy, fully aware of the election violence and fraud, continued its hands-off attitude. It never contradicted when throughout the campaign the Lon brothers asserted that United States aid was conditional on the marshal's election. Privately, American officials and high-level visitors like Henry Kissinger and Vice President Spiro Agnew, who made Phnom Penh a brief stopover — no overnight stays — on trips to Saigon, urged Lon Nol to "broaden his government," which meant bringing back Sirik Matak. But Lon Non, now a brigadier general, had undermined his brother's confidence in the prince and convinced him that Sirik Matak wanted to restore the monarchy and would allow himself to be "used" by the Communists. Sirik Matak, on the contrary, had publicly renounced his princely title in 1970 and called for a republic immediately after the coup against Sihanouk.

In an open affront to the United States, Lon Non requested that I interview him in March 1973. He wanted to put his views before the American public through my newspaper because he had no contact with the American embassy. "How do you think the Americans can bring Sirik Matak back into government?" he asked rhetorically. "Do you think my political group would accept Prince Sirik Matak? Do you think Parliament would accept him?" I asked whether this was his brother's view. His reply made clear who was in charge of Cambodia in 1973. "The marshal never says anything," the general said. "He must choose: on one side his friend, on the other his country. He will choose his country."

Lon Non had Sirik Matak's house ringed by a heavy military guard, nominally to protect the prince, and cut off his telephone. Inside this outer ring was a genuinely protective smaller circle of troops commanded by a major loyal to Sirik Matak. One of the prince's sons smuggled me into the house. "There is only a slight margin of difference between the 'protection' they are giving me and house arrest," the prince said with a smile as he greeted me. Avoiding harsh words, the man who had long been considered as America's best hope for effective use of its money and matériel in Cambodia, which by that time exceeded $200 million a year for military and civilian purposes, for the first time broke openly with Lon Nol and voiced his pain over United States policy. Portraits with gracious dedications by Nixon and Agnew, souvenirs of his Washington visit, occupied places of honor in the spacious living room.

"I understand America's attitude of not wanting to interfere in our internal affairs," he said. "But if the United States continues to support such a regime we will fall to the Communists. You give help to a people that wants to live freely. But when you support a regime not supported by the people you help the Communists." Sirik Matak called American help generous. "But the government uses it all to establish a military dictatorship in contempt of the people." Ambassador Swank had been to his house for dinner two months earlier, but not once during the critical period of Lon Non's agitation against him and his virtual house arrest had Swank or any other embassy official demonstrated

American interest in him, the prince said, at pains not to let his bitterness show. He would telephone Swank if he could, he added.

As he spoke, a witch-hunt atmosphere against suspected "royalists" had gripped Phnom Penh, which added poignancy to the prince's implicit appeal for a measure of American protection. On the third anniversary of the coup, in March 1973, a disgruntled military pilot, who had once had an affair with one of Sihanouk's daughters, made off with a T-28 at Phnom Penh airport and, aiming two bombs at the Presidential Palace, where Lon Nol was holding a rare cabinet meeting, hit a housing area for government employees and killed more than fifty persons, mostly children. The regime distorted the act into part of an invented "royalist" plot and declared a state of siege. Hundreds of arrests followed, and many members of the two branches of the royal family, the Norodoms and Sisowaths, were detained.

On the same day, agents of Lon Non, who was now in command of the largest of the army's four divisions and had been promoted to ministerial rank, "in charge of edification (rural development), mobilization, and rallying [guerrillas to the government side]," broke up with grenades the most important open act of dissatisfaction with the regime, a month-long, nationwide strike of twenty thousand teachers, that had closed the schools and added fuel to student restlessness. At least two persons were killed when the grenades were thrown at a strike meeting in Phnom Penh. On the pretext that the assailants were Communist agents, the government ordered the teachers back to work under the state of siege but closed all schools and universities at the same time.

Sirik Matak did not hold back on his criticism of the regime that had grown out of the coup he had led three years earlier. "I believe that this regime must not survive and will not last," he said, his soft voice hardening. If free and honest elections were held opposing Lon Nol to his cousin, Sihanouk, the prince he had overthrown would win easily, Sirik Matak said. He proposed that contact be established with Sihanouk, the nominal leader of the Cambodian resistance. "He counts for something in this country," Sirik Matak said. "He is a Cambodian, too. If the people wanted him, I would accept." Three months later, at our meeting in Romania, I told Sihanouk about Sirik Matak's change of heart. He answered in a burst of rage. "Sirik Matak is one of the worst reactionaries and traitors of the history of Cambodia. That man, we are going to hang him, quite simply hang him, hang him, hang him." Sirik Matak's brother, Prince Sisowath Methavi, who was Sihanouk's chief of protocol in his exile years, was in the room. He let no emotion at Sihanouk's outburst show on his face.

As I left Sirik Matak, the prince put his hand on my arm to detain me for a moment. "Present circumstances indicate that I should wait here until the storm passes," he said in his soft Indochinese French. "Man is born to die. I will not move. I shall stay here and face everything that happens. They can arrest me. If they kill me, what of it? I stay for my country." Two years later, it was in a similar vein that he wrote to Ambassador John Gunther Dean to decline an invitation to be evacuated with the American embassy staff as the Khmers Rouges were poised to enter Phnom Penh:

"I cannot, alas, leave in such cowardly fashion. . . . I have committed only one mistake, that of believing in you, the Americans." And when some days later the French consul, in whose embassy compound foreigners and some Cambodians had taken refuge, told him that the new rulers had demanded that all Cambodians be surrendered or the foreigners, too, would be seized in their temporary sanctuary, Sirik Matak took leave quietly and walked out of the embassy to certain death.

While the Lon Nol government put an end to the minimal vestiges of democratic rule, it was the United States Air Force that kept at bay the guerrillas, who were by now fighting with minimal Vietnamese help. "In 1970 and 1971 we had the help of the Vietnamese," Sihanouk told me in Romania in 1973. "But since the second half of 1972 we are autonomous. Arms and ammunitions deliveries have been finished since January 1973." American intelligence confirmed the assertion.

In Paris, in January 1973, the United States and Hanoi concluded the agreement committing both to the restoration of peace in Vietnam and the ending of their military operations in Cambodia and Laos. Foreign Minister Long Boret was invited to Paris to be briefed before the signing of the agreement by a member of the Kissinger negotiating team, Deputy Assistant Secretary of State William Sullivan. Long Boret came to dinner at my house that evening, before he was to return to Phnom Penh the next day. What had most impressed the foreign minister was Sullivan's profession of high American confidence that Hanoi would persuade its Cambodian and Laotian allies to stop fighting, even though they were not party to the American-Vietnamese agreement. At American request, Cambodia would unilaterally suspend offensive actions on the strength of that assurance. Sullivan, known for his often cynical skepticism, could have had few illusions that the Vietnamese Communists would or could keep their promise. Most of the Vietnamese Communist troops had been withdrawn, and occasional armed clashes and persistent tension between the former allies were not unknown to Washington. Sullivan knew that Hanoi retained slight influence over the Khmers Rouges and that the Cambodian Communists, knowing the weakness of the Lon Nol regime, would hardly stop short of victory. But Washington clearly wanted no critical voices from its allies to interfere with the signing of the Paris Agreement.

By mid-February 1973 the cease-fire, which remained unilateral, ended, and the United States resumed bombing. Since only Phnom Penh and some provincial capitals were under government control, almost all of Cambodia became an aerial free-fire zone. And since as a result of the Paris Agreement the U.S. Air Force was no longer active over Vietnam and Laos, it concentrated all its bombers on the Cambodian countryside to devastating effect upon the civilian population and the country's rudimentary infrastructure.

"American air power is necessary and indispensable," the chief of the Cambodian general staff, Major General Sosthene Fernandez, told me in March 1973. "Yes, you can say indispensable." The general, observing the government's fiction that few Cambodians had joined the guerrillas, insistently called the enemy "the V.C." or "Vietcong." At that time, North Vietnamese units were in place largely in the little-populated northeast, where they maintained the Ho Chi Minh Trail network. Fernandez differed with the official American line that the Air Force sent in its B-52s and fighter-bombers only when its own forward air controllers determined that a target was purely military. On the contrary, the general said, most of the information was supplied by Cambodia. He described how readily his commanders called for the B-52s: The "V.C." mix with the villagers, and the villagers flee and ask that the village be bombed, he said. "They themselves come to ask us to destroy everything, because they hate the V.C. Of course the villagers are sad about their belongings, their houses, their lands, but they want us to bomb everything to drive out the V.C. We do all we can to avoid civilian casualties, but one cannot always be certain that all civilians have fled."

With the callous disregard of the interests of the Cambodian people that marked all of America's wartime involvement in that country, and in full knowledge that Cambodia's demented and corrupt regime could only prolong their people's suffering, America did all that it could to drag out senselessly the life of a hated government and a war that Washington knew was lost. Congress forced the Nixon administration to end the bombing in August 1973. But military supplies kept flowing, and so did hypocritical words about eventual victory. The war dragged on, now entirely a Cambodian civil war. The government held Phnom Penh and the principal towns to the west, each bloated beyond its normal proportions by masses of uncared-for refugees from the countryside. They fled from the fighting and the forced recruitment of the young by the Khmers Rouges. Famine was widespread among the displaced, and child mortality frightful.

The regime's corps of civilian and military officials was disgraced with ever more greedy and corrupt members. Provincial governors and commanders began denuding the forests, Cambodia's greatest riches, a practice that continues to this day, and selling its timber to equally dishonest Thai officials and merchants, as happens today. Wholesale selling of American-furnished arms and ammunition to the enemy enriched many an officer briefly, until their customers massacred them at their victory. Cambodia's society was in dissolution well before the Khmers Rouges destroyed it.

The end of the bombing in 1973 allowed the Khmers Rouges to tighten their noose around Phnom Penh and make the random rocketing and shelling of the capital a constant terror. It claimed countless victims among the swollen population at any time of day or night. Sadly, once the United States had stopped waging its cruel war in Indochina, the justified humanitarian outcry throughout the world, which had contributed to the American withdrawal, ended. The world of the compassionate seemed incapable of considering the reality: that the side that had been victim of American destructiveness was also making victims among the innocent. In March 1974 I used the occasion of a meeting with Prime Minister Olof Palme of Sweden, who had shown a serious interest in Indochina and led his nation in effective protest against America's war, to ask him to make a public appeal against the continuous indiscriminate shelling of Phnom Penh by by the Khmers Rouges. After listening thoughtfully he said he would seriously consider making such a plea. But no humanitarian appeal was issued from Stockholm.

The United States continued keeping the Phnom Penh government supplied for war and provided with minimal food for its people. When the Mekong River route became totally unsafe in the last months of the conflict, only an airlift could feed the city. Washington's policy was to urge Lon Nol to conduct a more effective war, clean up and rationalize his government and military, and, thus strengthened, seek to negotiate for a peace that would leave at least a marginal role for non-Communists. But Lon Nol was clearly past becoming what he had never been, a vigorous leader, and the Khmers Rouges, certain of victory, rejected all conciliatory approaches. Unconditional surrender was their unfaltering stand.

In a last-minute effort, the United States, which had always viewed Sihanouk as a puppet in the hands of the Communists — Cambodian, Chinese, and Vietnamese — turned to Sihanouk as the possible least objectionable way of ending the war. But Washington's original estimate of Sihanouk's range of independent options had been correct. The prince told me himself in June 1973 that he considered his role as nominal head of the "Royal Khmer Government of National Union" to be as a spokesman to the outside world for the resistance movement inside Cambodia. He said he had told Khieu Samphan, Pol Pot's front man as chief of the guerrillas, "Tell me what the resistance movement wants, so that I can say things in conformity with what it wants."

At the end of March 1975, in one of the bizarre happenings in which Sihanouk's biography is rich, he opened the door to direct contact with the United States Liaison Office in Beijing, headed by George Bush. He asked a special favor: would the Americans send him the copies of his films that he had stored in Chamcar Mon, his modern Phnom Penh residence? Kissinger ordered the embassy to do so and Bush to use the opening to arrange a meeting with Sihanouk. But Sihanouk refused what Kissinger considered a last-minute chance for a negotiated end to the war, a settlement in which the Khmers Rouges would not be placed in sole control of the country. The Khmers Rouges knew that militarily it was already theirs for the taking. Their rejection took both Sihanouk and any representative of the American-backed side out of Cambodia's equation.

Frantic, at that point hopeless, American efforts to remove obstacles to negotiations that might save a remnant of American prestige continued. On April 1, 1975, Lon Nol was finally persuaded to leave, on the pretext that only his departure would ensure the continuation of American aid to Cambodia. He left with a gift of what was variously reported to be between $200,000 and $1 million in American-provided pocket money, to end his days in the United States after a brief stop in Indonesia. An ultimate American appeal for Sihanouk to return failed.

Early in the morning of April 12, Ambassador Dean sent his invitations to the highest Cambodian officials to join him on the helicopters that were to take the envoy and his remaining staff members to a ship standing by in the Gulf of Thailand. Lon Non, who had not accompanied his brother, and Long Boret, the last prime minister of the Khmer Republic, both constantly vilified in Khmer Rouge broadcasts as traitors to be condemned to death, declined the invitation. Both were killed, as they must have known they would be, on April 17, 1975, the day the Khmers Rouges made their vengeful entry into Phnom Penh.

It was typical of the American disregard for Cambodians that the final helicopter evacuation included only 159 Cambodians. They were largely high officials and their families. Some hundreds had been evacuated earlier in transport planes. When a similar curtain-down rescue operation was staged in Saigon two weeks later, nearly six thousand Vietnamese who had collaborated with the United States or been employed by American government or private agencies were lifted out. Tens of thousands of such Vietnamese had left under American auspices in the preceding weeks. As in the five years of war, Cambodian lives didn't count for much to the superpower that had taken over their fates without accepting ultimate responsibility for them.

11

"The Cambodian No Longer Exists":
1975–1979

C AMBODIA'S LONGEST NIGHT began on the morning of April 17, 1975. Gradually the Khmer Rouge guns and rocket launchers, which had continued to hail death and fire onto the defenseless city of Phnom Penh through the night and into morning, fell silent. The longtime residents of the capital called their children inside and locked the doors. The majority of Phnom Penh's people at the end of the five-year war, the countless refugees from the zones of fighting who were not favored with the luxury of fixed homes, clustered around pagodas, schools, ministries, and other public buildings. Soldiers of the government army ditched their weapons and blended into the population. The few remaining foreigners — diplomats, journalists, aid workers — gathered in the Hotel Le Phnom, which they had declared a neutral safety zone under Red Cross auspices, or in the spacious grounds of the French embassy. The city waited nervously, its people trembling when an occasional burst of small-arms fire crackled nearby.

And then the Khmers Rouges came. Silently marching in

single file, dressed in black, shod with sandals cut from tires, arms, mainly Chinese-made or captured American rifles, at the ready. What struck the people of Phnom Penh most, according to firsthand accounts of those who escaped, which I began gathering shortly after the event, were the youth of the conquering soldiers and their fierce, unsmiling, automatonlike demeanor. Their grimness was frightening. Whatever fears the citizens may have harbored of the Khmers Rouges before, their coming meant to many Cambodians the end of the five years of war, and that was cause enough for gladness. That a Communist regime was arriving was certain, and to most Cambodians no cause for rejoicing. But even to them it meant not merely a future under a regime of unforgiving rigor but also an end to the violent lawlessness and corruption that the Lon Nol government and the war had visited on Cambodians.

But on that very first day of what was so romantically called the "liberation," came the stunning order to all to evacuate the city. The old and the young, the healthy and the invalid, those who had secretly wished for the victory of the Khmers Rouges as well as those who until the last moment had served the Lon Nol regime, whatever their beliefs — all were driven out. For weeks the roads of Cambodia were clogged with masses of wretched men, women, and children heading away from home, far from where they wished to be, from where they wanted to begin their lives anew in a time of newfound peace. The new rulers drove them to distant places, whose principal attribute was as often as not unsuitability to sustain life.

Some were spared the long march. Cabinet ministers and generals who failed to escape did not survive the "liberation" long enough to join the exodus. They were summoned to appear in front of the Information Ministry, and it is presumed that those who did — they included Lon Non and Long Boret — were killed on the same day, without even a sham trial. Reports I have never been able to confirm said the slaughter of Lon Nol's men, and perhaps their families, took place behind the ministry at the Cercle Sportif, the club of the Cambodian and French elite, between the tennis courts and the swimming pool.

The news that officers were to report to the new authorities reached my friend Am Rong, the frustrated cinéaste and most unmilitary of military spokesmen, who had unaccountably risen to the rank of brigadier general, a day or two after he had set out with the wretched flow from the city. A witness told me years later that, guileless to the end, Am Rong turned back and, walking alone against the stream, made his way to Phnom Penh to report. He was taken to a shoddy hotel on the main avenue, apparently a gathering place for the doomed. His trace ends there. Whenever I now walk past that hotel, I feel a plaque should be put up at its entrance to commemorate the credulous naïveté that led a nation into unending catastrophe.

In early July 1975 I traveled along the Thai-Cambodian border for five days to seek out Cambodians who had succeeded in escaping. About six thousand had by then made it to safety after treacherous treks through uncharted jungles, avoiding known roads or paths. How many failed and met a cruel fate cannot be known, but from almost all of the dozens of refugees I questioned at length in three widely separated camps along the long border in July I heard accounts of others who had left with them and never reached Thailand. The first stories that had given an inkling of what the new, Khmer Rouge Cambodia would be like came from the journalists who had found sanctuary in the French embassy and were finally allowed to leave in a truck convoy two weeks later. Their reports were necessarily limited to what they experienced in the first hours of the new regime, until they were shut up in the embassy, and what they saw from their open trucks as they crossed the country under heavy guard to the Thai border. The occasional reports that drifted out of the new Cambodia, whose nameless rulers had expelled all foreigners and sealed the country against the outside world, were too horrifying to credit at second or third hand. My purpose was to hear of the experiences and observations of Cambodians themselves, particularly those who had most recently made good their escape and had lived under Khmer Rouge rule for long weeks.

What I was told in the three camps, which had no communications with one another, surpassed the worst that I had heard before. The accounts were strikingly uniform and consistent with one another, wherever I heard them and whether they came from Cambodians typical of the majority of the refugees, ordinary peasants or common soldiers from the border regions, or the rare educated men and women from Phnom Penh or Battambang. They were all too credible. The very composition of the mass of refugees was a kind of corroboration of the radical leveling of an entire nation that they related. They represented a fair cross section of Cambodian society. Most were, like the great majority of Cambodians, of the unlettered and unfavored mass, overwhelmingly rural. The number of men whose torsos were heavily covered with Sanskrit tattoos to protect them from evil by their magic was remarkable. It indicated a preponderance of the uneducated and superstitious. There were also urban laborers, petty government employees, and a smattering of the French-speaking educated class.

The essence of the horrors that became manifest four years later in 1979, in monumental piles of skulls and bones, artfully constructed by survivors after the Khmer Rouge regime was driven from power by the Vietnamese invasion, was already contained in these earliest accounts. When my 1975 report, written in understatement and moderation, was published, it met with considerable incredulity, often antagonism, from those who during the war had not only condemned, justly, I believe, the American role and Lon Nol's absurd regime, but had gone beyond that to give emotional verbal support to the revolutionary cause. In the prosperous Western world of the 1970s, "revolution" was deemed good, whatever its results, as long as it happened in distant countries.

Some academic and journalistic specialists in Southeast Asian affairs were particularly stern in their rejection of what they considered propaganda from those who would not forgive the revolutionaries for having defeated the American-supported side. There were even those who defended the pitiless uprooting of the urban populations, either because they said it was inspired by the new government's humane striving to lead the millions from the foodless cities to places where rice was growing and fish were swimming, or because they believed the leaders harbored well-grounded fears that the vengeful Americans were about to bomb Phnom Penh and other towns.

Oddly, many of the writers on Cambodia who since the downfall of the Khmers Rouges have become the leading recorders of their crimes were also among their most uncritical defenders until their regime fell. It is a pity that their earlier ideology made them arrogantly reject the truthful voices of humble victims. I suppose that as a refugee from a rather abominable regime myself I am short of sympathy for those who shut their ears to the experiences of the few who escape. It was as though the lesson of those who in the face of ever-mounting evidence persisted in regarding Stalin as a benefactor of mankind had no relevance.

Of the many accounts of life under the Khmers Rouges that I gathered, particularly in the five years from 1977 until 1981 when I had returned to live in the region, the story of Chan Serey Monty struck me as representative of what happened. There clearly were regional differences; some accounts were even harsher, few less so. Hers was a generally valid description of life under the Khmers Rouges, though I heard variations on its basic theme from men, women, and even children from various regions of the country. The similarities of detail were often striking. The young woman's patient and modest testimony, as flat as her soft voice, contained all the most telling features that marked the hundreds of such narratives that I heard over the years.

Serey Monty was eighteen years old when I met her in a temporary refugee camp — two open fields bare of any roofs for more than six hundred people in the monsoon season — next to a Thai police station in the border village of Ta Phraya in 1978. She had crossed to safety less than a month before our long conversation. With characteristic Cambodian modesty and politeness, she dwelled only reluctantly on details of her family's immense suffering that she thought might shock me and my interpreter. She would look up apologetically as if she wished to take the painful edge off what she said.

Serey Monty's father had been a minor government employee and she had been a high-school student in Phnom Penh. In 1975 the announcement of the beginning of her new life came in the raw voice of a black-clothed soldier, which rang up the stairway of their apartment house in the center of the capital to order all inhabitants to leave immediately. With her parents, two brothers, her sister, and brother-in-law she crowded into the family car. They took whatever food was in the house, a few clothes and the women's jewels, Southeast Asia's most common form of family savings. Even on that first day, Serey Monty witnessed roadside shootings, of men she thought had been recognized as soldiers or officials. They trembled for her father, but his job had been mediocre and anonymous and he was not identified as a government worker. On the second day, at the first river ferry — bridges over Cambodia's wide streams are exceedingly rare — they had to abandon the car and join the mass of marchers. Grim teenage soldiers lined the road, shouting at them to move more quickly, beating those who lagged because they were carrying the ill or their young children. Other people were shot at the roadside, she said, but she didn't know why.

Four days out of Phnom Penh, the girl's nineteen-year-old brother, who had been ill with malaria for several months, could go no farther. Three soldiers pulled him from the others' supporting arms and shot him dead on the spot, Serey Monty said, in full view of the family. The killers pushed the others onward, and the youth's body lay on the road. Those who followed stepped over it. The girl stopped a moment in her recounting to wipe her eyes with a bare hand and apologized. For a month they marched, in the hottest time of the year, until they reached the western provincial capital of Pursat, 130 miles from Phnom Penh. The killing and the dying continued, day after day, and often she had to walk around bodies on the road. Once in the course of that month the family was given a small can of rice, no other food.

They entered the "liberated zone" not far from Phnom Penh. It was territory long held by the revolutionaries, whose people had not been driven from their villages. The marchers traded their belongings with them for food. At Pursat the survivors of the long column were jammed onto a train and rode for three days and nights, halting frequently for no apparent reason in the middle of nowhere. When they were ordered to get off at Sisophon, a district town near the Thai border, their car was no longer so jammed, Serey Monty said. Death from hunger and illness had taken a heavy toll.

At Sisophon, which the Lon Nol government had held until its collapse and whose people had been expelled, the family was separated and split among different work brigades. The girl and her surviving brother were assigned to a group of young men and women and sent into the jungle to clear the ground for new rice fields. Her sister was put to work weaving cloth, her sister's husband to repair bicycles, which were the soldiers' main means of transport. Her father built fish traps and her mother threshed rice.

The girl's workday began at 5:00 A.M. She poured some water over herself, put on her only set of clothes once again, and set out for the fields without breakfast. When there was no seasonal labor to be done in the rice fields, the young were put to work to build earthworks and dig ditches for irrigation projects. Work stopped at 11:00 A.M. for the first of the day's two identical meals: a thin soup of rice, sometimes some greens and salt. No fish, no meat, no eggs, no milk, rarely some fruit. In a country where food was once abundant, where hunger was the one misery of underdevelopment rarely known, now Cambodians went hungry all the time. Hunger and untreated illness were, by all accounts, responsible for even more deaths than the brutal killings that from the outset of the Khmer Rouge regime were virtually daily tragedies. Work resumed after a half-hour break and continued until 6:00 P.M., the time of the second meal. On moonlit nights the labor continued until 11:00 P.M., and sometimes older men and women were pressed into service to hold torches to allow work to proceed even if the night was dark. On other nights the evening meal was followed by an indoctrination session.

During the first year the family slept in the open, under trees, even during the monsoon rains. Then its members, each with his work brigade, were moved to a nearby village. They remained living apart. Although she lived near her parents, Serey Monty saw them only once during the year that preceded the family's escape. "You have to learn to tremble," a Khmer Rouge chief told her group. "You have to live as we lived during the war." Like others from Phnom Penh, Serey Monty felt that Khmers Rouges of all categories, from senior officers who occasionally visited the village to the humblest boy or girl guard, were driven by implacable hatred of the people of the capital. They believed or had had it drilled into their minds that the people of Phnom Penh had led "American" lives of luxury while those under Khmer Rouge control suffered not only complete deprivation but also American and, to a far lesser extent, Cambodian bombing.

Fear dominated life, and immediate death was constantly at hand, the girl said. They lived in terror under the unceasing watchfulness of fiercely suspicious and hostile teenagers who held arbitrary, apparently unlimited power over the "new people," those who had remained under the Lon Nol regime's authority until the war ended. They feared also the spying eyes of equally hostile younger children, who reported them to their guards for such real or invented infractions as resting for a moment at work, eating a fruit fallen from a tree, or pocketing a snail or large insect to be eaten later. Severe beatings were the punishment. There was deadly fear of falling ill, whether from hunger, overwork, or the three principal "natural" causes that plagued the "new people." These causes were malaria, long bouts of diarrhea, and colds that quickly degenerated into grave respiratory illnesses. For people chronically exhausted from overwork and insufficient sleep, without decent food or shelter or any form of medical care other than herbs, leaves, tree bark, or roots of uncertain value, such treatable illnesses often ended in death, particularly among children and the aged.

And the recurrent abrupt disappearances of people, sometimes because they were suspected of association with the Lon Nol regime, often without apparent reason, created fear of being "taken away." The Cambodian phrase is *chap teuv*, and in the years of terror these words took on the sinister sense of "never to be seen again." Serey Monty witnessed only one scene of the full meaning of *chap teuv*. Late in the afternoon on the day that she and her family made their escape, she walked out of the forest in which her brigade had been clearing ground. She had been given a rare leave to visit her parents for a few hours. Emerging into an open field, she saw no more than ten yards ahead three black-clad guards savagely plunging their knives into a group of eight persons. They were mainly women and children, the girl said, and their hands were tied. A child cried for its mother, but Serey Monty said the mother already lay motionless on the ground. "I knew before that the soldiers killed people, because they told about it," she said. "They are very happy when they kill them. They tell us their names. One said, 'It is very easy to kill children; we only have to tear them apart.'"

On that day all the Monty family members had permission to be in the village — Serey Monty, her parents, brother, sister, brother-in-law, and the sister's fourteen-month-old child. The decision to take the lethal risk of making their escape was made. They stole away separately and then began walking toward the

Thai border. All through the night and the next day they walked through the forest. Exhausted, the family stopped to rest. Only Serey Monty had the strength to continue at dawn. She wanted to remain with the others, but her mother insisted she continue while it was still possible. They feared discovery because they sensed that they were very near the border, an area patrolled with particular watchfulness. The girl crossed to safety only about two miles ahead. Nearly a month later, when I met her, Serey Monty said she was still waiting for the others, but the infinite sadness in her eyes and voice told more than she dared say.

The regime of terror was a reality of unknown origin for Cambodians. They knew only the oppressors whom they saw. They knew that those were the local representatives of a remote higher authority. They knew it was a sterner authority than any they had ever before felt, because even their local tyrants sometimes fell victim to it. Purges were frequent, indicating serious divisions in the ruling group, and local chiefs, often with all their staff, disappeared. They were replaced with new men who usually came from a distant region. In May 1978 I met Sen Smean, who had escaped from the village of Koil Moun Om near the border in January of that year. He recalled that the village, in Battambang province, had lived under three district chiefs in little more than one year. The first whom he recalled was Tem. Shortly after he had vanished, his successor, Nan, told the people at the Cambodian New Year in February 1977 that Tem had been killed because he was still under the influence of the governments of Sihanouk and Lon Nol. There were fifteen thousand people in the district, Nan said, and ten thousand must be killed as "enemies." He said six thousand of them were already dead. "We must burn the old grass and the new will grow," Nan said, according to Sen Smean. Nan's successor was Van. Nan had been killed as an "enemy," Van told the people shortly before Sen Smean fled.

But Cambodians knew of no definite connection of a specific person or identifiable group with the unforgiving high authority. They knew, of course, that Prince Sihanouk had headed the resistance forces in the five years of Cambodia's participation in the Indochinese war, but it had not escaped them that since the Khmer Rouge victory his name was no longer mentioned. They did not know that the prince and his consort were under house arrest, in constant danger of being "taken away," in the Royal Palace in Phnom Penh. Many knew that Khieu Samphan had figured as the leader of the "forces of the interior," while Sihanouk represented them on the international scene. Some had heard the name of Pol Pot, although none seemed to know that he was identical with Saloth Sar, his real name, who in the war years headed the "military activities committee" of the guerrillas. The name of Ieng Sary was known to a few. But no one knew who was Number One, or indeed whether he might not be someone whose name had never been heard.

To most Cambodians the center of absolute power over their lives was known until the end only as Angkar or Angkar Loeu, the "organization" or "high organization." Until 1977, even in the political indoctrination sessions, the Communist party was never mentioned. The dogma that was instilled was above all self-reliance, first to create a strong agricultural base, later to proceed to industrialization. The self-reliance that was preached was xenophobic and extreme — Cambodia would accept nothing from foreign countries. They were told that much of what had come from abroad in the past was intended to subjugate Cambodia to alien interests and must be destroyed. That included books, musical instruments, cassettes, films, air conditioners, and the like. Some refugees told of bonfires of such objects in the outskirts of Phnom Penh.

Sadly, the forbidden goods also included modern medicines. Cambodian traditional herbal nostrums could cure all ills, the people were told. "Today we have nothing but our hands, but in three years we will have our own cars and machines, and you will be allowed to drive them," an instructor told Hong An Khieng. Khieng was twelve years old when I spoke with him and his family after their extraordinarily dangerous escape by rowboat along the coast to Thailand in 1977.

One constant theme of indoctrination was that the new Cambodia would be a classless society of absolute egalitarianism. It was a lesson that was belied daily by what people saw around them. The Khmers Rouges lived quite apart from those whom they tyrannized. They had better housing, ate a richer and more varied diet, received occasional changes of clothing and sandals, worked far less hard, and were accorded priority in the rudimentary medical service that was dispensed. They also had access to radios, and those who knew how to read received occasional printed matter. But because of the high frequency of purges, reaching from leaders at the top of the party structure through local chieftains down to their lowest minions, the Khmers Rouges themselves were not immune to the workings of the savage system instituted by Pol Pot and his closest associates — Ieng Sary, Khieu Samphan, Nuon Chea, and Son Sen, as well as two sisters, Khieu Ponnary, the wife of Pol Pot, and Khieu Thirith, Mrs. Ieng Sary in private life. They secured their places at the summit in murderous power struggles that made Stalin's elimination of all imagined rivals seem like a civilized political process.

In September 1977 Pol Pot disclosed that Angkar was in fact the Cambodian Communist party. It had been created in 1960, and he was secretary of the Standing Committee of its Central Committee, top man in the Stalinist-style structure. Pol Pot had been named prime minister in 1976. But all this news reached only a handful of privileged Cambodians, even though it was announced on the daily Phnom Penh radio broadcasts. Closely monitored by interested countries' intelligence organizations and news agencies based in Bangkok, the principal listening post for Cambodia watchers, its news rarely reached its own people. Cambodians lived isolated in their communes, deprived of radios or newspapers; their sole source of information was the political education sessions that punctuated their lives, which were otherwise devoted only to work. There was no time free from communal obligations. But the low-level watchdogs who constituted their principal contact with distant authority were as a rule no better informed than the people they watched.

"Each Cambodian remains enclosed in his village," said Seng Horl, who had been a law student and a Phnom Penh high-school teacher of French. I met Seng Horl, then thirty-eight years old, shortly after his escape in 1978. "I have no idea what goes on inside or outside my country. They don't even honor us with propaganda."

The Cambodian people never knew that in March 1976 nationwide "elections" were said to have been held and that a People's Representative Assembly of 150 members had existed since then. Pol Pot was "chosen" as a "representative of the rubber-plantation workers." Even in the long history of elections without choice in Communist countries, there exists no precedent for an election held without the knowledge of the electors. In fact, in the nearly four years of Khmer Rouge rule, Cambodians were unaware of the existence of a government or administration. There was no currency. There was no school system, except for some vocational-training institutions, in which children of trusted "old people" received a minimal education while they learned how to operate simple machines. "The ignorant have become an honorable and inviolable class," said Seng Horl. "Ignorance is good for the country, they believe. Our children learn only to work, and most of the work they do is gathering dung and digging ditches."

Hen Soth, a thirty-eight-year-old former chief of a district agricultural-extension service, whom I met days after he reached Thai safety in 1978, spoke of his family, which he had had to leave behind when word reached him that he was about to be "taken away" for having worked for the Lon Nol government. The youngest of his five children was only one month old when he fled. He was desperately worried, with good reason, about what would happen to them and his wife as a result of his escape.

"We don't dare tell our children what Cambodia once was," he said. "My oldest boy asked me to continue to teach him to read and write, now that there are no more schools. But I didn't dare, and there are no books. I just told him to work harder, just a little harder, in the fields, so that he will survive." I asked the boy's age. Soth looked at me sadly and said softly, "Ten years. Ten."

"We grow ignorance," the agronomist continued. "No schools, no books, no newspapers, no radio, no television, no pagodas. There are no more traditions, no festivals. I don't know how it will continue. My homeland is finished, I think. The Cambodian no longer exists. Another animal, yes, animal, which I cannot recognize, has taken his place."

12

The Genocide and Its Perpetrators:
1975–1979

THE REGIME'S LIES WERE MONSTROUS, of dimensions to match Goebbels's, but because of the total absence of public information they did not reach the Cambodian people, those who would have been best able to measure Pol Pot's spectacular perversions of the truth. "We lived like frogs at the bottom of a well," an agricultural engineer said after the liberation, describing the state of ignorance in which Cambodians were kept, ignorance even of their leaders' infrequent public pronouncements.

Speaking to a group of rare foreign visitors, a "delegation" of Yugoslav journalists, in March 1978, the despot who ruled over a country where untold numbers of people were dying daily of hunger and malaria asserted brazenly that the problem of rice production had been solved and there was "enough rice to feed our people." And, Pol Pot continued, "We have eliminated malaria." He went on to boast of one more fictitious achievement: "Another outstanding result is the basic elimination of the illiteracy, which was a blemish in the former society." This from the head of the regime that had abolished the entire system of education. The unwritten conventions governing journalistic good manners between "brotherly" Communist nations, applied even by the less orthodox Yugoslavs, barred the unbelieving "delegates" from following up with skeptical questions. They did not raise the fundamental issue of whether there was truth in the harrowing descriptions of life in "Democratic Kampuchea," as the regime had renamed the country — they asserted "Cambodia" was a colonialist term — that the testimony of refugees had presented to the world. Privately my Yugoslav colleagues told me that they were horrified even by the prettified glimpses of reality that lurked behind what they were shown during their carefully staged, constantly supervised visit.

What motivated the Pol Pot regime to set in motion and continue in the face of appalling results its unique, murderous experiment in social engineering, will, I believe, remain forever an enigma. Not being intellectuals or theorists, Pol Pot, Ieng Sary, Nuon Chea, Son Sen, and the others have provided no writings that might explain their thought. The 1959 Sorbonne doctoral dissertation of Khieu Samphan, another Pol Pot disciple, on the outlook for industrialization in Cambodia is, to say the least, of little relevance to the economically destructive rustication of an entire nation that the Khmer Rouge government imposed. There was nothing resembling Mao Zedong's collection of moralizing platitudes bound in red, although the Cambodian leaders had probably read it and nodded approvingly at its revolutionary banalities.

Pol Pot's extremely rare public declarations in his four years in power were couched in the wooden language of ill-digested Marxism-Leninism. They were reminiscent of Stalin's paternalistic pronouncements and writings while millions of Soviet citizens were dying of starvation in the countryside or in the terrors of his gulag, either blatant lies or verbiage conveying no meaning. Whether Pol Pot's statements were intentionally obscurantist or an authentic reflection of an intellect dulled by decades of hearing and speaking only theoretical revolutionary claptrap remains a mystery.

I have had a half-dozen or so substantial conversations with Pol Pot's deputy in government, Ieng Sary, in various capitals, in jetliners, and in a jungle encampment, between 1973 and 1997. He is the only member of Pol Pot's inner circle who has spoken extensively to outsiders and given an image, however self-serving, of how the Khmer Rouge leadership functioned. Our conversations disclosed little to elucidate the political philosophy of the deputy prime minister in charge of foreign affairs, if there ever was one other than paranoiac hatred of Vietnam, where he was born. Immediately after the Vietnamese had driven Pol Pot's regime of Democratic Kampuchea from Phnom Penh, Ieng Sary made his first admission of some of the gravest charges that had been laid against it. He had rejected them indignantly in the past.

"In the early days there was certainly much killing," he told me a few hours after he had fled into Thailand as the Vietnamese columns neared the border region in January 1979. A Thai commercial flight was taking him from Bangkok to Hong Kong on his way for a visit to Beijing. A few months later, when again I had occasion to travel with him, on a flight from Bangkok to Sri Lanka, he said dismissively that the number of those killed in the four Khmer Rouge years was only "a few thousand." When the hostess came pushing her wagon of duty-free goods into the first-class compartment, a touch of surrealism entered with her. The radical revolutionary, right out of a Khmer Rouge encampment in the deep forest, took considerable time in choosing among various perfumes, questioning the stewardess about their qualities. He made his purchase with some of the American currency that China was providing to keep Khmer Rouge militancy buoyant.

Early in 1980, Ieng Sary was far more loquacious and seemed to draw closer to at least a partial truth during a two-hour conversation. I had accepted an invitation to spend two days at a secret jungle base in northern Cambodia, near the Thai border. We sat alone and talked by the light of a smoky kerosene lamp deep into the night, after a banquet offered by him and Khieu Samphan. "There were political errors," my host said in his lisping voice. "We recognize there were errors in going too far to the left. We moved too rapidly. We did not think enough about the organization of the state. We emphasized the political consciousness too much and had too little experience in the management of the state. We did not choose our public servants well and lost some control. Each region constituted a small kingdom. They ran their own affairs."

The deputy prime minister made a far from credible or creditable attempt to dissociate himself from the expulsion of the city populations. "Phnom Penh was liberated on April 17, and I arrived from China April 24," he said. "The city was already evacuated. It was a collective decision. If there had been two or three who think like me the decision would not have been taken." He added that Pol Pot had been "the leading personality" in the making of the decision. His implication that so fundamental a policy had been decided not well in advance by the party leadership but at the very last moment — the expulsion was decreed on the day that Phnom Penh was conquered — is impossible to credit. Ieng Sary was certainly part of the inner council that ruled on matters of such importance. (He was not, however, the second in command in the all-important Communist party of Cambodia. He held that rank only in the Khmer Rouge government. I asked him at a meeting in Phnom Penh in 1997 what his real place had been in the party hierarchy. He had defected the year before from the Khmers Rouges and been recognized by Hun Sen, Cambodia's latest strongman and a much earlier defector, as an independent warlord in a particularly rich border area. "Number Six," he replied modestly.)

Ieng Sary made it clear that the inner council around Pol Pot, whose title was party secretary, actively discussed important policies, and Pol Pot did not rule alone. He said that he had "raised many questions" about the abolition of money but had been told by Pol Pot that Cambodians did not know how to handle it. He grew agitated in his rather ignoble effort at white-washing himself by pushing the guilt for the most cruel policies on Pol Pot and others close to him, exempting himself. "I defended the intellectuals and was accused of being a rightist who knew nothing of the country because I had lived in exile," he said. He was referring not to his student days in Paris but his 1970–75 assignment in Beijing as the Khmer Rouge "ambassador" to Sihanouk, the wartime nominal chief of the anti–Lon Nol alliance. "There was no real discussion between Sihanouk and me," he told me. "He regarded me as a spy," a valid testimony to the prince's political acumen.

I met Ieng Sary again at the end of 1980. By then he was ready to concede that the regime's "errors" had been on a large scale. "We made a revolution," he said, in a hotel room in Jakarta. "The revolution in Vietnam and in France made many errors, too; many good things and many errors. We tried." When I asked him to describe some of the "good things," he was at a loss and finally called on an associate to fill the awkward gap. "Agricultural progress," was the best Minister for Economy and Finance Thiounn Thioum could think of, a claim belied by the state of the country that I had toured earlier in the year.

By 1997 Ieng Sary had advanced sufficiently in his divorce from his ideological past to give further insights into relations within the leadership. He sought to separate himself more emphatically than earlier from Pol Pot. He said that his differences with the party leader, who was as we talked a prisoner of his comrades Nuon Chea and Ta Mok in a northern redoubt, had begun after both had returned from government scholarships that took them to Paris after 1945. There, from 1951 until 1956, Ieng Sary had been head of the cell of the French Communist party for Cambodian students. Pol Pot was "a simple member," Ieng Sary said. Pol Pot returned to Cambodia in 1953; his scholarship had been canceled after he failed to attend his courses in electrical engineering regularly. Ieng Sary returned home in 1957. "There was a very important political discussion between Pol Pot, Son

Sen, and myself in 1960," he said. Son Sen, the Khmer Rouge defense minister, had also belonged to the group of Cambodian Communist students in France. The issue was "national democracy," which Ieng Sary said he advocated. "But Pol Pot was against democracy," he said.

They shared a common past in France, where the anticolonialism and republicanism of the young Cambodian nationalists found a facile theoretical basis in Communist ideology and an organizational home in the French party. A strong bond was forged, and apparently considerable freedom of speech prevailed among Pol Pot, Ieng Sary, Son Sen, Khieu Samphan, and a handful of others who became the leaders of their country. Some ended as victims at Tuol Sleng, the torture and assassination center in Phnom Penh. The group also included the Khieu sisters: Khieu Ponnary, Madame Pol Pot until he divorced her and married a younger woman when she began to suffer from depression, and Khieu Thirith, who remains Madame Ieng Sary. As an example of the candor that prevailed among them, Ieng Sary recalled that, annoyed at Khieu Samphan's slavish devotion to Pol Pot even while Samphan held the title of head of state from 1976 until 1979, Madame Ieng Sary said to him, "You should talk back to him. You act like the head of his office, not like the head of state."

Living in the stimulating and highly politicized atmosphere of Paris of the 1950s must have been an overwhelming experience for young people at a most impressionable age from sleepy Phnom Penh. They had had a thoroughly French education through high school, which equipped men and women of their generation in former French colonies with an admiring view of France as the intellectual center of the world, even while they resented France's colonial dominance in their countries. They had learned far more about French geography, history, and literature than about their own countries and tended to see the world through assimilated French eyes and sensibilities.

I have always been struck by the readiness of Cambodians,

far greater than that of their Vietnamese or Laotian neighbors, to adopt and make their own foreigners' ideas, particularly when delivered in French. Their French comrades in Paris, with the perennial readiness of the left-wing French "intellectuals" to construct radical theories and order the lives of others, must have played an important role in shaping the radicalism of Democratic Kampuchea. At the very least they must have heightened the readiness of Pol Pot and those around him to absorb Soviet, Vietnamese, and Chinese revolutionary prescriptions.

Back from France, most of the Cambodian Communists found teaching jobs in Phnom Penh and busily organized revolutionary cells among students and urban workers. They remained barely ahead of the persecution of Sihanouk's brutal secret police, supervised by Lon Nol. In 1963, Ieng Sary recalled, Pol Pot, by then acting head of the Khmer Workers party, said the time had come for the leaders to go into the "maquis." Indochinese Communists all use the French World War II term "maquis" when they talk about creating or joining a resistance movement in the jungle. Ieng Sary, as a member of the Central Committee, had urged staying in Phnom Penh, saying "we could still work underground there." But Pol Pot insisted, and Ieng Sary accepted "on condition that we stay inside Cambodia." He feared Vietnamese control over the Cambodian Communists; Hanoi was the revolutionary center of Indochina. Pol Pot learned many revolutionary lessons from the Vietnamese on his visits in 1965 and 1970, Ieng Sary said, "above all his secretiveness."

Was the suffering of the Cambodian people under the Khmer Rouge regime a secret to Ieng Sary? When did he learn of it? "From my children, in 1976," he replied. "All four lived in communes around Phnom Penh and were often sent to the countryside to gather herbs for traditional medicines. They came to me and said, 'Papa, people are dying of hunger. They are eating gruel, not rice.' I confronted Pol Pot, not at a meeting but in tête-à-tête and questioned him. He said I was against the regime. From then on, whenever I came back from a foreign trip, when the plane approached Phnom Penh, I asked myself, 'Will I go home or to 21-A?'" He was referring to the notorious Tuol Sleng by its party code name, which was S-21 or 21-A.

His apologia for his political life reminded me of the self-justifications that I had often heard in Germany at the end of World War II. People who clearly knew better claimed time and again they didn't know about concentration camps. Yet when asked why Hitler and the Nazis met no opposition, the same people replied: "How could we oppose them? We were all afraid of being sent to a concentration camp."

How much did Ieng Sary know about Tuol Sleng? I asked. "I thought it was a reeducation center, and after reeducation people would be sent back," he replied. "But later I noticed they didn't come back. I knew people were accused there without justification." And Pol Pot? I asked. Ieng Sary shrugged. "I don't know if Pol Pot knew. Only two people knew for certain, because they must have been there: Nuon Chea, who was responsible in the party for security, and Son Sen, who was responsible for state security." Those who have studied the rich archives of interrogation transcripts left behind at Tuol Sleng have no doubt that Pol Pot was fully aware of what purposes it served. Did Pol Pot intend the wanton mass killings, the starvation, the inhuman mistreatment? I asked Ieng Sary. Was he aware, while living in Phnom Penh, which was empty of people except those who served the party and government, of what life was like for Cambodians? Ieng Sary suggested that the leader may not have known the full truth or cared to know it. "Pol Pot spoke only in theory," his Number Two in government, Number Six in the Communist party, replied. "He was a master of words. He spoke convincingly at meetings."

With all their self-justification, Ieng Sary's words contain some plausibility. Like his direct predecessor, Lon Nol, Pol Pot traveled little outside the capital and had scarce direct knowledge of how Cambodians lived under his rule. I doubt that his

underlings ever reported to him facts that would have contradicted the brilliant results of his policies that he claimed as his
achievements. Nothing that Pol Pot has said publicly, in or out
of power, indicates that he was interested in the effects of his rule
on the Cambodian people. What motivated Pol Pot and mattered most to him, according to Ieng Sary, was "the fear of losing
his power."

I will never know whether Ieng Sary's account of his conversation with Pol Pot about starvation in the countryside, where
all Cambodians were forced to live, is true. But Pol Pot would
not have been the first dictator in history to reject an associate's
unpleasant report and accuse him of opposition.

The collective culpability of the Khmer Rouge leadership in
the genocide of their own people is beyond doubt. Since 1979 I
have not met a Cambodian, including ministers of the Khmer
Rouge regime, who did not mourn the death of members of his
family between 1975 and 1979. Nor is there any doubt that the
executions without trial of entire classes of men and women were
acts of determined policy.

Pol Pot's leadership is responsible also for having stirred up
the insane and lethal hatred of many of the "old people," those
who had been "liberated" by the Khmers Rouges earlier in the
1970–75 war, toward the "people of 1975." These were Cambodians of Phnom Penh, Battambang, and other towns and villages, the great majority of the population, who remained under
the Lon Nol government's rule until the Communists' final victory. The youngest of the oppressors were the generation of
malevolent children — mindless, brutal servants of the Pol Pot
regime, who starved and worked to death hundreds of thousands
of their compatriots, made countless others die of unattended
maladies, and turned the lives of vast numbers into nameless terror from which they will not recover.

But I suspect that innumerable deaths and an infinity of suffering resulted also from the tendency of Cambodian leaders to
give no thought to the ultimate results of policies that they dic-

tate and the dangerously fatuous words in which they are communicated to those responsible for carrying them out. In such circumstances, a central decision to make the "people of 1975" experience the hardships and deprivation that the "old people" suffered during the war against Lon Nol and the United States Air Force; to make them obedient servants of Angkar, like the "old people"; to teach them to live like "true Cambodians" rather than as pampered "running dogs of American imperialism," could easily be translated in its transmission to half-educated regional chiefs and by them to the brainless automatons of their creation into a license to brutalize and murder by all means at their disposal.

13

A War Left Unfinished: 1979

IT WAS PRINCE SIHANOUK and Ieng Sary who disclosed to me that all was not well between the Khmers Rouges, whom the prince served as figurehead leader of the anti–Lon Nol Front, and their Vietnamese Communist allies. This was in an interview in June 1973, at the height of the 1970–75 war, when nothing was publicly said to suggest that any discord marred the harmony among all national liberation forces — the Vietnamese, Cambodian, and Laotian Communists.

Sihanouk was on a visit to Nicolae Ceausescu. The Romanian dictator was the only follower of the Soviet Union who recognized the prince's wartime exile government. Ieng Sary accompanied him to make sure Sihanouk stuck to the Khmer Rouge line in his public statements. Ceausescu had grossly slighted his visitor by telling him within minutes of his arrival for a ten-day stay that he was leaving the following day for a state visit to West Germany, a more important power for Romania than the Cambodian guerrilla movement. He installed his guest in one of his luxurious mountain chalets in the Carpathians and left it to Sihanouk to find something to keep himself entertained.

Like many journalists, I had many times asked the resistance movement's representatives in Paris to be invited to Beijing, Sihanouk's exile headquarters, to interview the prince. I was invited instead to Transylvania, to Predeal, a resort in Dracula country, to help the sulking Sihanouk to pass the time in the alien Balkan setting. He greeted me warmly and informed me that he had reserved a hotel room for me. He counted on my company for more than just an interview. Our interview was so important, I begged off with flattery, that I had to rush to my typewriter and the telephone to New York, available only in Bucharest, to pass on his words to an eager world.

The interview lasted the entire morning and Ieng Sary sat next to Sihanouk for a good half of it. Sometimes he took an active part, at others he whispered counsel into Sihanouk's ear in a soft lisp. The scene was theatrical, the black Mao-suited Khmer Rouge a caricature of a diabolical Mephistopheles luring Faust to his soul's perdition. By excessive courtesy to the man whom he called "the Ambassador of the Forces of the Interior" to his court, Sihanouk made plain how annoying he found Ieng Sary's guidance. He excluded him from lunch. Seated next to the prince, I had to explain to him, his wife, Monique, his mother-in-law, and his chief of protocol, Prince Sisowath Methavi, Sirik Matak's brother, the Balkan cuisine that was served. (Prince Methavi, in one of the tragic ironies produced by Khmer Rouge paranoia, shared his brother's fate, although, unlike him, he had joined Sihanouk's exile regime. While Pol Pot placed Sihanouk under house arrest at the Royal Palace from 1975 to 1979, Methavi was tortured to death at Tuol Sleng. So was Huot Sambath, Sihanouk's ambassador to Yugoslavia and Romania and former United Nations representative, who drove me from Bucharest to Sihanouk's mountain chalet. It was the fate of many a "Sihanoukist" under the Khmers Rouges.)

The Paris Agreement between the United States and the Vietnamese Communists had been in effect since January 1973. Both sides had undertaken to cease all military action not only in

Vietnam but also in Cambodia and Laos. But since February the Nixon administration had resumed bombing in Cambodia, concentrating with devastating effect on one country the planes that earlier had sown destruction also in Vietnam and Laos. The administration justified the bombing by telling a critical Congress that the North Vietnamese were continuing to supply arms and ammunition to the Khmers Rouges and directing them in battle.

Throughout the long interview in Romania, Sihanouk and his guardian devil returned repeatedly to their dissatisfaction over Hanoi's attitude. "Naturally the evolution of their policy, which is becoming friendly to the United States, worries us a little," the prince said. "They don't help us; they have completely lost interest in Cambodia." When Cambodia entered the war, Sihanouk said, the Vietnamese Communists pledged "to fight against American imperialism to the end." He continued mockingly, "Who could foresee that afterward they would stop before us? And suddenly you would see Kissinger smile and Le Duc Tho smile at Kissinger, they shake hands, they go arm in arm and leave us alone?" Le Duc Tho was North Vietnam's negotiator who concluded the Paris accord with Henry Kissinger.

Sihanouk and Ieng Sary complained that since January Vietnam had stopped delivering to the Khmer Rouge guerrillas the Chinese-supplied arms and ammunition that had kept them fighting. This had left them dependent on weapons captured or bought from the Lon Nol army. Hanoi was not living up to the Paris Agreement in many other respects, the prince said, alluding to the Communists' continued warfare in South Vietnam, but it was living up to its letter and spirit in Cambodia. "I wish the North Vietnamese weren't so correct," he said. "Unfortunately for us they don't violate the Paris Agreement."

The prince stepped across the Khmer Rouge party line in speaking openly about tension between the Vietnamese and Cambodian Communists, who consistently belittled Vietnamese help, often to the point of accusing those who had built their fighting forces in the first phases of the war of being a hindrance.

"The Khmers Rouges don't allow me to speak these truths," Sihanouk said. "I told them, 'I can't respect all your discipline.' According to them, one must never admit that the North Vietnamese helped us. We must say how it really was. In 1970 and 1971 we had the help of the Vietnamese. There were two things that were given to us at my request: There was help to our young resistance. They helped us to structure our people's army. And second, there were naturally some North Vietnamese units that helped us. But since the second half of 1972 we are autonomous." Ieng Sary hastened to assure me that the Khmers Rouges were "not at all" under Vietnamese influence, not at all like the Laotian Communist forces. "We don't have any Vietnamese advisers," he insisted.

In the two years before the end of the war in Indochina, reports impossible to verify drifted out of the secretive Communist world telling of friction that sometimes rose to the point of armed clashes between Vietnamese and Cambodians. In liberating themselves from Vietnamese influence, the Khmers Rouges were also eliminating their comrades who had spent many years in North Vietnam and had returned to help the Vietnamese organize the Cambodian resistance movement.

Khmer Rouge secretiveness reached absurd dimensions. When I was working in Pakistan early in 1977, when Ieng Sary happened to be there on an official visit, I phoned his hotel room. Thiounn Prasith, the regime's leading diplomat and United Nations representative, curtly rejected my request to interview the deputy prime minister or himself but volunteered to give me a written statement. An hour was fixed for me to pick it up from him. When I asked for him at the appointed time, the receptionist informed me he had just checked out. The statement the Cambodians had left for me was a tirade of hatred against the United States, rejecting reconciliation on any terms.

In the summer of 1977 I was told by well-placed officials in Washington that detailed, credible reports, substantiated by the accounts of recent refugees from Vietnam interrogated in camps in several Southeast Asian countries, had told of major attacks launched throughout the month of May from Cambodia on several widely separated border areas of Vietnam. So serious were the raids that witnesses reported that two sizable towns, Ha Tien on the South China Sea and Chau Doc farther inland, had been temporarily evacuated because of shelling. It was not known whether the attackers were Vietnamese resistance fighters supported by Cambodia, or the Cambodian military. Large numbers of Vietnamese military and civilian casualties were said to have been seen by the witnesses.

My report again raised the hackles of those who, having supported with equal enthusiasm all Indochinese "liberation" movements, found it difficult after the war to be challenged by having to make a choice. By the end of the year, the enmity between the former allies could no longer be hidden. A major Cambodian raid causing many civilian casualties hit Tay Ninh province north of Saigon. Vietnam countered with an attack deep into the province of Svay Rieng, the "Parrot's Beak" in American military parlance, a narrow, pointed salient of Cambodia that juts deeply into Tay Ninh.

On the last day of 1977 came the bombshell that broke the silence shrouding the hostilities. Phnom Penh radio announced that Cambodia had broken diplomatic relations with Vietnam, accusing its neighbor of "ferocious and barbarous aggression." Khieu Samphan, then bearing the title of President of Democratic Kampuchea while Pol Pot, the undisputed Number One, was Prime Minister, read a government declaration calling the Vietnamese Communist troops an even more cruel enemy than the South Vietnamese who had fought against the Khmers Rouges in the past. It accused Hanoi of many attempts to seize Cambodian territory and of trying to stage a coup d'état. The break in diplomatic relations was extraordinary in the history of Communist governments. Even at the height of their strident ideological hostility, the Soviet Union and China maintained formal diplomatic links.

In 1978, bloody Khmer Rouge border raids continued, causing heavy Vietnamese civilian casualties. At the same time, the Vietnamese Army enlarged and consolidated its hold on strategic border areas, in the "Parrot's Beak" and to the north, in the once French-owned rubber plantations. Phnom Penh rejected a Vietnamese truce proposal and replied to invitations to negotiate with ever more bellicose propaganda. In Vietnam, large numbers of Cambodian prisoners seized in the fighting, as well as defectors who took advantage of the border war to change sides, were being reindoctrinated and trained in several camps.

Clearly Vietnam was preparing a Cambodian cloak to cover its eventual invasion to replace the ferociously hostile Pol Pot regime with a pro-Vietnamese satrap. The glaring disproportion in military power left no doubt that Vietnam could capture any place in Cambodia that it desired and put into focus the irrationality of the challenge thrown out by the Pol Pot regime. Did it count on decisive help from China, with which Vietnam's relations had descended into bitter hostility as a result of Hanoi's embrace of Moscow?

Early in December 1978, Hanoi announced the formation of a "Kampuchean United Front for National Salvation" in the "liberated zone," the part of Cambodia Vietnam had occupied since 1977. The front then called on the Cambodian people "to rise up for the struggle to overthrow the Pol Pot–Ieng Sary clique." History was repeating itself. In 1970, following the coup against Sihanouk by what was then called "the Lon Nol–Sirik Matak clique," the "Khmer National United Front" was created in Beijing by the Khmers Rouges and Sihanouk as a curtain covering the invading Vietnamese Communist forces. The front grew quickly in numbers and combativity to become the nucleus of the Khmer Rouge guerrilla army. By 1972 it was able to fight its own war and win it three years later.

The Hanoi radio named the leader of the new front as Heng Samrin and identified him as a former Khmer Rouge political commissar and division commander. The front's own radio, broadcasting no doubt over the same Vietnamese transmitter, set forth a political program that struck themes identical with the refugee accounts of the horrors of life in Democratic Kampuchea. It pledged to undo all the revolutionary innovations of Pol Pot's vision of Cambodia. It promised to dissolve the agricultural communes, repopulate the cities and towns, allow families to reunite, reintroduce a currency, and restore education and the practice of religion. "Pol Pot and Ieng Sary have put their heads in a noose," Radio Hanoi declared. "They are now in a predicament and on the verge of collapse." They were, and who would know it better than the Hanoi government, which had decided to open a full-scale invasion of Cambodia?

It began before the year was out and led in a few days to a replay of the Vietnamese advance against Lon Nol's army in 1970. The Cambodian northeast, including the provincial capital of Kratie on the Mekong River, a region that Nixon in 1970 had called the "headquarters for the entire Communist military operation in South Vietnam," fell quickly to Vietnam, as it had nearly eight years earlier. On January 7 Phnom Penh was in Vietnam's hands, and Pol Pot and his comrades fled by road to the Thai border. "The regime of dictatorial, militarist domination of the Pol Pot–Ieng Sary clique has completely collapsed," Radio Hanoi declared in its first announcement. The Khmer Rouge hold over Cambodia had indeed been broken, but with the support of most of the international community the regime remained alive and recognized as the legitimate government of Cambodia or a component of it, occupying its seat at the United Nations, alone or in coalition, for another decade.

Pol Pot's remaining forces controlled only unpopulated jungle enclaves along the four-hundred-mile Thai border, usually in mountain areas of difficult approach for an attacker. They survived there only because of Thailand's readiness to supply them and to allow the leaders of the widely separated Khmer Rouge camps easy contact with one another by the use of Thai roads. China supplied them with arms, delivered to the Cambodians via the Thai military. Unwillingly, the international community, through various official and nongovernmental relief organizations, provided the Khmers Rouges with food and medical care. This happened because Thailand took firm control of channeling all the international aid to the hundreds of thousands of Cambodians who had rushed to the border. Some went to escape from the acute food shortage caused by the inefficient agriculture practiced under the Khmer Rouge regime, exacerbated by the disruption of the Vietnamese invasion. Others fled to the border in hope of being accepted as refugees in Western countries. Yet others sought asylum from what they feared would be a long war.

They all needed to be fed, but none of the providers of aid was allowed to do so directly. Relief goods had to be turned over to the Thai government and its politically powerful military, who in turn decided how much assistance would be channeled to each camp. Thailand, for political reasons, granted the highest priority to the Khmers Rouges. Western governments and the United Nations and other international organizations protested, invoking the generally established rule that military forces should not benefit from foreign food aid supplied for humanitarian reasons. Thai blackmail was effective: either you provide food and we distribute it as we see fit, or we will accept no food aid at all for any Cambodians. The hapless civilian refugees were made hostage to Thai insistence on supplying the Khmers Rouges.

Thailand sided with Pol Pot and his enclave regime not because it admired him or his record. In Thai realpolitik, it was fear of Vietnam that dominated, and with its invasion of Cambodia, Vietnam had arrived on Thailand's border. To a lesser degree, this view was also held by Thailand's partners in the Association of Southeast Asian Nations (ASEAN): Singapore, Malaysia, Indonesia, and the Philippines. The "domino theory" of the Eisenhower years — that the fall of one country to a Communist foe endangered all its neighbors — was not dead in Southeast Asia. Supporting the Khmers Rouges was also doing a favor to China, the giant that all of Southeast Asia wants to placate, to advance its economic interest in China's giant market and to assure itself of a budding superpower's goodwill. China, too, having changed policy from revolutionary zeal to economic modernization, was not supporting the Khmers Rouges from sentiments of radical Communist brotherhood. China's motivation was rooted in its animosity to the Soviet Union. To the Beijing regime, Vietnam was not only a client state economically dependent on the Soviet Union but also a Soviet military and espionage base at its southern border.

The Western world, led by the United States, supported the Pol Pot regime's claim to legitimacy because it had been overthrown by a foreign invasion, a clear violation of sovereignty and international rules of conduct. Faced with a choice between upholding the most tyrannical and bloodthirsty regime since the days of Hitler and Stalin, or a puppet regime put in place by an invader, it backed the tyrant's claim to legitimacy. The elevation of sovereignty to the pinnacle of international virtue is a damning comment on the sincerity of the Western democracies' constantly proclaimed advocacy of human rights. Vietnam did not march into Cambodia to free its people, and it deserved no praise. But the invasion restored to Cambodians some basic human rights that they felt at that stage of their immense suffering to be more precious than sovereignty. It allowed the survival of a great number of Cambodians who had felt that they were doomed.

No visitor to Cambodia in the months following the Vietnamese invasion could fail to grasp that truth. That does not mean that Cambodians were grateful to Vietnam or changed their minds about regarding it as their historic enemy. They were painfully aware that among the freedoms that they were denied was that of being allowed to choose their liberator. I could easily put myself in their place; I waited long years in my native Germany for another country, any other country, to come and free me from a tyrannical ruler. It took World War II to end

Hitler's dictatorship. Uganda's dictator Idi Amin was overthrown by an invasion from Tanzania at about the same time as Vietnam's; few eyebrows were raised. The Soviet Union had invaded Hungary in 1956 and Czechoslovakia in 1968, occupying both countries, toppling exceptionally popular governments and installing puppets in their places. The Western democracies moaned but accepted the results. Realpolitik, pragmatism — call it what you will — coexistence with the mighty Soviet Union proved more important than the principle of sovereignty. But the survival of Cambodians, as the United States and all Vietnamese governments had proved in the recent past, was not important enough to sacrifice a principle.

Three days after the fall of Phnom Penh to the Vietnamese, I was told by an acquaintance in the large American intelligence community in Bangkok, which was glued to its monitoring equipment to keep abreast of a war that was proceeding in isolation from the non-Communist world, that Ieng Sary had managed to send a letter from Cambodia to the Thai government asking for permission to cross Thailand on the way to China. The Thai government denied receiving any such message. Late the following day, the acquaintance called to suggest that I would find it interesting to be on that evening's Thai International flight to Hong Kong. I can take a hint and so reserved a first-class ticket.

No exceptional passengers had arrived when I boarded. I feared that Ieng Sary, if indeed the Thais delivered him to the flight, might spot me and wish me to be removed so as to avoid the press. So I chose a seat in the last row of the first-class compartment and held a newspaper ready to hide behind until the plane was airborne. The only encouraging sign was that the cabin crew had been instructed to keep the right-hand front row seats free. They were not told for whom. It was past takeoff time, and the seats remained empty. I asked the hostess to let me know when the cockpit ordered the passenger doors to be closed. I might want to get off at the last moment, I told her. She looked at me strangely, but hostesses are used to bizarre passengers, particularly in first class. I stood in the aisle to be ready to hop off.

Suddenly a short motorcade drove up to planeside, preceded by a lead car with a howling siren and a rotating blue light. I rushed into my seat and hid my face behind the *Bangkok Post*. Ieng Sary, accompanied by two men and a woman, was conducted to the front seat. His male aides were seated behind him, and the woman sat beside him. Then four men and three young women boarded, dressed identically in white shirts, with black pants or long black skirts with bare feet in open sandals. They marched through the front section and disappeared silently behind the curtain. The Khmer Rouge chief refused a glass of champagne and was brought the *Bangkok Post*, which he scanned intensely. He had, of course, seen no newspaper since his flight from Phnom Penh.

His frustration must have been keen — he speaks no English. So once the plane was safely in the air, I went to greet him and offered to translate the articles that might interest him. He professed joy, rose to greet me, and asked the woman aide next to him to give me her seat. He introduced her as Yun Yat, minister of culture and education, surely one of the least active Khmer Rouge cabinet posts. But she was the wife of Son Sen, the movement's chief military planner, and in her own right an important leader. Pol Pot had her killed eighteen years later, along with her husband, children, and other relatives, during an internecine leadership conflict within the Khmer Rouge remnants in 1997. In an extra measure of gratitude for decades of devoted service to him, he had their bodies run over by a truck.

Ieng Sary was delighted to hear that the United States had condemned the Vietnamese invasion. "I thank you very much," he said, looking at me. I did not acknowledge his gratitude for an American policy from which I greatly differed. "We appreciate very much the attitude of President Carter and his principles," he said. To hear the Khmer Rouge leader fawn over the attitude and principles of a president of the United States was as astounding a reversal as I have ever experienced. It made me queasy. Perhaps he had noted my surprise, because he added, as if to prove his ever-doubtful sincerity, "The hatred of Cambodians for the Vietnamese is even greater than that for the Americans during the war." Pol Pot was in good health and thoroughly optimistic, Ieng Sary assured me. He had seen him that very day, just before leaving Cambodia. They had left Phnom Penh about two hours before its fall, Ieng Sary said, while heavy fighting was under way. "There were many dead," Madame Yun Yat interjected.

"The war will continue, and we will win victory," Ieng Sary said. He said the situation at that moment was no worse than "temporary difficulties." The Khmer Rouge army was far from defeated, he said, and correctly, as events proved, he reported that many units had been withdrawn intact. "What do you want?" he continued. "When tanks arrive with cannon, why keep the towns? Why stay there? We think it is normal to retreat before tanks. But the Vietnamese have taken only the towns." This, of course, was a considerable understatement. The Vietnamese quickly gained the upper hand throughout the country in 1979, despite occasional small-scale Khmer Rouge raids, and the bulk of the Cambodian troops, thanks to Thai connivance, was reduced to some easily defensible redoubts along the border.

We were flying over Vietnam, and I asked him his thoughts about Cambodia's former ally. "We have known the perfidious nature of the Vietnamese for a long time," he replied. "We hoped after the war they would let us live in peace, but you see . . ." His sentence trailed off. He belittled Vietnam's help during the Khmer Rouge war against Lon Nol. "They helped us on condition that we become their puppets," he said.

A delegation of six members of the French parliament, on their way to Beijing, asked me who it was that I had been talking to. They had never heard of Ieng Sary and were not interested. "We were interested in Indochina in the past," one parliamentarian explained in remarkable testimony to the impermanence of national interests. Two other passengers were very interested, however. "What did he say?" one, an American, asked as I made my way back to my seat before landing. I thought, correctly, that he was the CIA man "covering" Ieng Sary. "I work for the *New York Times*," I said. "Read all about it tomorrow. Who do you work for?" "Oh, you know, for 'the institute,'" he replied, smiling. He introduced his neighbor, clearly a Briton. "And you work for the British 'institute'?" I asked. "Of course," he said.

A heavy security guard, rifles at the ready, awaited the Cambodians on the tarmac. They were whisked into waiting cars and rushed off into the night, into China, the best remaining hope for the Khmers Rouges.

On February 17, 1979, Chinese guns opened up on northernmost Vietnam, and China's punitive invasion began. It continued for sixteen bloody, destructive days, with heavy losses to both sides. Deng Xiaoping, China's supreme leader, had signaled his country's intention to deliver "an appropriate limited lesson" to the country that he described as China's and America's foe. But it could be only a "lesson." Nothing could budge Vietnam from Cambodia until the Soviet Union, whose unceasing flow of military and civilian assistance sustained Vietnam's capacity to maintain its large expeditionary force in the neighboring country, pulled out the rug from under its main Asian ally. Mikhail Gorbachev's priorities were centered closer to home. In 1989 the last Vietnamese troops crossed the border toward home, to the immense relief of the Cambodian and Vietnamese peoples. The Vietnamese had rejoiced at the end of war with the West in 1975, only to find themselves three years later sending off their husbands and sons into renewed carnage.

They left their mission unfinished. Pol Pot had survived.

14

Meeting the Murderers: 1979

T HE FIRST TIME I SAW THOSE whom I had known only
from the chilling accounts of Cambodians who had
made their perilous escapes was after Vietnamese control over the country had been fully established.

The Chinese Army had withdrawn from its spiteful invasion
of Vietnam. It had been costly to both sides and destructive of
Vietnam's northern border provinces. But it did not lessen Hanoi's
determination to maintain its hold over what had been Beijing's
only Southeast Asian client state. Pol Pot's remaining troops, a
considerable force, were establishing themselves in early 1979 in
sanctuaries on the Thai border, and I often went to the border to
look for them. They were being rearmed by China and nour-
ished and nursed by the food and medicine shipments from
Western countries that had been intended for starving Cambodian civilians. With the full knowledge and connivance of the
Western governments and Thailand's Southeast Asian neighbors, the Thai military handled this clandestine traffic, not
without benefit to their pockets. They chaperoned the Pol Pot
forces and their leaders, ferried them between their enclaves

inside Cambodia on Thai roads, and provided their communications and contact with the outside world while officially denying everything.

The world was fully committed to upholding Democratic Kampuchea's violated sovereignty, because the release of the Cambodian people from a genocidal regime was the result of a Vietnamese invasion and occupation. America's unforgiving stand against the Vietnamese Communists, whom it had failed to defeat in war, was even stronger than its distaste for the Khmers Rouges. That the deposed Pol Pot regime was the greater evil by far did not matter.

With a few journalists, mainly Thai, guided through mined fields by a local peasant, I made my way through an unattractive landscape of stubble and sparse woods in southeastern Thailand. Near the malodorous remains of a cow that had stepped on a mine while grazing, our path took a steep downward turn to a narrow stream, and there they were: the Khmers Rouges. The opposite bank was Cambodia. Men and women in regulation Pol Pot black, with the traditional red-and-white checkered *khramas*, peasant scarves, on their heads or about their necks, were encamped along their side of the river, which was shallow in the dry season.

Their appearance and behavior confirmed the descriptions that refugees had given to me over the four preceding years. Dark, unsmiling glares were the response to the waves and shouts of greeting from my Thai companions. Men armed with Chinese automatic rifles stared suspiciously at us from behind bushes and trees. One, sitting on a branch, now and again raised his rifle against his cheek and trained it on a cameraman. In the stream, men and women scooped water into plastic buckets and blackened pots. Two armed men stood guard over three foraging cows. Two girls led a pony from the stream up the bank, back to the bivouac. A boy soldier walking down the riverbed, proud of his shiny rifle, met my look with an unsmiling stare at what may have been the first European face he had ever seen. Two soldiers lolled in hammocks without suspending their watchfulness or laying down their rifles.

Earlier that day, a Thai district officer had told me Vietnamese troops had just captured Poipet, the Cambodian border town on the Bangkok–Phnom Penh road, and had planted on the guard post on the Cambodian side of the border stream the red-and-yellow flag with the five stylized towers of Angkor Wat of the new, Vietnamese-installed regime of President Heng Samrin. The Khmer Rouge combat unit and their families facing us had evidently avoided combat and escaped to this spot about twenty-five miles to the south and set up their camp, backed up against the Thai border. The war was going badly for them, and they might well need Thai help for food or refuge if the Vietnamese moved southward along the border. It was clearly this concern that made them put aside their hostile reticence. An unarmed emissary waded across to us. His right arm was withered; he said he headed his unit's medical team.

There were ten thousand of them in the area, he said, and they were going to do battle against the *yuon*, that contemptuous word for Vietnamese that was common to Cambodians of all political camps. They had everything they needed and did not intend to ask for Thai asylum. Pressed on this point, the emissary said he would have to consult his superiors before replying. He waded back to the Cambodian side, climbed up the steep embankment, and consulted three men who, sitting behind a bush, had been watching his every move. They were emphatically spelling out a precise response. He crossed the river border once more to our side. Thai authorities had assured the Khmer Rouge leaders that if necessary the unit would be allowed to cross, he reported. But eleven of the Cambodian group had crossed the day before to let their cattle graze and had not returned. They must be sent back, he told us. Why doesn't he go ask the Thai authorities? the Thai journalists asked. Once again the messenger crossed to his camp. The consultation with his three chiefs took longer. He came back to us and drew from his pocket a sheet of paper listing the eleven missing. His superiors demanded their return.

The emissary was restless. His comrades were staring at him. Clearly he had been instructed to end the conversation. He had smoked continually, avidly, the cigarettes the Thais had been offering. But when they held out their open packs for the messenger to take along, he rejected the offer firmly. They needed nothing, he repeated. Only when our small group turned to leave did two or three of the Khmers Rouges respond hesitantly to the farewell waves of the Thais. No smiles. Angkar's discipline over its automatons held firm, even in defeat and full retreat.

Cambodians by the thousands made their way to the Thai border, taking advantage of the confusion of war to escape. Many among them hoped that Thailand would be a way station to permanent asylum in a Western country. Faced at home with a choice between the remnants of a Communist regime whose exceptional cruelty they had endured for four years and new Communist rulers under Vietnamese domination, they looked for a third alternative — emigration. Many thought they had relatives in America or France, Australia or Canada. They were not sure because they had been cut off from the world and didn't know the whereabouts of those they hoped to join. But Thailand, the principal country of first asylum not only for Cambodians but also Laotian and Vietnamese refugees from the new Communist regimes, had always been a reluctant host. (The quality of mercy that met seekers of temporary asylum in Asia was distinctly strained. The Philippines was the sole charitable exception.)

A young, British-educated colonel at Supreme Headquarters in Bangkok, a specialist in Cambodian affairs, explained the Thai policy to me. Thailand would continue to allow armed Khmer Rouge soldiers to traverse Thai territory to evade pursuit by the Vietnamese and reenter Cambodia in border regions easily defended against the invader. However, Thailand would not allow civilian refugees to remain. The military would make them return at places where it believed the refugees would be safe from Pol Pot's troops, who might kill them for having sought to escape. The Khmer Rouge remnants continued their mindless cruelty against other Cambodians even after their defeat by Vietnam.

The Thai colonel, who thought of himself as a realistic geopolitician, said foreigners, particularly the United Nations High Commissioner for Refugees, who protested against the forcible return of asylum-seekers, were hypocritical "bleeding hearts" who failed to understand Thailand's legitimate security concerns. He criticized the United States for complaining about Thai policy while failing to take as many refugees to the United States as Thailand wished. Thai refugee transit camps were crowded at the time with about 150,000 Laotians, Cambodians, and Vietnamese hoping for asylum in Western countries. The cost was borne by the international community through the United Nations refugee agency. "Ideally we would like to build a ten-meter-high steel wall all along the border," the colonel said. "But since we can't do that, we will have to provide for our national security another way."

There also was another reason, the colonel explained. Cambodia must retain a maximum population, because underpopulated it could not fulfill its role as a buffer state protecting Thailand from Vietnam. "We don't want a Cambodia that has become a lebensraum for Vietnam," he said, using a favorite Nazi term for vital national living space. This explained the appalling scenes of Cambodian civilians, starved and ill, who had sought refuge from the war on the border and been seized by the Khmers Rouges. Pol Pot's troops pushed and shoved them along Thai roads, removing them from areas of Cambodia conquered by Vietnam to reenter Cambodia at points inaccessible to the invaders. International aid workers and refugee officials who witnessed such scenes will always be haunted by the victims' pleading eyes and the indifference of the Thai military who protected the operations. The Khmer Rouge needed a civilian population to support their internationally recognized claim that they were Cambodia's legitimate government.

The results of Thailand's policy were horrific. A total of about forty-five thousand Cambodians — children, women, and men — were rounded up in temporary refugee camps along the border in June 1979 and transported in buses to a point opposite a desolate, heavily forested region of Cambodia's north. There, at gunpoint, they were pushed back into their country. Early one morning, a French friend who had long lived in Cambodia knocked at the door of my Bangkok home, an emaciated, frightened Cambodian at her side. He had been among those who had been forced back into Cambodia but had escaped again and was now hiding in the Thai capital. He told me his story, and the Thai colonel and many Cambodian survivors subsequently confirmed it was typical.

The buses carrying the refugees had halted at the entrance to a narrow mountain pass, and Thai soldiers forced their passengers out at gunpoint. The terrain, near the ancient temple of Preah Vihear, which in 1962 the International Court of Justice awarded to Cambodia over Thai objections, is a rocky plateau on the Thai side atop a high cliff that drops precipitously into a densely forested, nearly roadless and uninhabited region in Cambodia's Dangrek Mountains. The desperate refugees had to make their way down the cliff into the edge of the forest at its foot, while Thai troops fired their rifles to urge them on. Most lost whatever possessions they carried as they clung to creepers growing out of the cliff face. Often they had to hold still for what seemed like hours because the knowledge that the ground below was heavily mined slowed the advance of those ahead. The mines had been sown by the Khmers Rouges to prevent escapes from the country during their reign. In bitter irony, many who had succeeded in avoiding them while escaping were now falling victim to these explosives on their forced return.

The refugees did not dare to penetrate far into the forest to forage for water or something edible because too often they heard the blasts of exploding mines. Immobilized, many were dying of hunger and illness while clinging to the edge of the forest or taking shelter from the drenching monsoon rains under rocky outcroppings. The smell of death hung over the area, the trembling Cambodian said. The ground was rocky, and the dead could not be buried. How many thousands remained could not be estimated, he said in his halting French, because the jungle was dense and the frequent mine explosions discouraged the refugees from leaving the safe spots they had found. But he said smoke from cooking fires could be seen rising over a large area.

The saddest I heard of the many individual tragedies of what the United Nations refugee agency described as the first mass expulsion of refugees at gunpoint in its history was told to me by Kim Kok Hoai and his sister, Huong, Sino-Cambodians. Kim, twenty-six years old, had rushed to Thailand from Paris when he received word that Huong, whom he had last seen as he left Cambodia in 1970, had escaped and made it to a Thai camp. She was nine years old when he left, and he feared he would not recognize her at eighteen. He waited at the camp that sheltered about thirty thousand while others went to search for her. When they met, together with a sister who had rushed in from Hong Kong, Kim told me their emotion overflowed, and the older sister could not release Huong from her embrace because she had fainted in her arms. "There was a terrible coldness in her eyes, and they were deep, very deep," Kim said in describing the woman that the child had become.

They asked her the question whose answer they dreaded: "Where are our parents, where is our sister?" Their father was the first to die, Huong told them after a long pause. "She washed his body, rolled it into a mat, and buried him by herself," said Kim. "He cried in pain for hours before he died." That was shortly after they had reached the grim destination of their long march from Phnom Penh. Their grandmother died next, and Kim buried her. Then it was their mother, and two months later their youngest sister. "For the fourth time, my sister had to bury one of our family," Kim said, no longer trying to hold back his tears. "Then my sister was all alone. She was fifteen years old and indescribably sad."

Kim rushed to Bangkok after their meeting and obtained French assurance that his sister would be welcome in France. He went to the United Nations refugee organization, who requested the Thai authorities to release her to a transit camp in Bangkok to await a flight to Paris. I met Kim ten days later. He had just been told that Huong had shared the fate of those pushed down the cliff back into Cambodia. A broken man, he returned to France.

And yet not all Cambodian odysseys ended in tragedy. Three months later, after Thai policy had become more accommodating at international urging, I visited another huge border camp. As usual, I looked for refugees who spoke a foreign language to help me question others. Amazingly, the bright-eyed eighteen-year-old speaking fluent French was Huong. Kim was back from Paris, hoping once more to take her with him. "Are you sure I will not be pushed back again?" she asked repeatedly. "Will the United Nations protect me? Do you think the French will really take me?" The answer to all her questions proved to be "yes."

This is how Huong told me she made good her second escape: The Vietnamese troops in the area into which the Thais had expelled the Cambodians ordered the rejected refugees to stay put until they had cleared a path through the border minefields. Then, for about ten days, an endless column of perhaps twenty thousand starved Cambodian refugees had finally been trooped by the Vietnamese on a long march to the provincial capital of Kompong Thom. Many dropped by the wayside, Huong said, and some were buried there. It was never learned how many of the remaining refugees had managed to make their own way or how many of the forty-five thousand who had been forced back had died. Huong was determined to escape once again. In return for some gold for which she had exchanged a watch that her Hong Kong sister's husband had given her before she was forced back into Cambodia, she got a ride on a Vietnamese Army truck heading westward. For five chickens another truck took her to Siem Reap, the town near Angkor. Another lift advanced her to Sisophon, close to the Thai border. Then, dodging Khmer Rouge and Vietnamese soldiers, wading through flooded fields in the wake of three smugglers heading for the border to buy food, Huong reached Thailand for a second time, not far from the spot where she had crossed the border on her first escape. "I never want to see Cambodia again," she said. "Never."

By October 1979, famine throughout Cambodia grew desperate. Warfare and the breakup of the Pol Pot communes following the Vietnamese conquest had grossly disrupted the agricultural cycle. Cambodians were not cultivating their fields but wandering across the country to return to the places from which the Khmers Rouges had uprooted them. Rice had been left in the fields; the Khmers Rouges retreating before the invaders had destroyed it to deny it to the Vietnamese. In increasing numbers, skeletal victims trudged across the Thai border hoping for food and medical care. Malaria of the most lethal strains was making ravages. Some crossed into Thailand on their own, while others were marched through Thai territory, with Thai tolerance, under Khmer Rouge control to be settled in Khmer Rouge border enclaves.

The southeastern Thai village of Ban Laem, opposite an area remaining under Khmer Rouge control, became a major crossing place. Their heads gaunt, their eyes sunken, their bodies burning with malaria, Cambodians walked unhindered across the border. Yet even in Thailand they remained largely under the stern discipline of the Khmers Rouges who had led them there. Many, particularly children, limped on feet swollen from the severe illnesses of malnutrition that beset them. The Khmer Rouge soldiers with them were in better health and much less starved. "We let a part of them go, but most must stay in Cambodia," their leader told me. There was not enough food for them in Cambodia. Famine, malaria, and other illnesses raged among the population, he said, and many, particularly children, were dying every day. Children are born, the Khmer Rouge leader reported matter-of-factly: "Some live, some die." I spoke with him near the headquarters of a company of Thai marines stationed at Ban Laem.

The Khmers Rouges — about fifteen men and ten women — had come to pick up from the marines rations of rice, fish sauce, peppers, and blankets, which they carried across the border on their backs and in a caravan of seven oxcarts. The Thai feeding program for the Khmers Rouges was in full swing. "I am faithful to Pol Pot," the twenty-three-year-old chieftain told me. "Everybody, military and civilian, is for Pol Pot, because in his day all was well."

Cheam Sok, a fifty-eight-year-old Cambodian refugee, said fewer than four hundred refugees had arrived the day before after walking for two days and three nights. They had been 525 when they set out, but many fell by the wayside and probably died, Mrs. Sok believed. Her husband was among them. Now the Thai marines had camped them in an open field around a humble wooden pagoda, about one thousand altogether, waiting. They weren't sure for what. The scene of the mass of black-clad, suffering, apathetic men, women, and children camping in the open field resembled a Goya painting of the horrors of war.

A young woman held up to me a thin bundle wrapped in a filthy kerchief. An infant's face, resembling that of an old man, stared at me from blank eyes in deep hollows. Its arms were little thicker than a man's thumb, and loose flaps of skin hung from fleshless limbs. The infant stared but didn't move. Her son was three months old, the twenty-five-year-old woman said, and she had no food for him. Her breast was barren. Palm sugar in foul water had kept him alive until then, but she knew he couldn't live much longer. I asked a Thai lieutenant to let me take the child to a doctor. "Come back tomorrow," he said. "I'll ask the admiral."

When I went back for him the next day, about a dozen mothers were there, pleading with me to take their babies. All the infants' eyes looked as though they were seeing death, and all the mothers knew it.

A little girl, six years old perhaps, or ten or twelve — who could tell in her state of malnutrition and infinite sadness? — sat alone on the steps of the pagoda. I passed again hours later. She still sat there, exuding solitude much as more fortunate children convey the joy of life. Her head was large and bald, her belly protruded, and her feet were so swollen with malnutrition that a finger touching their top left a deep indentation that seemed to take an eternity to rise again to bloated smoothness.

A girl of twelve lay on the ground, trembling with a fever that burned my hand even through her black shirt as I touched her bony body. Her older sister squatting by her side in a gesture of silent accusation unfolded a rag wrapped around the only nourishment that had sustained them for days: tamarind leaves, often used to flavor soup but never eaten. At the edge of the camp, a woman who resembled a child although she was twenty-eight years old sat alone stoking a small wood fire. Her husband had died during their flight, she said, and then their six-week-old baby. She had waited alone in the forest for six weeks, she said, because the Thai soldiers wouldn't let her cross into Thailand. A man of middle years told me that he, too, was alone now. His wife and four children, aged from ten to twenty, had died on their way. "They ate leaves and whatever we could find," he said, as if in apology for having survived. "It was not enough."

The mingling of hardened Khmer Rouge soldiers and their suffering victims, whom on Thai soil they could not control as firmly as on the Cambodian side, was one of the anomalies of the border scene opposite Khmer Rouge sanctuaries. The victims hoped to be allowed to stay in Thailand and managed to do so as long as foreigners, usually from private aid organizations, were about. But most were eventually forced back into Cambodia by the young Khmer Rouge martinets.

I came upon a frail, desperately exhausted boy of six or seven years lying on a jungle trail on the Thai side. A car of a medical team of the International Committee of the Red Cross was parked nearby while its members were working in the area. I decided to wait to make sure the child received care. Two Khmer Rouge soldiers ambled up the trail, eyed the boy and me, and urged the child to return to Cambodia with them. He couldn't rise to his feet. They made a motion to carry the boy, and I told them to let him rest. The hard-faced youths consulted with each other and squatted down next to the boy and me, clearly waiting for me to leave. The child moaned now and again but made no move to rise. They talked to him in urgent tones; he replied with wan, negative gestures, looking expectantly at me. The face-off lasted for about ten minutes. Then the two exchanged brief words and without a further look at the child or myself trudged on toward the Cambodian side. The Red Cross team picked up the boy.

The Khmers Rouges, who from 1975 to 1979 had lived in complete isolation from the outside world, had been indoctrinated to hate most of it, particularly Vietnam and the United States. Yet after their defeat by Vietnam they began to enjoy attention and tender care from unexpected quarters. The West provided most of the food that the Thai military, over Western objections, passed on to the Khmers Rouges and with which they fed their troops and their families rather than the people they had forced under their control. Western aid organizations manned the camps in which the Khmers Rouges were housed and where they continued to impose their fanatic will upon unwilling Cambodians. The Thai military arranged the camps to favor Pol Pot's cause. The nations that provided assistance felt that they had no choice but to give aid on Thai terms or not be allowed to help anybody. Some, perhaps, believed, with Thailand, that any force that opposed the Vietnamese invaders merited support.

Malaria and other ills had not spared the Khmers Rouges.

In the sick wards that occupied large parts of the camps on the border their "cadres" lay, suffering and dying alongside other Cambodians, their victims. Swiss, American, French, and other volunteers of various aid organizations, in the best tradition of impartial charity, bestowed equal care on both. They nursed them, fed them, and carried them to the latrine ditches. So did the wives of Bangkok's diplomatic corps on their well-meaning volunteer weekend outings. Turning the other cheek reached an absurd climax when Rosalynn Carter, on behalf of her husband, the President of the United States, paid a highly publicized visit to a refugee camp in November 1979. Did she know that many of her encouraging smiles, pats of the hand, and friendly words were directed at ruthless and unrepentant servants of a genocidal machine? And did they know that the kindly foreigner was the First Lady of the country that until recently had been in their minds the imperialist devil incarnate?

15

Life Starting Anew: 1979–1980

*V*IETNAM GRADUALLY REOPENED CAMBODIA to the outside world after the years of Pol Pot's hermetical borders. It did so slowly, limiting access first to delegations
from Communist countries of Soviet affiliation or to persons of
proven sympathy with their cause. Selected international relief
agencies were next. As the need for food and medical assistance
mounted, more critical outsiders found admittance for brief
stays.

One of the briefest was an eight-hour visit accorded in November 1979 to a group of six American congresswomen and
three women members of Australia's parliament. Their purpose
was to persuade the new Vietnamese-imposed authorities to ease
the food crisis more rapidly by allowing international assistance
to arrive at all possible points of entry to Cambodia, particularly
by opening truck routes from the Thai border. Most of its four-
hundred-mile extent was not under firm Vietnamese control.
Vietnam, like the Khmers Rouges, was exploiting the wish of
Western countries to feed hungry Cambodians. Recognition of
its occupation and the puppet regime that Hanoi had installed in

Phnom Penh was Vietnam's objective. It refused to allow the opening of truck routes from Thailand, which would have been the most effective and economical way of transporting large quantities of food throughout Cambodia, and it limited deliveries to points of entry under firm Vietnamese control. These were Phnom Penh's airport and river port and the seaport of Kompong Som. The Western powers objected to Vietnam's rejection of the land route. They believed that if they accepted the limitation of shipments to points under Vietnamese control they would be granting implicit recognition to Hanoi's occupation of Cambodia.

Along with a handful of other journalists, I accompanied the nine legislators. Their plane bore the legend "United States Air Force" in huge letters on its sides, a surprising sight in Phnom Penh four years after the last American ambassador had left, the folded Stars and Stripes clutched under his arm.

The Phnom Penh that I returned to after an absence of six years had become a depleted city of unoccupied houses crumbling from neglect. But life was once again beginning to stir, life of a grievously impoverished character. About seventy thousand people had settled in Phnom Penh or were halting there temporarily on their way elsewhere that November 1979. In 1975, before the Khmers Rouges drove them out, it was believed that up to two million people were living in the city. Now, some had come back to homes from which they had been expelled; more had come to find what the countryside could not provide — food, shelter, and care for their ills. Many were merely on their way through, east to west or north to south, in all directions, undoing the demented redistribution of the population that had been part of Pol Pot's grand scheme. They were hungry and dressed in tatters and seemed infinitely weary despite their obliging smiles for foreign visitors.

Food and the unending search for it was their principal subject of conversation. But those with whom I spoke on my first stroll through familiar streets refrained politely from complaining about their hunger. "It is still a little miserable," a teacher said when I asked whether there was enough. "A little enough," said a man driving a truck, and a port worker replied, "It is not complete." Most of the food that arrived at the permitted points of entry was distributed to the new civil servants in lieu of money. The void left by Pol Pot's abolition of currency — unneeded in a country that had abolished all commerce — had not yet been filled. The basic unit of exchange was a small, used condensed-milk can filled with rice, and the price of such rarities as slim loaves of French bread baked with Soviet-supplied flour, or meat, fish, vegetables, and fruit was fixed in cans of rice. Limited electricity and water supplies had been restored.

The guided tour on which two pleasant Cambodian Foreign Ministry officials, surviving members of the pre–Khmer Rouge middle class, took us touched on the principal themes of the new regime's intense and unvarying propaganda — the evils of the regime that Vietnam had overthrown. What else could a government that owed its existence to Vietnam, a disliked foreign power, and could not yet provide its people with what they needed most, food, invoke to give it legitimacy? In a newly reopened school, a group of smiling, cheerful children, dressed in dirty clothes because they owned nothing to change into, sang what seemed a gay song. Sunshine, perhaps, and orchids? But what they sang was, in rough translation, as follows:

> Pol Pot committed genocide,
> He massacred our parents,
> He forced us to slave in the fields,
> He made us gather human excrement for fertilizer,
> He did not allow us to go to school.

We were taken to view what remained of the former National Bank. It had been blown up to symbolize the Khmers Rouges' total abolition of capitalism. Out of its gutted interior, scraps of banknotes of the past were still being blown onto

Norodom Boulevard. On a singed pile of rubble on the sidewalk lay charred banknotes and remnants of the alien cultures that Pol Pot had banished — a novel in Vietnamese, scraps of a Chinese film, and phonograph records. The next stop was an empty grassy plot opposite the old Hotel Royal and the fashionable Lycée Descartes. Not a single stone remained of the building that had stood there, the Roman Catholic cathedral. It had been razed to express Pol Pot's rejection of religion and all foreign influences.

Awful as is a void of wanton destruction that was once filled by stones, the final landmark of the tour of what Pol Pot had left behind was incomparably the most shocking. It was a place where persons of public or professional stature of former regimes — foresters or doctors, professors or senior civil servants — had been tortured to extract false confessions of participation in imaginary conspiracies with the CIA or the KGB. They had all been murdered. A first wave of victims were nonpolitical persons of prominence under the Sihanouk and Lon Nol regimes, and whose wives and children often suffered the same fate. Next had come supporters of Sihanouk who had joined the prince in alliance with the Khmers Rouges but were considered "class enemies." They were killed while Sihanouk and his wife were confined in the golden cage of the Royal Palace. Finally, when Pol Pot's paranoia turned on his own comrades, the Tuol Sleng death factory devoured also some of the worst of the Khmers Rouges, who had confessed to fictitious collaboration with Vietnam against Democratic Kampuchea. The bodies of these last victims were still chained to beds or lying in their cells when the Vietnamese troops captured Phnom Penh. Sixteen thousand is the approximate number of those tortured and slain at Tuol Sleng.

Tuol Sleng had been a school in a residential area of Phnom Penh, a long, two-story central building flanked by shorter side wings, forming a rectangle open at its front. Many of its classrooms were divided into sixteen brick cubicles each, so small that merely to be confined in them was torture. Their sole furnishings had been left in place — an ammunition case and a plastic can, into which the prisoners relieved themselves. Other classrooms were left undivided and served as interrogation rooms. Each contained an iron cot, to which the prisoners, stripped naked, were chained, and a desk and chair for the interrogator. The instruments of torture were varied, and fiendish beyond the traditional whips and electric generators to shock and burn victims. A special gallows-like machine was designed to hang prisoners by their feet while their heads were submerged into jars of water.

Like the administrators of the Nazi death machines, the Khmers Rouges kept meticulous records of their victims and protocols of their interrogations. They are monuments of their manic imaginings of enemies in their midst. They photographed their victims as a form of receipt that they had been delivered to Tuol Sleng. Now hundreds of these photos line the walls of the interrogation rooms. Terrified faces, some bearing the marks of brutal beatings, look upon visitors as if to pose the poignant question of why the world let it happen and then condemned those who made it cease. Others were photographed after death had released them from terror.

I have searched for photos of friends who I know perished at Tuol Sleng and, stupidly, I felt momentarily relieved when I did not see them among the frightened faces on the walls. Strange self-delusion, as if my friends had not shared the fate of those whose ordeal was made visible. No photo is displayed of my friend Suon Kaset, the country's Belgian-educated chief forester. Shortly after the 1970 coup, his wife, Sokhomaly, who had been the editor of Sihanouk's foreign-language magazines, asked me to have a word with Kaset. She had failed to persuade him to consider going into exile with their three children. She was convinced that under Lon Nol's lunatic regime Cambodia was destined for tragedy. "Perhaps he will listen to a friend more than to his wife," she said. Kaset heard me out. Smiling knowingly to suggest that he knew on whose behalf I was speaking, he replied, "You may be right. But Cambodia is a country of forests, and I am its chief forester. Whoever wins this war will need a good forester. That is why we have to stay. We shall live through what the other Cambodians will live through." He finally consented to let Sokho and their children leave eight days before the collapse, just before Phnom Penh airport closed for good.

On my first visit to Tuol Sleng, I found Kaset's name on a list of engineers murdered there, after having "confessed" to being the CIA chief of the Agriculture Ministry. He was a first cousin of Nuon Chea, who was probably the second most powerful man of the Khmers Rouges. But even that did not save this unpolitical patriot, who thought more of his country's forests than of its leaders. It was he who early in the war had told me in bitter anger that Lon Nol's corrupt military chiefs in western Cambodia were deforesting the country by opening vast tracts to Thai loggers associated with the Thai military. This crime, an economic and ecological disaster for Cambodia, has continued through all the regimes since then and enriched holders of political and military power of all factions.

The acute food shortage and the Vietnamese refusal to accept relief shipments by road from Thailand led to a controversial program of delivering food to the border. There it was distributed to Cambodians who made their way to the edge of Thailand from all parts of the country, some from hundreds of miles away. Some settled down there, others carried home on their backs, on bicycles, or on occasional oxcarts sacks of rice and rice seed donated by the world community, which were distributed in a joint operation by UNICEF and the International Committee of the Red Cross. However necessary the provision of food by all possible means, this distribution helped to create astride the border huge temporary settlements, bigger than any Cambodian town of the time. At certain moments, the numbers at single settlements that had sprung up, sometimes overnight, reached 300,000. Hygienic and sanitary conditions were what was to be expected when open, uninhabited fields suddenly become home to anarchic masses of men, women, and children. These were people weakened by hunger and illness and demoralized to the point of apathy by memories of a recent past of inhuman travail, a present of wretched dependency, and the fear that no future at all lay ahead.

The settlements unavoidably became places of crime of all kinds. Cambodian and Thai smugglers and black market operators preyed upon the unfortunates gathered there to extract from them the last links of gold chains that usually represented their life savings, hidden in the earth in 1975 and dug up when people were free to return to their original homes. The camps became places where treasures of Cambodia's cultural patrimony — temple sculptures vandalized at Angkor or bronze Buddhas hidden from the Khmers Rouges — passed into the hands of unscrupulous Bangkok antique merchants, who did not lack for equally avid Western dealers or collectors. Outbreaks of gang warfare, in which at times Thai military equally involved in unsavory business dealings played a decisive role, were common and made many innocent victims. Half-educated men declaring themselves leaders over frightened men and women accustomed to obedience to anyone claiming authority issued bombastic declarations of high political aims. They entered alliances with shady traders of all sorts and took charge of the all-important and profitable distribution of relief goods. Some of them wound up with a competitor's bullet in their heads. The border camps were unhealthy places in all possible respects, and it is a tribute to the heroic work of the doctors and nurses of various international and voluntary relief organizations, largely from Western countries, that the danger of fatal epidemics, always present, was contained.

But even more harmful to the people who had come to the border for food and medical care were takeovers of individual refugee camps by dubious political factions. They had in common only opposition to the Vietnamese occupation and the unconcern of Cambodian elites for ordinary Cambodians.

Among the anti-Communists, the most serious political force that emerged was the Khmer People's National Liberation Front, a nationalist, conservative group given to wildly anti-Vietnamese rhetoric not free from racial slurs. It was headed by Son Sann, one of Sihanouk's most competent prime ministers before the war. This group more than the others was beset by factionalism and rifts based on personal and commercial rivalries. However, Son Sann himself and those closest to him shunned corruption. They had returned from exile in France and accepted spartan lives in dangerous border zones, while Sihanouk and his son, Prince Norodom Ranariddh, led their resistance group from safe exile.

Without doubt, the Khmer Rouge bastions were the most potent of the border encampments. They owed their strength to the constant support of the Thai military, a steady flow of money, arms, and military equipment from China, and the undiminished rigor of their fanatical discipline. In their enclaves the men were soldiers and their families porters or furnishers of other services to them. Thailand made sure that in the distribution of food supplied by the international community and destined for Cambodian civilians, Pol Pot's forces enjoyed undisputed priority. Son Sann's and Sihanouk's factions also shanghaied men into armed service but with less ruthlessness and efficiency than the Khmers Rouges. Their relations with the Thai military, who held the trump cards by their control over access and supplies of all kinds, were subject to constantly shifting personal relations and individual bargaining. Their relative military ineffectiveness compared to Pol Pot's guerrillas lessened their bargaining power with Thailand.

I had occasion to see a Khmer Rouge redoubt early in 1980. Convinced that Pol Pot's men would never receive Western visitors, I had not asked to be invited. But one day their Bangkok representative, who was accredited to the United Nations office in the Thai capital, phoned asking whether I could find two or three free days "for a little trip" the following week. We met at one of Bangkok's lesser hotels around midnight and were loaded into two tarpaulin-covered trucks. Our group consisted of three or four Western correspondents, a young American enthusiast for the Khmer Rouge revolution, a Japanese or two, and a Yugoslav correspondent of remarkable Communist dogmatism. Yugoslav Communists, haunted by the possibility of Soviet aggression against their nonaligned Communist country, saw a frightening precedent in Vietnam's invasion of Cambodia — a large Communist nation attacking a smaller one of differing ideological persuasion — and staunchly supported Democratic Kampuchea.

We were driven northward through the night. Near the Cambodian border we were stopped at several Thai military roadblocks. Clearly the trip had received official Thai approval; we were waved on. The paved road turned into a bumpy dirt track; we had arrived in Cambodia. We halted at dawn in what seemed the middle of nowhere, a clearing in a dense forest.

From then on, reality was suspended. It became difficult to keep in mind whose guest I was, that I was in a remote jungle hideout that represented what was left of a regime that had raised to the nth power its absurd, unique idea of communism. My hosts were murderers of their own people and possessed by a pathological hatred of foreigners. They had banished all common comforts of life, such as medicines to cure their people's ills, as privileges of a decadent society. They had condemned an entire nation to starvation. They had, of course, largely excepted themselves from such rigors. Under the Khmers Rouges, Cambodians were allowed to consume only a little of what they produced, working with virtually bare hands. Nothing was imported, nor did Cambodia produce anything that could raise money with which to pay for badly needed foreign goods, like medicines. Their Cambodia, not they, lived in autarchy at starvation level.

"Welcome to Democratic Kampuchea," said a smiling and suave man, who introduced himself as "Minister without Portfolio Keat Chhon." (He has since changed sides and is now finance minister in Hun Sen's government.) The minister led us to a table decorated with flowers and greenery, placed under a handsomely thatched, vaulted roof resting on newly felled tree trunks. He offered hot coffee to refresh the travelers. It was served with shy smiles by young Khmer Rouge soldiers in jungle green, Chinese-style uniforms. The youths, yesterday's ogres, had left their weapons out of sight. A courteous young man, speaking flawless French honed in his student days in Paris, collected our passports to issue us visas. Mine was returned bearing the only visa in longhand I have ever received.

The border formalities completed, the minister invited us on a walk farther into the forest. Polite Khmer Rouge soldiers picked up our bags with kind smiles and firm insistence. In the manner of a gracious host cautioning his guests not to trip over ornamental features of his gardens, the minister urged us not to stray from the path on which he led us. He pointed out sinister devices near the edges that at the release of ingeniously hidden trip wires would discharge arrows aimed at the chest of the unwary, set off explosive charges, or cause one to step or fall onto keenly sharpened bamboo sticks. I asked Ambassador Pech Bun Ret, the representative at the United Nations in Bangkok, whether the tips were poisoned. "No, that would kill them, and a dead man you put in a hole and forget," the diplomat replied. "A wounded man takes four others to carry him, and then he cries and cries and cries. It makes the others begin to think." So much for the finesse of Khmer Rouge diplomacy.

"Did you hear the mine explosion a minute ago?" the minister without portfolio asked cheerfully as he led us on. "We have a system of defense." The nearest Vietnamese positions were only twelve miles away, said Khieu Samphan, then prime minister of Democratic Kampuchea, as he greeted us in the camp, which we reached after a half-hour's jungle hike.

The Khmer Rouge guest camp was the very latest in jungle luxury. It was clearly modeled on the sumptuous hunting lodges to which French planters of the past invited guests for weekend shoots. The Khmer Rouge urban planners had respected the environment. They had cut down only enough of the banyan saplings to create spaces for four guest bungalows and paths linking them to the bath houses, toilets, dining pavilion, meeting lodge, and communications shack. Local materials had been tastefully used. Each of the bungalows had four beds, made of bamboo and wooden planks and equipped with homemade mattresses. Blankets, pillows, and mosquito nets were provided. The floors were raised, and gravel was spread on the walkways to hold down the dry-season dust. Soldiers swept the entire camp daily to keep the falling leaves from cluttering.

In front of each bungalow there was a handcrafted simple table, on which our attentive hosts had placed trays of glasses, a thermos of hot water, a packet of Chinese tea, and packs of American cigarettes, a rarity even in Thailand at that period. Vases of bamboo were attached to the pillars of the bungalows and filled with fresh flowers. They must have been brought from Thailand; I saw none growing in the surroundings as we toured the redoubt. An elaborate floral arrangement also decorated the prime minister's banquet table. The plates of fruit brought from Bangkok were renewed each day. Ample supplies of freshly laundered towels were laid out in the bathrooms, next to new cakes of Lux soap, and replaced by unseen hands immediately after a single use. Hammocks were strung between saplings for siestas. Nowhere was there a weapon to be seen in the visitors' part of a heavily armed guerrilla encampment. The songs of birds and the chirping of the insects were the only sounds that came out of the jungle.

If the war seemed far away, so did the famine of Cambodia, so painfully visible all along the four hundred miles of Thai border. Indecent quantities and varieties of food brought from Bangkok were the visitors' fare. Meals were of French inspiration except for Khieu Samphan's banquet at the end of the first day. That evening the soldier-waiters filled the table with platters of Cambodian, Chinese, and Western dishes of infinite variety and saw to it, following the prime minister's discreet, silent commands, that the visitors' plates stayed filled. The best Thai beer, Johnnie Walker Black Label scotch, American soft drinks, and Thai bottled water were served; the ice to cool them, which also must have been brought from Bangkok hundreds of miles away, never ran out.

The contrast between the real Cambodia and the holiday resort atmosphere created out of nothing in a particularly beleaguered and deprived part of the world by the very men who were responsible for their country's dire reality was shocking. The reason for the theatrical decor was evident: Democratic Kampuchea, with its back to the wall, needed to make itself appear as a fit partner for its Asian neighbors and the West in its fight for survival against Vietnam and dominance among the Cambodian resistance groups. That was the reason for the meticulously staged visit and the theme of speeches, conversations, and interviews by Khieu Samphan, Ieng Sary, and two other ministers, as well as a troop of high officials whose job it was to mingle with the visitors and engage them in conversation. Banishing the hostile rhetoric of earlier years, when they were masters of their nation, the Khmer Rouge chieftains adopted anew the courteous, hospitable ways of Cambodian tradition. They did it skillfully, but who could forget that these hard men of soft manners were the very ones who had set out to destroy those traditions at the cost of untold innocent lives?

The message was simple: the Khmers Rouges had changed not only their methods but also their goals and wanted the West, particularly the United States, to help them in their present objective — to repel Vietnam. "Our main duty is not to make the socialist revolution or to build socialism," Khieu Samphan said. "Our main concern is to fight to drive all the Vietnamese forces out of Cambodia and defend our nation, our people, our race." Before the year was out, Ieng Sary made it even more definite. "The construction of socialism is rejected," he told me in his hotel room in Jakarta, where he had stopped off on his way back to the jungle from the General Assembly of the United Nations in New York. "We abandon the socialist revolution." As part of the campaign for Western approval, Khieu Samphan had replaced Pol Pot as head of the border government of Democratic Kampuchea and announced that Brother Number One would be in charge only of military affairs. It was a cosmetic operation that diminished in no way Pol Pot's predominant power. "I believe his name is badly accepted by world opinion," Ieng Sary said in considerable understatement.

Speaking as though the Khmers Rouges had been the aggrieved party, not the perpetrators, the new prime minister counseled the world to let bygones be bygones. "If we talk about the past we will never, never finish," Khieu Samphan said. "Everybody has a past."

We were taken to see a company or so of soldiers display their arms and go through warlike maneuvers. A young woman, clearly Eurasian and of urban bearing, sat to the side. Over her dark brown shirt and folded black ankle-length traditional skirt, she wore a canvas musette bag marked with a red cross. I asked her in English and French whether she was a doctor, and she replied in both languages. Her French was Parisian, her English that of a French high-school student.

Her name was So Kantha, she said, and she was twenty-four, her father Cambodian, her mother Eurasian. Her family had always supported the revolution, she said, and she left her high school in the Paris suburbs in 1971, when her parents took the family to Beijing to join in the struggle against the Lon Nol government. She had studied for one year to become a Chinese-style "barefoot doctor" in the revolutionary cause. She said she marched down the Ho Chi Minh Trail from Vietnam to the "liberated zone" to join the struggle in 1972. In 1975, a few days after the "liberation" of Phnom Penh by the Khmers Rouges, she returned to the capital, her native city, which she had left in 1965. She had not questioned any of the regime's policies, she said, including the emptying of the cities. "What went on in the countryside I did not know," she said. "But the decisions were correct." I asked whether she would still support Pol Pot's cause if she learned that the crimes of which the regime was accused had really happened. She thought for a while and then, smiling gently, she replied, "We will meet once again, and I will tell you."

I have learned that Kantha was called Catherine, was a daughter of Thiounn Prasith, Pol Pot's representative at the United Nations, and has now resumed her life in Paris. Her father, a Pol Pot advocate to the last, is reported to have found a home in the United States. Worthier Cambodian applicants for refuge in America have been rejected.

A month after stepping through the looking glass into Khmer Rouge wonderland in 1980, I traveled for two weeks through the real Cambodia, unfree and occupied by the Vietnamese invader, grievously wounded, lacking in everything, above all food and medicines. Yet there was a beginning of hope. With the sparsest of means, Cambodians were restoring their everyday lives to resemble the normality of prewar years. Families were reuniting after the unnatural separation of the Khmer Rouge labor brigades that had replaced the family as the basic unit of life in society. Schools were functioning and pagodas being restored. Traditional festivals, the days that bring moments of joy into the monotonous lives of the 85 percent of Cambodians who live in the countryside, were being revived. The Vietnamese Army was omnipresent and disliked, but its soldiers were disciplined and observed orders not to interfere with normal Cambodian life. The Cambodian puppet regime was not admired but was accepted as a burden Cambodians had to bear. They accepted the view that the Vietnamese Army was their only protection against the return of Pol Pot, and the Heng Samrin regime an unavoidable by-product. They fretted about how long the Vietnamese might stay. Would they ever leave?

I traveled for more than a thousand miles over much-abused roads. They had not enjoyed the benefit of even minimal maintenance in a decade of war. And again, I encountered hunger, illness, and poverty wherever I went. I heard individual tales of the Khmer Rouge genocide until I ran out of even perfunctory words of sympathy. Not that Cambodians readily burden guests with accounts of their sorrows. But mourning was so omnipresent in Cambodian lives that the recollection of irreplaceable loss could not be avoided. No matter what the subject, any conversation would lead to the frightful, standard phrase, "killed by Pol Pot."

I dropped in on the National Library and met Youk Kun, the only person working there. He was rearranging the few books that the Khmers Rouges had left, so that the humble colonial building would again deserve the high-flown title engraved on its facade. We chatted, and I asked what food rations he received for himself and his family. His voice neither rose nor fell when he answered quietly, "My wife and my six children were killed by Pol Pot." "Killed by Pol Pot," in French or English or in the voice of my interpreter, still resounds in my ears many years later. I dreaded the moments in conversation when suddenly the fatal phrase became once again unavoidable. And rare were the villages I visited where I wasn't taken to a field where the murderers had done their work and where I was shown the macabre arrangements of remains, skulls placed apart from lesser bones, that survivors had erected as memorials after their liberation.

I drove through towns that I had known, but so little was left of their buildings that I did not notice their former sites until it became evident that I had driven past them. Mounds of rubble were all that was left of the provincial capital of Kompong Speu, once a neat town thirty miles west of Phnom Penh. The same was true of Skoun, to the north. A few tawdry new shacks had replaced an especially pleasant district town.

But towns leave traces. Paved roads remain, amid shells of houses or piles of wreckage. That was not true of many villages that Pol Pot's men ordered razed by their populations before banishing them, sometimes only to a few hundred yards from their old homes. Destruction was for its own sake, punishment for having lived under the Lon Nol regime. Along the road I saw fruit trees and coconut palms in neat clusters. But the houses were no longer there. The mind's eye had to restore them to imagine the harmony with nature in which Cambodia's rural majority had once lived. The concrete stilts on which wooden houses once stood along the roadsides were there, and so were the steps that once led to the entrances. But the houses themselves had vanished. Concrete arches were standing, and from them paths, now overgrown, once led to village pagodas. Now they ended in limbo.

Passing through Dey Eth, a village fifteen miles from Phnom Penh on the road to Saigon, I heard the singsong of Buddhist prayer from a pagoda. As soon as I stopped, my car was instantly surrounded by men. They had come running to invite me to join them at a meal at a long outdoor table. They were teachers celebrating the opening of a school that they had rebuilt. Their pupils were largely orphans, 190 under communal care, many others living in the large village of eight thousand people with members of their extended families. The prayers came from the pagoda on the other side of the road. It had just been restored after having served as a rice mill. They commemorated the teachers who had been killed by Pol Pot. How many? I asked. "Most," a survivor replied. He said the teachers had preferred to build a new school rather than restore the old. It was still standing, but Pol Pot had turned it into a storehouse for cow dung, which the children had had to gather. "In the Pol Pot era, the people were more miserable than the beasts," said Nong Kim Srorn, a teacher. "The beasts had enough to eat."

16

"Below the Level Required by Their Task": 1980–1987

*I*T WAS BY ITS CAPACITY TO MEET the primary needs of the hungry and debilitated survivors of Pol Pot's reign of terror that the Heng Samrin regime was judged when I returned to Cambodia in April 1980. The judgment of the Vietnamese, who had assumed responsibility by invading Cambodia and installing a government of Khmer Rouge defectors of their choosing, was damning. "What we see here does not please us," said a high Vietnamese official who supervised the Cambodian Foreign Ministry in its relations with non-Communist foreigners, such as representatives of relief organizations or journalists. "It could be catastrophic." And Ngo Dien, the Vietnamese ambassador to Cambodia and a principal architect of Hanoi's policy toward Phnom Penh from the beginning to the end of the Vietnamese occupation, made the accusation specific. The Heng Samrin regime was inadequate, he said. "They are below the level required by their task."

The principal task at the time, when Cambodia's own stocks from the last rice harvest were being rapidly depleted, was to see to it that the foreign assistance was efficiently received and fairly distributed. International and voluntary relief agencies were working to prevent another major food crisis. They knew that before the monsoon rains began in June, food and seed had to be distributed to the many villages that would become virtually inaccessible after that. The government's poor record in receiving and distributing food was worrisome. The failure was due in part to the limited absorption capacity of the Kompong Som and Phnom Penh ports and the poor state of the roads. But the Heng Samrin government's lack of concern and foresight, as well as incompetent management, were equally worrying. Few Cambodian officials seemed to be aware of the individual problems; nobody in central authority, relief officials said, recognized the potentially disastrous implications of their combined effect.

I visited Kompong Som, the principal point of entry. The port was congested; ships waited for weeks to dock and unload at its six berths. Every berth was occupied, but only one ship was discharging rice. Its Filipino second mate told me it had waited twenty-four days before it could dock, at a cost of about two thousand dollars a day wasted. In the eight days since then it had unloaded 2,512 tons of its 4,000-ton cargo. At any other port the entire cargo would have been unloaded in three days, he said. Vladimir, the first mate of a Soviet freighter, complained that his ship had waited thirty days before docking and would not be unloaded in less than seven or eight days. It would take two or three days in a Soviet port. "The problem is the workers and the technique." A Soviet stevedoring crew had worked for three months and raised the unloading rate to fourteen hundred tons daily. They left their equipment for the Cambodians, the harbormaster said, but still the rate had dropped to below half.

Distribution was equally slow, despite the 1,100 trucks that had been donated by various aid organizations. Rats were getting at the undistributed supplies. On a five-hundred-mile journey on the principal east-west roads, I encountered only three of the relief trucks. They were visible in large numbers only around Phnom Penh. Those I saw on the road were transporting people, not food. In every village in which I stopped I heard the same tale: hardly any rations and no seed had been distributed. The fact was that the government, instead of doling out the relief food equitably, was still using it to pay its employees. Cambodian ministers ate better than their counterparts in Hanoi and received more meat in one month than a Vietnamese in a year, a Vietnamese adviser told me. Government employees drew a regular and adequate ration of at least thirty-five pounds of rice or corn a month. Vietnamese officials said that they had strongly urged the government to redress the imbalance of distribution and deliver more food to the countryside. There, many were already stretching their stocks by eating a thin gruel rather than solid rice, Cambodia's staple. Ngo Dien called it politically unwise to create widespread rural discontent in an overwhelmingly agrarian country.

The ambassador said that despite the Heng Samrin government's poor performance, the Vietnamese hesitated to involve themselves actively in making decisions on such internal matters. I reminded him that this was no different from the American attitude when Cambodia was its client, and he smiled a bit ruefully. Seven years later, in the same embassy, this was Ngo Dien's judgment of the state of Cambodia: "There is too much passivity. Energy is low. They have hospitals but no personnel, schools but not the right teachers. They cannot yet live by their own hands. They are fatalist. The fear of a return of Pol Pot remains very strong, but they don't do enough to transform that into an attitude of resolution. Vietnam cannot do that for them." When again I drew the comparison with America's position in its day in Cambodia, when the Nixon and Ford administrations richly supplied and financed the Lon Nol government while despairing at its incompetence and corruptibility, Ngo Dien seemed at first to take umbrage. Then, excellent diplomat that he is, he smiled and lifted his glass of Coca-Cola to me in acknowledgment of a point taken.

Vietnamese officials were advising the government of

poorly educated Cambodians that Hanoi had installed in every ministry. One adviser told me that for Hanoi to take a more active rather than discreet role would perhaps raise the level of performance but would also increase international criticism over Vietnam's dominance.

In the provinces, Vietnamese officials were less tactful or sensitive to Cambodian self-esteem than in the capital. When I arrived at the Grand Hotel Angkor in Siem Reap, the man who came to welcome me to the very heart of the glory that was the Khmer Empire was not a Cambodian but the Vietnamese provincial "adviser for information." The Cambodian staff watched this egregious tactlessness with sullen resentment and shared their feelings with me later in the day. The Cambodian curator for the treasures of Angkor, an archeologist, arrived moments later, and the Vietnamese lectured him condescendingly through an interpreter on how to arrange my visit. That evening, the top Vietnamese for Siem Reap province — in America's years of comparable dominance in South Vietnam he would have been called the "province senior adviser" — drew up at the hotel in a large black Mercedes-Benz, a more ostentatious car than his American equivalent would have used. He was received with the reverence reserved for potentates and accepted it as his due.

The Cambodian government seemed unable or unwilling to face the huge problems of its suffering people. In interviews, senior officials offered perfunctory replies to questions on food, medicine, and social problems; they preferred to be grandiloquent and vague about the future and eloquent about their own very real suffering in the Pol Pot past. The government's insouciance passed the bounds of understanding of international relief officials. Midway through my stay, on a Sunday, all work stopped for three days to celebrate the Lunar New Year. The stoppage included the unloading and distribution of food relief. Work was resumed on Wednesday, but only for one day. Thursday, April 17, was a national holiday, "Liberation Day." It

marked, under the thoroughly misleading name, the fifth anniversary of Pol Pot's victory. Cambodia had also celebrated
three months earlier another "Liberation Day," the first anniversary of Vietnam's defeat of Pol Pot. (I was delighted to learn in
1997 that April 17 remains a public holiday but is now called
"Day of Hatred.") The following week was more rigorous; only
one holiday stopped work, Lenin's Birthday. It is no longer celebrated.

Even such critical matters as the desperate shortage of medicines did not interfere with the government's obsession with
holidays. An international medical official hastened happily to
the Health Ministry when he was advised that a much-delayed
planeload of badly needed medicines for country infirmaries had
just arrived. The ministry was less enthusiastic. It was already
Friday, an official explained, so the job of distribution could not
begin before Wednesday because of the New Year. But he said it
would certainly begin next Friday, after Liberation Day. And yet
the need for medicines in the provinces was urgent. I visited
provincial hospitals and district health stations throughout the
country and found largely unsupplied, dirty places, crumbling
from years of neglect, full of suffering people and short of
everything else — doctors, nurses, medicines, equipment, and
food. Only eight of the eighteen provincial hospitals were
headed by a doctor.

In the western province of Pursat, the chief was a Viet-
namese-trained medic. A male nurse took me to see a teenaged
boy who a few days earlier had lost his right leg from above the
knee to a mine. The wound was gangrenous, the nurse said. "We
are irrigating the infection," he said. I looked from the oozing
bandage up to the bottle that was linked to it by a plastic tube. It
was empty.

Dr. My Samedy was dean of the reopened Faculty of Medicine, the only university branch operating in the early stage of
post–Pol Pot Cambodia. A recent convert to communism, the
member of the old Phnom Penh bourgeoisie opened our con-

versation, perhaps by obligation, with the self-criticism that had been part of his conversion process. In the past, Cambodia's doctors had been interested only in making money instead of serving the people and had practiced largely in Phnom Penh, neglecting the countryside. But minutes earlier Dr. My Samedy had told me matter-of-factly that of the fifty-four doctors who had survived the Pol Pot years and remained in the country, thirty-two worked in the capital. Despite the urgent need for trained medical workers, in their first two years of study, students, together with their teachers, were devoting a full day each week to "political education," dispensed by Cambodian and Vietnamese teachers.

With marked condescension, the Vietnamese adviser to the Foreign Ministry spoke of the low level of Cambodians' political consciousness. They were being given "in a very relaxed way very soft political courses," he said. Their purpose was "to show them where we are going." The assumption that Cambodia would have to go wherever Vietnam went was unspoken but clear. In fact, political indoctrination could be seen in progress everywhere in Phnom Penh, mainly in empty shops. The sight of haranguing agitprop lecturers and somnolent audiences more interested in watching street life than in the speaker raised doubts over how far along ordinary Cambodians were on the road to communism. What was clearly lacking was a concerted government campaign to mobilize people to cope with the great needs of the nation or even an open discussion of the needs.

Self-satisfaction among officials in Phnom Penh seemed often to be based on closing their eyes to what was happening outside the capital and the fact that their own needs, plus a little extra, were reasonably fulfilled. But not only in the capital: in the district of Sisophon on the Thai border, I sat with Chap Koy, the district chief, in front of his office. We faced the road, on which moved steady countercurrents of people heading to the border or returning from it carrying sacks of rice. The chief insistently argued that feeding at the border should stop, and all international aid should be delivered to Phnom Penh or Kompong Som. He said only pro-Western Cambodians and supporters of Prince Sihanouk went to receive aid on the border. I suggested that maybe hunger also played a part. He agreed readily. People were eating gruel instead of rice in his district, he said. But he added that as an official he received enough. He and his family were eating rice.

The problems were not only of Cambodian origin. The assistance from European Communist countries was not always what was most needed. In the port of Kompong Som, with berths to unload vital relief goods scarce and ships carrying food waiting at anchor, I saw a Russian unloading large crates from a Soviet freighter. What is inside? I asked. "Teapots," he answered. I looked incredulous. "Yes, *chainiki*, teapots," he repeated. I looked at an open crate in the warehouse. It indeed contained great quantities of aluminum kettles, not a primary need at the moment. I met members of a delegation of doctors from European Communist countries who had been dispatched on a brief mission to inoculate people in Phnom Penh against a number of illnesses. These included yellow fever, never encountered in Cambodia. However, the vaccines had been left behind in Hanoi. An Indian doctor, late in arriving to join the group, saw them at Hanoi airport and had them loaded onto his Vietnamese flight. But a Soviet diplomat ordered them taken off and refused to let them leave on anything but a Soviet plane. The delegation left to return home after some days of sightseeing trips; their vaccines were still in Hanoi.

In 1980, well over a year after the fall of Pol Pot, Cambodians were still crisscrossing the country in search of missing family members or a place to settle down or simply something better than what they had at the moment. At night, the sidewalks around Phnom Penh's railroad station became the capital's biggest bedroom. Entire families cooked, slept, fed, or nursed their children and lived their everyday lives in a city that could offer them no livelihood. They were waiting for the next train out, ceding their places to new arrivals from the train that would carry them westward, to indefinite destinations.

At the Thai border in that year's rainy season, foreign medical workers reported increasing incidents of severe malnutrition and the diseases associated with it. People with whom I spoke on the forest trails on the Cambodian side leading to the border told me of people in their villages dying, the old and the very young in particular. "The government of Heng Samrin doesn't give us the rice," said a twenty-five-year-old man in halting school English. He had pedaled his bicycle for two weeks from the eastern province of Kompong Cham. Carrying about eighty pounds of rice on his baggage rack, he was starting to push it back to Kompong Cham. It would take more than two weeks, he said, and his family was waiting for him.

Reacting to the Vietnamese occupation, China and ASEAN, with Thailand and Singapore in the lead, were twisting the arms of non-Communist, anti-Vietnamese Cambodian factions to join forces with the Khmers Rouges. The United States and most of the West supported the pressure. Sihanouk and Son Sann, the leaders of the most important non-Communist groups based on the Thai-Cambodian border, squirmed uneasily under the pressure to form so odious an alliance. I took advantage of a stay in Beijing, one of the few places from which it was possible to telephone to reclusive North Korea, to call Sihanouk, who in exile was dividing his time between Beijing and Pyongyang. Both capitals had been places of asylum for the prince in his earlier exile, after Lon Nol's coup in 1970.

It was on March 18, 1981, the eleventh anniversary of the event that plunged Cambodia into its bottomless descent, the overthrow of the prince. He had just received a visit from the Khmer Rouge prime minister, Khieu Samphan. Sihanouk had had to bow to Chinese pressure for a coalition of all Cambodians opposed to Vietnam and had begun talks with his Khmer Rouge enemies. The talks with Khieu Samphan had left him convinced that there was no chance of forging an alliance. "They say they have given up communism, but they are not sincere," the familiar high-pitched voice shouted over the creaky phone line. "The Khmers Rouges do not want to give the slightest guarantee of security to the population that they will not again begin their massacres." The root of the divergence was the insistence of China and the Khmers Rouges on continuing the war until the Vietnamese were driven from Cambodia, Sihanouk said. The prince maintained that there must be a negotiated solution, because Cambodians were too traumatized to pursue an unending war. "Then there would be nothing left to negotiate about," he said. "War, war to the end — it is madness!"

The people preferred "a Vietnamese protectorate" to the risk of renewed Khmer Rouge "genocide," the prince said. "Many people enjoy family life again, no longer slave at forced labor, and observe Buddhism. The Vietnamese have brought relative peace." But he said that under unrelenting Chinese pressure to join all forces in a war against Vietnam he would continue negotiations with the Khmers Rouges. He hoped that in return Beijing would supply arms not only to the Khmers Rouges but also to a small pro-Sihanouk force based on the Thai border. They would do no good against Vietnamese power, Sihanouk, ever realistic, said. "But my partisans demand it. I am too realistic to believe in it. It is a very bitter, sad irony."

The ebullient prince, clearly bored out of his wits by his solitude in austere, ultra-Communist North Korea, was reluctant to let me end the conversation. He waxed enthusiastic about his life there. "My friend Kim Il Sung gives me rights of extraterritoriality. My palace is on a lake, and I can ride in a motorboat. I go for walks in my big park. The personnel waits on me marvelously well; the cuisine is good. And I even have American films, I mean it, American films, Monsieur Kamm, imported especially from Japan and Hong Kong." Still Sihanouk was unready to give up the call that must have been that day's only entertainment for him. "But you haven't talked to Princess Monique." He called his wife. "*Monique, Monique, c'est Monsieur*

Kamm au téléphone." I doubt the princess knew who I was, but dutifully we exchanged the courtesies of the day before I could hang up.

Despite Sihanouk's reluctance, shared in even greater measure by Son Sann, the conservative anti-Vietnamese leader, by August the screws on both had been sufficiently tightened to move on to the shotgun wedding *à trois.* Sihanouk told me, speaking this time from his house near the French Riviera, where he was under medical treatment, that he would soon go to Singapore, where the vows were to be sealed. "It would be saying too much," he said ironically when I asked him whether he was ready to make peace with the regime that had killed three of his sons, several grandchildren and other relatives, and most of his former entourage. "If the Vietnamese were not there and the Khmers Rouges won, they would liquidate me," he said. Antagonism also existed between the two anti-Communist leaders, Sihanouk and Son Sann. Son Sann had resigned the prime ministership in 1968 in protest against Sihanouk's tolerance of corruption within his family and entourage and his break with the United States.

On September 3, 1981, a joint statement of intention to form a three-party coalition government was concluded. "Warm as always," Sihanouk replied when I asked him how his meeting with Khieu Samphan had gone. "He didn't try to kill me yet." At lunch after the signing the following day, Sihanouk spoke at length about the intensity of Chinese pressure. He said Beijing wanted "bourgeois" like himself and Son Sann to serve as a cover over the Khmers Rouges to facilitate their acceptance by the West and keep Cambodia's United Nations seat out of Vietnam's hands. The deal he had just signed, he said, proved that John Foster Dulles was right when he told him in 1958 that he could not be neutral. Dulles had said: "Prince Sihanouk, you are very young. You must choose." He continued with heavy irony, "Today I pay homage to his grave. John Foster Dulles was right. There is no nonalignment." At press conferences the following day, Sihanouk and Son Sann spoke bitterly of the Khmers Rouges and their distrust of them. And the prince added, "I support Son Sann because certainly Son Sann is better than the Khmers Rouges — or less bad." Khieu Samphan slipped out of Singapore at dawn, without taking leave from his new allies.

In 1981 the Coalition Government of Democratic Kampuchea was formed, the hybrid child of the shotgun marriage. Sihanouk served as its president, Son Sann as prime minister, and Khieu Samphan as vice president and foreign minister. In the years that followed, the sponsors of the unholy alliance spent a great deal of effort and exerted considerable pressure to keep the feuding partners together. Of course, the outside powers, supported by the United States, held all the cards. China and Thailand, keeping the anti-Vietnamese pressure in high gear, saw to it that the disciplined Khmers Rouges remained the most potent military force, causing Vietnam to commit considerable might to keep western Cambodia under government control. Son Sann's movement never grew into a military counterweight to the Khmers Rouges. On the contrary, most of its generals split from Son Sann's leadership. This greatly reduced the organization's military and political weight. Sihanouk's supporters fielded only token military strength. They remained a factor prized by all parties concerned because all shared a belief that Sihanouk's political stature, among Cambodians and in the international community, made the prince the key figure in lessening the role of the Khmers Rouges and reaching an accommodation with Vietnam and its main supporter, the Soviet Union, to take the sting out of the festering Cambodian wound.

In the occupied country, material conditions gradually improved to allow Cambodians to live at a survival level. Life was in all respects immeasurably better than it had been under the Pol Pot regime. Starvation had yielded to widespread malnutrition. A vigilant, often brutal police state under Vietnamese military occupation had replaced Pol Pot's rule by murderers. After a long absence I returned for a visit in 1987. So great was Cambodia's isolation from the world, which recognized only the Coalition Government and shunned contact with the Vietnamese-imposed regime, that only the Soviet and Vietnamese airlines flew to Phnom Penh. I arrived on an Aeroflot flight from Moscow on which all but six seats of the more than one hundred were occupied by young Cambodians returning from various training courses in the Soviet Union. Five were taken by Soviet technical experts. I was clearly the only passenger who had paid for his passage. In Cambodia, a "national" airline flew internal routes. That was pure fiction: planes and crews were Russian.

The country's dependence on outside assistance remained great, and the assistance was provided mainly by the Soviet Union and its European allies, either directly or via Vietnam. What was even more disturbing was that this did not disturb Cambodians. They would have preferred, of course, that Cambodia's protection against a return of Pol Pot were not in the hands of the Vietnamese Army; any other foreign force would have been preferable.

Phnom Penh was a shocking sight. The city that in 1980 had seemed on the way to returning to its prewar state had become by 1987 an overgrown rural settlement. The superficial boom of the 1990s had not come yet; it was a Communist capital. The pigs, poultry, and occasional cattle that had been driven to the popular quarters were now comfortably roaming the city, even in the center. Cows rested in the shade of main boulevards. The litter of years lay ungathered everywhere, breeding rats, flies, and sickness. "The streets are still dirty," agreed Madame Chhey Kanha, the deputy health minister. "Most people here are new to the city. Life is hard for them. We are trying to educate them, especially in sanitation, but we are short of trained people. The culture and education of the people are limited." Medical relief workers had told me that no more than one percent of the people had access to safe drinking water. The deputy minister said few people were heeding advice to boil the water. She seemed to give no thought to the evident fact that a population that had barely enough money to ward off starvation had none to spend on firewood to boil what they drank.

A sense of immense human depletion was my dominant impression, one shared by many in the small foreign community. My awareness was of irreplaceable human loss on a scale comparable with that of other groups mourning terrible depletion — Jews and Armenians after genocide, Europe immediately after World War II, sub-Saharan Africa after disastrous famine.

In an important way the sense of loss in Cambodia was keener: Jews and Armenians had had a vast mass of educated men and women of competence in other than menial tasks, and of that elite many survived; the African famines touched few in the small educated elites. In Cambodia, the limited pool of people of education had been a particular target of genocide. The losses from the eradication of the fittest were apparent everywhere. Cambodia was paying the price, and is paying it to this day, of all the reckless human waste of its recent past — the destructive war; the steady outflow of well-educated people who foresaw that the incompetent Lon Nol regime, with American backing, was leading their country to disaster; the Pol Pot genocide; and the subsequent renewal of the brain drain of many of the educated survivors across the Thai border to exile in the West after 1979.

There was a ready way by which to take the measure of the loss. Before 1975, French had remained the language of education beyond the elementary grades. Cambodia had lacked the time to nationalize fully its school system in the scant seventeen years of independence and peace from 1953 until 1970 that it was accorded. Throughout the country, persons with skills other than those of basic agricultural labor spoke French that ranged from rudimentary to perfect. I had never needed to engage an interpreter in Cambodia; there was always a speaker of French handy. By 1987, however, French seemed largely to have disappeared. For the first time, Cambodia's principal leaders — President Heng Samrin and Prime Minister Hun Sen, elevated from foreign minister — spoke no French. With the second language, there had disappeared also the skills and knowledge that had been learned in it. The only area in which Cambodia was nearing its prewar level of attainment was agriculture; the competence of its accomplished growers of rice suffered fewer losses than that of its mechanics, physicians, or teachers.

The international community in Phnom Penh, including Vietnamese and Western, shared deep concern over Cambodia's lack of progress. These were the causes: a lack of qualified people in all fields, lassitude throughout the administration in meeting the basic needs of the population, and suspiciousness and foot-dragging by the bureaucracy. Foreign officials were disturbed by the Cambodian people's all-too-great, fatalistic readiness to accept a deprived and diminished life as their due.

Cambodians were fed with an unremitting flow of ideological cant, in nonresponse to the real questions about their impoverished lives. "Attending political courses seems to be the first requirement for all workers," a western European relief official said. "In hospitals they are called away to attend them at any moment, even doctors during operations." A West German doctor working at Takeo's provincial hospital said his Cambodian colleagues were required to hold frequent lectures on Marxism-Leninism for the staff but didn't believe a word of their own words. "One came out of the lecture room, and the first thing he said to me was, 'Can you lend me your copy of *Newsweek*?'"

Ambassadors of Communist countries were patronizing and scornful about the state of socialist political consciousness of Cambodians and the government's stubborn attempts to make Communists out of a profoundly unpolitical people. The Hungarian envoy said, "They talk too much of Marxism, but the party is just beginning to seek a popular base. There are only leaders now. To start from the top like this is a little against the laws of nature." In private conversations, educated Cambodians made fun of the ideology that they were required to spout back in their classes. In official interviews, those questioned often covered embarrassment at being unable to speak openly by recourse to cant. I asked the vice dean of the Faculty of Medicine why students had to devote more than two hundred semester-hours to Marxism-Leninism. "To have an active basis for understanding the political line of the revolution," he replied, smiling sheepishly.

Kong Som Ol, an American-educated agronomist who in 1987 served as a minister in Prime Minister Hun Sen's office, agreed with my sense that morale was lower than it had been in 1979, immediately after the liberation from Pol Pot, when hopes ran high. "The younger generation, now in school, is okay," he said. "But the rest of the population is a little exhausted." Sadly, ten years later, that young generation, now out of school, seems quite as exhausted as its elders, and hope now lies with the not yet born.

17

Enter the United Nations:
1991–1992

I N THE DRY SEASON of late 1984 and early 1985, Vietnam mounted what proved to be its last all-out offensive to wipe out all the forces arrayed against it — the Khmer Rouge bases along the Thai border and those of the non-Communist resistance organizations of Sihanouk and Son Sann. Its initial success was great. When the monsoon season began in mid-1985, there was hardly a resistance redoubt left on Cambodian soil. The Khmer Rouge commanders withdrew into Thai sanctuaries, but their fighting units fled forward. They penetrated more deeply into western and northern Cambodia and kept up the struggle in a more far-flung area. The non-Communist guerrillas lost most of their effectiveness and ceased to be a military factor of importance.

The large encampments of civilians, numbering at any given moment between 350,000 and 400,000, settled along the Thai side of the border with reluctant Thai consent. Thailand, torn between its hostility to refugee settlements on its soil and its desire to deny to Vietnam and the subservient government of Prime Minister Hun Sen (who had replaced the incompetent

Heng Samrin) control over so large a segment of the population, opted for the alternative that contributed to Cambodian instability and let the refugees stay. But the military situation did not hold at that favorable state for Vietnam. The Phnom Penh government's army had greatly grown in numbers, but not in combat effectiveness. It could not hold all the ground that the Vietnamese offensive had gained, and the Khmers Rouges gradually edged back across the border to reestablish themselves on the Cambodian side.

The Vietnamese military are nothing if not tenacious. The fundamental decision that led eventually to their withdrawal in 1989 from what had proved an exceedingly costly military occupation without foreseeable end, heavy in battlefield casualties, material losses, and diversion of national energy, was not theirs. It was not initiated by Hanoi. The word that caused Vietnam to look for a way out from the Cambodian morass was spoken in Moscow. Since 1975 the Soviet Union had underwritten at a cost estimated at around one billion dollars yearly its dirt-poor, war-damaged but still warring, principal Asian supporter. Moscow had done so for the same reason that made it also foot Cuba's bills. Vietnam and Cuba were Soviet allies adjacent to Moscow's principal adversaries, China and the United States. They represented a foot in the door to hostile houses, a forward outpost for Soviet military intelligence, and a constant annoyance to Beijing and Washington.

Mikhail Gorbachev, who came to power in 1985, quickly concluded that the Soviet Union could no longer afford to pay the price of confrontation. He chose to seek accommodation with America and China and found them willing partners. It was not long after he became general secretary of the Communist party that Gorbachev sent word to Hanoi that Vietnam would have to find a way of doing without Soviet aid. It did. In 1986, Vietnam drastically changed its economic course. It encouraged its people to do what it had always prevented them from doing — use their considerable skills and energy to produce goods and services on their own and for their own benefit instead of being tiny cogs in a hugely wasteful and unproductive centrally planned, state-run economy. Financial aid from the international lending organizations and private foreign investment were needed to take up the slack caused by the stoppage of Soviet assistance and to advance Vietnam's development. The productivity and prosperity attained by most other Southeast Asian nations became the overriding national target.

To reach it and to enter into normal relationships with its region and the world beyond, Hanoi needed to get the onus of its occupation of Cambodia off its shoulders and assure the international community that it had forsworn aggressive foreign adventures. The motivation was political and economic; without Soviet support Vietnam could simply no longer afford to stay in Cambodia. It needed to scale down its ambitions. From domination over its Indochinese neighbors, Cambodia and Laos, it shifted to a policy of working to protect its legitimate security interests in two weak countries barely able to serve as buffers between Vietnam and its historic regional rival, Thailand. It clearly maintains ties with the military and an effective intelligence networks in both neighboring countries. The first contacts between Hanoi and Bangkok on settling the Cambodian issue came in 1986. Before the following year was out, Sihanouk, representing the Coalition Government of the Khmers Rouges and non-Communist resistance forces that had been reluctantly cobbled together under Chinese pressure in 1981, and Prime Minister Hun Sen of the pro-Vietnamese government in Phnom Penh opened conversations with a view to reaching a compromise.

The negotiating process was painfully slow, reflecting the enormous mistrust between the principal adversaries, the Phnom Penh regime of the People's Republic of Kampuchea and its predecessor, the Khmers Rouges of Democratic Kampuchea, a hostility that endured until, beginning in 1996, cracks opened in the once-solid Khmer Rouge structure. By 1998, after Pol Pot's "trial" by his comrades and mysterious death, the Khmers Rouges had been reduced to marginal importance on the political scene. What kept the negotiations alive and made them lead to an agreement in October 1991 was the determination of all the interested outside powers — China, Vietnam, the Soviet Union on its last legs, the United States, Japan, western Europe, and the members of ASEAN. Each for its own reasons hoped to put an end to a divisive issue of no great intrinsic importance to any of them except, of course, Vietnam. But Vietnam, too, was pursuing higher interests; Cambodia had lost its priority in Hanoi. The dispute over Cambodia hindered achievement of objectives that had become more important to each of the powers than its side in the Cambodian conflict. Above all, the United States, China, and the Soviet Union, because of the impending collapse of Soviet communism that was heralded by the decline in its international ambitions, knew that the time had come to put their mutual relations on a nonconflictual footing.

The first meeting of all four Cambodian factions — the Phnom Penh regime and the three ill-matched partners in the Coalition Government — took place in Jakarta in 1988. In 1989, with Communist governments tottering in Europe, Vietnam removed the principal obstacle to an agreement. It took the bull by the horns and unilaterally withdrew its troops. The distinctly Communist name of the Hun Sen government, People's Republic of Kampuchea, was neutered to State of Cambodia.

It took two more years of haggling. What followed was a peripatetic peace conference that involved the five permanent members of the United Nations Security Council and the most concerned Asian states, including the four Cambodian parties. They met at various levels of representation in Paris, New York, Jakarta, Beijing, Tokyo, and a Thai beach resort. The secretary general of the United Nations, Javier Pérez de Cuéllar, dispatched countless missions to Cambodia to study on the ground how a peace accord could be put into practice. In 1990, the State of Cambodia and the Coalition Government agreed to join in a Supreme National Council, which was to serve as the repository of Cambodia's sovereignty during a transitional period, in which the country was to advance to peace and reconciliation under United Nations auspices.

In 1991 Prince Sihanouk was named as the council's head. It was expected that he would eventually preside as the real or figurehead compromise leader over a country whose most powerful forces were the two unreconcilable Communist factions. He was seen as the only possible focus of mutual agreement. The negotiations culminated in a grand conference in Paris on October 23, 1991, with ceremonial speeches by Sihanouk, Pérez de Cuéllar, and the host, French president François Mitterrand.

What was signed by all four Cambodian groupings, the five permanent members of the Security Council, the six nations of ASEAN, Vietnam, Laos, Japan, India, Australia, Canada, and Yugoslavia, itself on its last legs as a unified state (it represented the Nonaligned Movement) was called "An Agreement on a Comprehensive Political Settlement of the Cambodia Conflict." Its stated goals were "to restore and maintain peace in Cambodia, to promote national reconciliation, and to ensure the exercise of the right to self-determination of the Cambodian people through free and fair elections."

A United Nations Transitional Authority in Cambodia was empowered, in effect, to govern the country in most essential aspects, until, following elections, a constituent assembly could approve a new constitution and a government could be installed. The powers that were conferred on the Transitional Authority, known by its acronym, UNTAC, were sweeping. "The SNC [Supreme National Council] hereby delegates to the United Nations all powers necessary to ensure the implementation of this Agreement," Article 6 stated unequivocally. Had UNTAC fully exercised the powers assigned to it, the United Nations would have become the effective government of Cambodia until peace and reconciliation were established and a freely elected government replaced it. This was not to be.

As a reward for Japan's considerable financial support of the operation, whose cost hovered near the unprecedented mark of two billion dollars, as well as Tokyo's readiness for the first time to match its enormous economic power with a concomitant sense of international political responsibility, the leadership of UNTAC was given to a Japanese. Yasushi Akashi was a highly regarded United Nations diplomat with many years of international experience. His skill lay above all in his tact in making conflicting views mesh into compromises that fully respected that holiest of holies in the glass-and-steel tower on New York's East River — the sovereignty of each member nation. The Japanese conciliator, a discreet and gentle man, never showed the will to use the muscle that he was given to carry out an agreement that expressly suspended Cambodia's sovereignty in the most sensitive areas of state power and transferred it temporarily into the hands of the United Nations. He was given more power than his temperament and experience inclined him to use. Presented with the might to hold sway as a czar, Akashi ceded to his inclination to manage by gentle persuasion. The two unscrupulous Communist forces whom he was meant to bludgeon into peace and reconciliation feasted on his soft diplomacy and subverted the high intentions of the Paris Agreement.

"In order to ensure a neutral political environment conducive to free and fair general elections, administrative agencies, bodies, and offices which could directly influence the outcome of elections will be placed under direct United Nations supervision or control," the all-important Article 6 continued. "In that context, special attention will be given to foreign affairs, national defense, finance, public security, and information. To reflect the importance of these subjects, UNTAC needs to exercise such control as is necessary to ensure the strict neutrality of the bodies responsible for them." This appointed, in effect, Akashi as superminister of foreign affairs, defense, internal security, and finance of all of Cambodia, mandated to supersede all Cambodian authorities in those spheres. It meant that Akashi was to replace

Hun Sen, who ruled with a heavy hand over most of Cambodia. To assume such power was simply not in Akashi's character; he was no Richard Holbrooke, who banged Yugoslav heads together in Dayton, Ohio, in 1996 to obtain an agreement on Bosnia.

The agreement called for an immediate cease-fire. It ordered all military forces of the four factions to gather in cantonment areas and hand over their arms, ammunition, and equipment to UNTAC's military contingents. There, 70 percent were to be demobilized. Those remaining under arms after the voting were to be placed under the command of the elected government and be reorganized into a single national army.

At least four-fifths of the territory and even more of the population were firmly under the control of the State of Cambodia, the Hun Sen regime, when the United Nations civilian and military administrators began arriving. It was a conventional Stalinist power machine, although in 1990 the ruling Communists had neutralized their party's name to People's party. Hun Sen's rule was intolerant of anybody deemed out of step with the rigid central authority and its local antennae. It tolerated, even encouraged, corruption at all levels but came down ruthlessly on those whom it suspected of being potential rivals for the spoils of power. Freedom of political choice and human rights had never been on its agenda, and with Cambodia's cowed, exhausted, and largely uneducated population, not a cry was raised in Phnom Penh or the provinces. Outside the Phnom Penh government's control lived only the small civilian populations regimented into their border enclaves by the Khmers Rouges and those of the less disciplined pro-Sihanouk and pro–Son Sann groups. The masses of civilians vegetating on international handouts in the Thai displaced-persons settlements, dominated by the same political factions, were to be repatriated under the Paris Agreement.

It was essential for Akashi to establish as quickly as possible UNTAC's determination to replace the Hun Sen government in the areas in which the Paris Agreement gave it "direct supervision or control." Only by taking over responsibility in Phnom Penh for "foreign affairs, national defense, finance, public security, and information" from the government that controlled most of the country could the United Nations hope to exact the same compliance from the Khmers Rouges in their remote border redoubts.

It cannot be said that under Akashi's tactful leadership UNTAC even tried to fulfill its mandate. Throughout the UNTAC period, which lasted from the last months of 1991 until September 1993, Hun Sen's government remained sternly in control, yielding no significant internal powers to those whom the international community had ordered to exercise them. The police-state hold over each citizen, down to the lowest level, remained fully in the hands of Hun Sen's corrupt and thuggish army, police, and security services. The Communist ideology vanished overnight, but the police state remained.

"There is only one ideology today; survival in the power struggle," said a central European ambassador, a newly converted former Communist. "They never were Marxist. They came out of the forest in 1979 with no education or experience. Most are still the same today."

In April 1992 I went to northwestern Cambodia to observe the beginning of the repatriations from Thailand. A European relief official who had long worked in the region told me that, contrary to the Paris Agreement, Interior Ministry and police officials were closely questioning newly arrived refugees on their political views and activities in the border camps from which they had come. They suspected that the refugees had come under the sway of one or the other of the anti–Phnom Penh factions, which dominated in the Thai camps. This was intimidating. And security officials in uniform and civilian dress surrounded the newcomers and eyed them with unconcealed suspicion, trying to overhear my conversations with them. Throughout my three-week stay, I encountered among ordinary people the same fear that prevailed from 1979 until in 1990 the

People's Republic officially forswore communism and became the State of Cambodia.

It was not until March 1992, four months after the signing in Paris, that Akashi and his military commander, Lieutenant General John M. Sanderson of Australia, were dispatched to Phnom Penh. By then the capital's profiteers were already gearing up for the inflow of men and money that the United Nations was bringing. The once-wealthier neighborhoods of the city had become large building sites. The villas of the former Cambodian elite and French residents of the past were being renovated for rent at exorbitant rates to the new international colony of UNTAC officials and embassies that were opening. The construction workforce consisted almost exclusively of illegal Vietnamese migrant workers. They found a profitable outlet for their skills and energy, qualities that were less pronounced among Cambodian workers.

Who were the greediest profiteers? Somehow, after having stood empty in the Pol Pot years and having been confiscated and nationalized by the Vietnamese-imposed regime, the luxurious residences had passed imperceptibly into the private hands of the State of Cambodia's privileged political elite. This outrageous plunder found general acceptance; questions about ownership were never raised. "Unbelievable corruption," said a Communist ambassador whose country had by then disposed of its Communist regime. Because of their common political past, he was on friendly terms with Hun Sen and his government and aware of their plunge into personal enrichment. "They are selling the country," he said. Another ambassador, whose country had remained Communist, said, "There are no rules, no laws, no sanctions. Corruption is very open and very extensive and reaches from the bottom to a very high level." The many cars and motorcycles that had suddenly made their way into what had been a pedestrian and bicycle city were rarely registered; minor clerks stole registration forms and sold them, leaving the owners to fill them out as they wished and avoid customs duties and other fees.

Carpetbaggers from the Asian economic powerhouses of South Korea, Hong Kong, Singapore, Malaysia, and Thailand were flocking in, drawn by the scent of opportunities opening up in the unfettered, dog-eat-dog mercantile liberalism that was replacing the Communist economy. They gathered in the only luxury hotel of Phnom Penh, the Cambodiana, on the banks of the Tonle Sap River. A vast, low, white structure, it had been left incomplete when war came in 1970, and its shell became home for masses of refugee squatters. Cleaned up and completed in 1990 by a consortium of overseas Chinese from Southeast Asia and managed by a French hotel chain, the Cambodiana reflected the hollow nature of the boom that had seized Phnom Penh. Hollow because little of Cambodia's exportable treasure, timber and gemstones was being officially traded and taxed under government regulations. These products were the merchandise of illicit deals.

Timber, in continuation of the wholesale plunder that my friend Suon Kaset, the chief forester, deplored in the days of Lon Nol, passed largely between State of Cambodia officials and the military and their Thai partners. As for Cambodia's sapphire mines, they had been seized by the Khmers Rouges, who held the western mining town of Pailin in a firm grip. Pol Pot's forces made of this trade with Thailand, along with the denuding of the forest, a rich replacement for the aid that had formerly flowed from China. (Chinese support had greatly diminished after the withdrawal of Vietnam's army and gradual normalization between Asia's largest surviving Communist powers.) The sapphire mines were exploited on behalf of Thai merchants by Thai and Burmese workers. The merchants paid the Khmers Rouges for the mining rights.

What the Cambodiana represented so symbolically was a commercial palace of super-air-conditioned luxury owned, managed, and occupied by foreigners. Almost everything that was provided, from sheets and towels to meat and bottled drinking water, came from outside Cambodia. Its managers were French, the middle level Singaporean, and only the menial work was done by Cambodians. Its customers were senior United Nations officials of many nationalities, diplomats, Thai, Singaporean, and Malaysian bankers, and representatives of varied foreign charitable organizations. They were there either to help restore peace and repair the devastation of the Pol Pot years and the neglect of the subsequent pro-Vietnamese regime, or to take out of Cambodia as much as they could of the inflow of foreign assistance that was expected to accompany reconciliation and peace.

The Cambodiana shielded its guests from the depressing realities of Phnom Penh life. Guests saw only the bustling main streets through the windows of air-conditioned cars. Those who lived away from the principal streets were the great majority of the people of Phnom Penh, those who did not share in what the United Nations economic adviser called the "miniboom." "Government outlays on central social services are much too small," said Roger Lawrence, the UN adviser. While the main streets throbbed with business activity, not far off masses of the underemployed, forever in search of a day's work, lived in hovels, among heaps of uncollected garbage, rich only in children. With annual inflation running close to 100 percent, they ate poorly and drank impure water. The illnesses of poverty were widespread and medical services scarce.

Hardly any of the two billion dollars invested by the international community in the "comprehensive settlement of the Cambodia conflict" went toward relieving the harshness of daily life of the eight million Cambodians. It was spent to pay for the transport to and from Cambodia of sixteen thousand soldiers and six thousand civilians, including administrators, policemen, diplomats, accountants, civil servants, and specialists in many fields. It went to pay for their housing, transport, communications, office equipment, and everything else that goes with the maintenance for nearly two years of a huge international deployment of forces in a war-devastated country with minimal infrastructure.

There had never been anything like it.

18

Elections Instead of Reconciliation: 1992–1993

*B*EGINNING EARLY IN 1992, there descended upon astonished Cambodians, who had lived in isolation from the rest of the world through the lifetimes of most of them, men and women of varied nationalities and occupations. The United Nations Transitional Authority comprised Hungarian policemen and Ethiopian diplomats, Uruguayan soldiers and French judges, human-rights specialists from the Ivory Coast and election organizers from Canada. They had been dispatched from more than one hundred member states of the United Nations in the most extensive peacekeeping operation ever. For the most part they viewed the Cambodians and their country with equal astonishment. The two sides found no common language, literally or figuratively. The foreigners tended to treat ordinary Cambodians with amused, somewhat condescending indulgence, and were content to find congenial company among the other foreigners.

The six thousand civilians of UNTAC — the abbreviation quickly became part of common language — collected, in addition to their regular salaries, a daily allowance of $130, roughly the annual income of the average Cambodian. For many UNTAC members this was more than their normal monthly salaries. "With $130 a day in their pockets, do you think they will go back to walking the streets of Budapest when they go home?" the Hungarian ambassador asked sarcastically about his country's police contingent. The policemen sent to Cambodia were earning far more than he as envoy of their nation. The sixteen thousand soldiers had to make do with $1.28 extra a day, unless their governments shared with them a part of the $988 per soldier per month that the United Nations paid their national treasuries for their services.

Not surprisingly, the $130 per diem caused bitter jealousy among Cambodian officials. They felt justified in their indecent grabs of whatever they could steal of national property. The ordinary Cambodian civil servant earned the equivalent of about twenty dollars a month, and his pay was usually months late. The well-subsidized international presence played a major role in driving up the prices of the necessities of life. Those who could least afford it suffered the most. "They come here to make dollars at the detriment of Cambodians," said Foreign Minister Hor Namhong of the Phnom Penh government. "Their spending doesn't benefit Cambodians." He said Akashi had turned down his request to oblige the United Nations staff to convert at least 10 percent of their earnings into Cambodian riels in order to inject some of their money into the national economy. The dollar became the currency of preference wherever foreigners went in the country.

UNTAC went everywhere, except into the Khmer Rouge areas. That is where the Paris Agreement broke down. The deterioration of respect for what had been signed began with the signature. The Phnom Penh government yielded none of its powers; the Khmers Rouges, with minor exceptions, barred their territory to outsiders, and both sides continually violated the cease-fire. Reconciliation was not on anyone's agenda. UNTAC "noted with concern" and issued protests. The breakdown that ratified the abandonment of two of the three overriding goals of the Paris Agreement, "to restore and maintain peace in Cambodia" and "to promote national reconciliation," occurred two months after Akashi and Sanderson arrived. On May 30, 1992, Khmer Rouge troops placed a bamboo pole across a road near Pailin and denied the head of UNTAC and its military commander the exercise of their right of passage. Akashi and Sanderson bowed to this act of defiance. Pol Pot's men justified their violation of UNTAC's mandate by accusing the United Nations of siding against them with Vietnam and the State of Cambodia. It was a case, of course, of the proverbial pot and kettle. Both sides were equally black; neither had ever had peace or reconciliation on its agenda.

Sanderson and Akashi explained their nonaction by a determination not to engage United Nations troops in warfare when their mission was to keep the peace. "We have no enforcement power," the general told me. "When you move into enforcement, your neutrality is gone. You have no one to talk to." And indeed, there was no specific enforcement power given to the military in the Paris Agreement. But UNTAC's mandate to make the agreement prevail was broad enough to allow for a much more activist interpretation. Surely Sanderson and Akashi would have come under considerable criticism from nations contributing troops if their forces sustained casualties. To die for Cambodia was not an acceptable proposition for a Bangladeshi or Ghanaian soldier or their governments. But what then was the purpose of sending sixteen thousand men who had chosen a military career to a distant country to implement an international agreement?

Akashi's and Sanderson's retreat before a bamboo pole and a handful of Khmer Rouge guerrilla fighters signaled clearly that UNTAC accepted the refusal of the Khmers Rouges to play by the rules that their leaders had signed in Paris. In the same fashion, UNTAC bowed to the State of Cambodia's equally obstructive insistence on keeping the prerogatives of sovereignty that had been temporarily assigned to UNTAC, with its government's explicit consent. The United Nations' surrender to the defiance of the two principal opposing forces at the very beginning of the peace process marked the end of any chance of achieving peace and reconciliation.

UNTAC and the international community that had created it did not acknowledge that they had abandoned the main objectives of the Paris Agreement. The opposing factions would not be disarmed, and guerrilla fighting, mainly between the army of Prime Minister Hun Sen's Phnom Penh government and the Khmers Rouges, continued. The need for peace of a people battered for more than two decades by the quarrels among their own leaders and by foreign intervention was put in the shade. Rather than own up to this failure, UNTAC performed an astonishing feat of diplomatic sleight of hand: it promoted the holding of "free and fair elections" to its primary goal. This, not peace and reconciliation, was made the objective by which success or failure of the two-billion-dollar mission was to be judged.

No Khmer Rouge detachment ever moved into a cantonment area to be disarmed. The three other forces — the Phnom Penh government army and the much smaller units of Prince Sihanouk and the conservative Khmer People's National Liberation Front of Son Sann — began a token cantonment but then followed the Khmer Rouge example of noncompliance with the Paris Agreement. Lip service to all the goals of the accord continued to be paid at UNTAC's seat in the former French government palace in Phnom Penh, at United Nations headquarters in New York, and in the capitals of the major powers that had engineered the Paris Agreement. But the opposing troops remained in the field. Skirmishes continued. Reconciliation was dead. Elections had been promoted to the be-all and the end-all of the Paris Agreement.

While the two principal hostile factions of the Phnom Penh regime and the Khmers Rouges maintained their war footing and sabotaged their pledges of peace, the weak Son Sann movement concentrated its politics on repetitious accusations that UNTAC was conniving at a vast presence of Vietnamese military and civilian invaders bent upon dominating the "Khmer race." "We are afraid of being invaded by the Vietnamese ants," the soft-spoken, ever courteous Son Sann told me. "They are seventy million, we are seven million." The Son Sann organization's newsletters abounded with charges of a "racist" Vietnamese plot to make Cambodian women marry Vietnamese so as to reduce within fifty years the Khmers to the status of a minority in their land. "In other words, the end of the Khmer race," declared an article believed to have been written by the leader's son, Son Soubert, a soft-spoken, courteous art historian.

There were indeed Vietnamese settlers and transient workers, probably as many as tens of thousands. Many were no doubt illegal immigrants. But they were farmers, fishermen, construction workers, and others in the manual trades looking for greener pastures than their own overpopulated and underdeveloped country offered. The notion of a racist plot, which was also often heard from supporters of Sihanouk, remained without evidence, then as now. "Xenophobia enters into the political discourse," Akashi told me in an interview.

It did more than express itself in words. More than one hundred Vietnamese farmers and fishermen, women, and children were murdered in armed attacks throughout Cambodia during 1992 and 1993, the UNTAC period. Most of the attacks were blamed, no doubt justly, on the Khmers Rouges. But no Cambodian in authority, none of the twenty political parties that participated in the elections, uttered a word of regret or condemnation. Sihanouk suggested that the Vietnamese return to Vietnam for their safety. For thousands of them it would not be a return home; they were members of the ethnic Vietnamese minority born in Cambodia.

In the worst single incident, thirty-three Vietnamese fishermen, their wives, and children were murdered in a Khmer Rouge attack on a floating fishing village on Tonle Sap Lake, near the monuments of Angkor. Twenty-nine more were wounded. Nineteen of the dead, mainly children, were mowed down in a large shack mounted on a fishing boat, where they had been watching a video show. The others were killed in their houseboats. I reached the lakeshore the morning after. Vietnamese fishermen were bringing the coffins of the victims, most of them pitifully little, to shore. They loaded them silently onto United Nations trucks, which were to take them to a nearby hilltop pagoda for burial. On or beside the coffins they placed trays of farewell gifts — flowers, plates of cookies, fruits, and incense sticks. As the coffins were brought ashore, Cambodians in a small market a few steps from the landing ostentatiously kept their backs turned and continued to play pool or a kind of roulette with a spinning top. "They are Vietnamese, but they are still human beings," was as far as the Cambodian interpreter for the UNTAC human-rights branch would go in expressing sympathy.

According to Brigadier General Klaas Roos, a Dutchman commanding the thirty-five-hundred-man contingent of international police that formed part of UNTAC, two nearby Cambodian police stations on the lake did not intervene. The raiders, who had arrived in stolen motorboats, were not pursued. Major Delwar, the second-in-command of the Bangladeshi infantry battalion in the area, had no intention of patrolling the shore. "But we informed the villagers to be careful," he said. "The people are very frightened." I asked General Sanderson what UNTAC troops would do to protect the Vietnamese. That was the responsibility of the army of the State of Cambodia, he replied. "Can they be trusted to protect Vietnamese?" I asked. "I am not going to answer that question," the general replied curtly.

The wounded were lying, largely uncared for, in the primitive provincial hospital. A well-equipped UNTAC field hospital of the Indian Army was nearby. Dennis McNamara, the head of UNTAC's human-rights component, asked the officer in charge, Lieutenant Colonel Pradeep Kumar, to go to visit the wounded.

He would go only if asked by local doctors, the Indian replied. "I'm not being bureaucratic; I'm being ethical," Kumar said. He finally went but returned, still insisting that local doctors would have to request his help. There were no local doctors or nurses to be found.

And while UNTAC lived up to its limited conception of its mission, unaided by the contending Cambodian powers, where was Sihanouk, the hope of the international community for persuading Cambodians to make peace and establish badly needed national solidarity? He ostentatiously neglected his chairmanship of the Supreme National Council, hardly honored his country with his presence, and sent a stream of sarcastic or petulant fax messages to Phnom Penh from abroad to give vent to his disdain for UNTAC. And further insulting the United Nations, the prince spent much of his time in the palace his friend Kim Il Sung had built for him in the North Korean capital. North Korea is the only country that has waged war against the United Nations and never concluded a formal peace.

I was at the airport to see Sihanouk arrive from Pyongyang the day before a 1992 visit of Boutros Boutros-Ghali, then secretary general of the United Nations. He was returning from North Korea, where he had celebrated Kim's eightieth birthday. The prince wasted no time in announcing, still at the airport, that he would be returning to Pyongyang immediately after Boutros-Ghali's departure. This time it was to celebrate the sixtieth anniversary of the North Korean Army. From Pyongyang he would go for two weeks of medical tests in Beijing, Sihanouk said. "It borders on irresponsibility," Akashi commented in customary understatement, asking not to be quoted. Wherever Sihanouk was seen in public, he was tightly surrounded by a squad of North Korean body guards, as rude and grim-faced a group of ruffians as I have ever encountered, a fitting, if unnecessary, gift from Kim Il Sung.

UNTAC detachments, multinational groups feeling understandably alien in a country about which they knew so little, were based throughout Cambodia. In my visits in various provinces, their members reflected openly on the futility of striving for peace and reconciliation in an atmosphere of such deep mutual mistrust. They were preparing for elections, despite their conviction that the "neutral political environment" in which they were to be held was unattainable. "We have not been able to achieve peace and national reconciliation," Akashi himself told me two months before the elections in May 1993. The Khmers Rouges, signers of the Paris Agreement, announced that they would boycott the voting. This made the campaign a contest between the Cambodian People's party of Hun Sen and the royalist party led by Sihanouk's son, Prince Norodom Ranariddh. The younger prince, a lecturer in international relations at the University of Aix-en-Provence, campaigned on the promise that a vote for him would be a vote to put Cambodia back into the hands of his father. Ranariddh's party is known by its acronym FUNCINPEC, derived from the French for United National Front for an Independent, Neutral, Peaceful, and Cooperative Cambodia, a full political program in abbreviation. Son Sann's Buddhist Liberal Democratic party played a minor role.

I asked Theo Noel, a Canadian election specialist who was organizing the voting in populous Kompong Cham province, about the outlook for peace and reconciliation. "At present, in practice, these goals no longer exist," he replied. Firmly under the control of Hun Sen's formerly Communist party, governed by the prime minister's brother, Hun Neng, the police and army were waging a campaign of terror against the royalists, the party's principal election rival. Intimidation takes many forms, Noel said, including "rifles pointed at people." The voting was still two months in the future, but eight local party officials had already been murdered in the province and one was missing, presumed dead, Noel said. "But it's very hard to come up with anything that would stand up in a court of law," said Berhanu Dinka, a former Ethiopian ambassador, who was UNTAC's deputy director for civil administration in the province. No court of law not under Hun Sen's control has ever existed. A Russian captain, serving as an UNTAC military observer, said, "Fairness is not a part of political life." He and an Indian major reported that the police and military had been illegally collecting voter registration cards in many villages. On returning them, they told their holders that their names and card numbers had been registered in a computer, which would show for whom they had voted.

In the remote northern province of Stung Treng, bordering on Laos, the UNTAC presence had something of the unreality of the Man on the Moon and illustrated the temporary distortions of normal life that accompanied the UNTAC phase of Cambodia's travails. There are not many regions in Asia that have been so out of touch with the outside world as this vast province of broad rivers, deep forests, and scarce population — sixty-three thousand people. Even in French colonial days, Stung Treng had little to attract foreigners, except the occasional party of big-game hunters, and enough malaria to discourage visitors. But the B-52s "interdicting" the western fringes of the Ho Chi Minh Trail blasted Stung Treng's tigers and elephants into extinction. Stung Treng was occupied by the North Vietnamese Army in 1970 over no resistance. The Vietnamese withdrew in 1975 and returned as conquerors in 1979. But even during the subsequent ten years of the People's Republic's close links to the Soviet bloc, Deputy Governor Koy Sarim told me that no Soviet or other eastern European "expert" had visited.

And then, in 1992, a battalion of Uruguayan troops landed. With them came a Belgian to head the UNTAC provincial detachment, with a Somali deputy and a Kenyan secretary. A Chinese officer commanded the team of military observers, which included officers from the United States, Cameroon, Malaysia, France, and Indonesia. UNTAC's hospital was run by Indians, the police by a Jordanian who had a Filipino deputy and a force from many nations. The elections were being organized by a Dutchman, and an official from the Ivory Coast was working to instill respect for human rights. "Ola, amigo!" the children in town greeted all foreigners, believing them to be Uruguayan. They didn't know the language was called Spanish.

The arrival of these outsiders had attracted another foreign element — prostitutes from Vietnam, at an apparent rate not very short of one per Uruguayan. Cambodians, by force of habit, blamed the Vietnamese, not the United Nations foreigners, for the rise in food prices, which had more than doubled with the inflow of UNTAC dollars. "UNTAC has made life a little easier for a few traders," said Johann B. Sünder, the Dutchman organizing the voting. "The man in the street suffers." Cambodian homeowners moved in with relatives and rented their houses, simple wooden buildings on stilts, for exorbitant amounts. The Blue Hotel, no better than primitive, billed the United Nations fourteen thousand dollars a month, which probably was not much less than the total monthly earnings of the employed among the eleven thousand inhabitants of the provincial capital. I asked the medical director of the province's only hospital what he earned. Calculating at the official rate of exchange, he arrived at $26.40 a month. His pay usually arrived two or three months late.

The UNTAC hospital did not treat his patients, Dr. Tann Theng Hor complained. There were almost none, because there was nothing with which to care for them. A young man, surrounded by four commiserating family members, writhed in pain on a filthy bed. He would not be operated on to remove his gallstones for four days, because the anesthetist was ill. To prepare for surgery, Dr. Hor said, they would build a wood fire in the front yard under the old Soviet-donated sterilizer, which was filled with fallen petals and leaves, to prepare his instruments. He hoped there would be electricity that day to give him some light. The UNTAC hospital, fully staffed, neat and well equipped, stood empty.

Hor Namhong, the Hun Sen government's foreign minister, called the United Nations operation a failure "never to be repeated." "They are here to pile up dollars and have no idea what their humanitarian mission should be." A Cambodian doctor told me, "With these enormous possibilities, with that budget, one would have to say the result is despairing."

But UNTAC achieved one triumph: despite crude Khmer Rouge threats to discourage participation, an astounding total of 4.8 million Cambodians in a very young population (estimated at around eight or nine million) registered to vote. Urged, or better commanded, by a stern letter from Mitterrand, cochairman of the Paris conference, Sihanouk finally consented to return to his country the day before the voting, giving by this act his long-delayed blessing to the event.

Fully 90 percent of the registered voters went to the polls. And despite the Hun Sen government's heavy-handed intimidation and tight control at local levels, despite its thugs' murders of about one hundred workers of the royalist and Son Sann parties, FUNCINPEC topped the poll with 45 percent of the vote. Hun Sen's Cambodian People's party won only 38 percent. Son Sann's Buddhist Liberal Democrats gained 3.8 percent. They and a small Sihanoukist party divided the seats in the Constituent Assembly among themselves in corresponding proportion. There is no doubt that without the People's party's pressures, particularly in the countryside, the royalists would have won a solid majority.

The Cambodian people had surprised all the experts, who expected them to vote obediently for the holders of authoritarian power, as they always had. A plurality had defied two unreconstructed, heavily armed totalitarian machines and voted with their hearts. They had chosen Sihanouk. In their collective memory, based on experience or the tales of the elders, the prince represented the last good days that Cambodia had known, days of peace and of life within their traditions, golden days compared with what had followed.

But the prince let them down.

19

Cheating the Voters: 1993

PRIME MINISTER HUN SEN'S PEOPLE'S PARTY was the surprise loser. Its leaders made rebellious noises and menacing gestures in the days when the votes of the week-long balloting were still being counted. As partial results were made public by UNTAC, and it became every day more evident that the royalists had received a strong plurality, People's party threats increased. Hun Sen and his coleader, Chea Sim, told Sihanouk to assume full powers. If he did not, they threatened that violence against FUNCINPEC, the royalists, would break out. No doubt the People's party leaders believed that their firm grip on the population would enable them, once the United Nations contingents had left, to manipulate the ailing and aging prince, who commanded no battalions, just as the Khmers Rouges had manipulated him from 1970 until 1979. Sihanouk and FUNCINPEC had neither an army nor a political structure that could compete with Hun Sen's organization, which blanketed the country.

The invitation for Sihanouk to put himself once more at the

head of the nation was like asking a child into a toy shop. The prince immediately appointed himself president, prime minister, and supreme military commander. At the same time, he announced the formation of a government, with Hun Sen and Prince Ranariddh as deputy prime ministers. He did so without consulting Ranariddh, the election winner. Placing winner and loser on the same footing, in defiance of the outcome of the voting, made clear that Sihanouk had, however unhappily, taken Hun Sen's side and was prepared to deprive Ranariddh of his triumph. He acted in the not unfounded fear that the People's party might unleash civil war if FUNCINPEC moved to strip it of its power. Would UNTAC have stood by idly? A moot question; the issue was not put to the test.

The irony was, of course, that Ranariddh, Sihanouk's son, owed his victory to his campaign pledges to return the country into his father's trusted hands. But not by Sihanouk's unilateral assumption of power and certainly not in collusion with Hun Sen, the opponent whom Ranariddh had defeated. The prince's appointment of himself was a coup d'état in defiance of the elections and the United Nations, which had organized them. His disdain for the voice of the people, ever an attribute of Cambodia's political elites, was rarely more blatantly displayed.

Ranariddh, fearing for his life in the ugly climate created by the losers, had left Phnom Penh for his party's small military base on Cambodia's northern border with Thailand. He sent a fax to his "venerated Papa" to protest against Sihanouk's nomination of himself, Ranariddh, and Hun Sen. UNTAC and the United States also opposed it. France supported the prince, whom it had always viewed as Cambodia's sole hope of salvation. Sihanouk, furious at this opposition, withdrew his proposal but urged his son to reconsider his rejection and agree to let "Papa" form a transition government.

The People's party did not wait for father and son to settle their differences. Ranariddh's hated half-brother and rival, Prince Norodom Chakrapong, Sihanouk's son from another of his many consorts (with at least five he produced children) had spectacularly defected from FUNCINPEC in 1992 and joined the People's party. Hun Sen rewarded the prince with a seat in the politburo and a post of deputy prime minister. Now Hun Sen used Chakrapong in an attempt to overturn the election by invoking a threat of rebellion. Chakrapong and his colleague Sin Song, Hun Sen's interior minister, left the capital in the direction of the Vietnamese border. From there, they theatrically announced the secession of six provinces in eastern Cambodia. They contended that fraud had deprived the People's party of victory. They hoped that Vietnam, which had created their party, would side with them and help to nullify the ballot. But Hanoi's decision to stay out of Cambodian affairs held fast; Vietnam accepted the election results. In the new "autonomous zone," People's party hoods went on a rampage against UNTAC and FUNCINPEC offices and assaulted opposition party workers. The secession ended five days later. It had worked, unlike Sihanouk's earlier attempt to preempt the outcome of the vote.

The People's party's coup de théâtre persuaded Ranariddh to bow to Sihanouk's power-sharing formula. It deprived Cambodia's people of the election victory they had given Ranariddh. Under Sihanouk as head of state, an interim coalition government was formed. It gave parity in ministerial portfolios to the winners and losers in the voting. Sihanouk obsequiously thanked Hun Sen and his secessionist son for their "obedience" and rewarded his son Chakrapong with the four stars of a full general. Ranariddh and Hun Sen were named co–prime ministers. UNTAC, pleased with its successful elections, offered no objection to this perversion of their result. But before returning once again to North Korea to await the drafting of a constitution and the completion of the Paris peace process, Sihanouk laid bare the ugly truth: he complained to interviewers that he had been blackmailed by the People's party.

The elected Constituent Assembly, working in undemocratic secrecy, drafted two constitutions, one for a monarchy, the other for a republic. By sending confusing messages from Pyongyang, Sihanouk kept the country guessing whether he wanted to resume the throne that he had abandoned in 1955. In any event, he declared, Cambodia must be governed by the two co–prime ministers. Ranariddh voiced his anger in private conversations, with frequent references to the fact that his father had never much liked him. Hun Sen used the period of the interim regime to retighten the slack in his party's hold over the country, which had been loosened by the tugs of international supervision over the election campaign. Shortly before the expiration of the three-month deadline between the voting and the adoption of the constitution, which was specified in the Paris Agreement, Ranariddh and Hun Sen took both versions of the draft charter to Pyongyang for Sihanouk's choice. No one was surprised when he opted to be enthroned once more.

On September 24, 1993, Sihanouk, back in his capital, signed the charter that made him a constitutional monarch and was installed as king. At his insistence, which sat none to well with Ranariddh and many others in FUNCINPEC, Princess Monique, to whom he is not legally married, was made queen. Of his many wives and concubines, Monique Izzi, daughter of an Italian-French father and a Cambodian mother, most enduringly captured the fickle Sihanouk's devotion, perhaps because she loyally shared his years of exile and palace arrest by the Khmers Rouges. She exercises considerable influence over his decisions. Ranariddh is known to blame the queen for his father's coolness toward him. Sihanouk, who announced just before resuming the throne that his Chinese doctors had discovered that he suffered from prostate cancer, has publicly indicated, before the 1997 coup d'état that drove Ranariddh into exile, that Ranariddh is the most likely next king. Monique, however, is believed to favor her own son, who bears the name of Sihamoni, a composite of his parents' names. He is a dancer and musician who represents Cambodia at the United Nations Educational, Scientific, and Cultural Organization in Paris. Cambodia's king is elected by the

Royal Council of the Throne, composed of political and religious leaders.

Two days after the promulgation of the constitution, Sihanouk's elevation, and the automatic conversion of the elected constituent assembly into a parliament, Yasushi Akashi and General Sanderson declared UNTAC's mission accomplished and departed. But not before the Hun Sen army and police had publicly shown their contempt for the international effort to bring peace and stability to their country. They set loose a nationwide wave of stealing as many as they could lay their hands on of the white four-wheel-drive Japanese cars and light trucks that had for ordinary Cambodians been the most visible emblem of the United Nations presence. Most of the thefts were fulfillment of "shopping" orders by generals or other dignitaries for specific models as status symbols for their personal use. By the time the UNTAC chiefs left for home, about two hundred of its expensive vehicles had disappeared, only to reappear without delay, brazenly parked in front of the mansions and offices of important government figures. Their continued presence in Cambodia may be the most lasting heritage of the two-billion-dollar international enterprise.

Because FUNCINPEC held fifty-eight seats in Parliament and the People's party fifty-one, Ranariddh was given the title of First Prime Minister (in French, which among the Phnom Penh bourgeois elite remains the foreign language of choice, the absurdity is emphasized by the designation "Premier Premier Ministre") and Hun Sen Second Prime Minister (Deuxième Premier Ministre). Ranariddh's primacy existed in title only; Hun Sen remained the wielder of maximum power. The reasons were twofold; they were institutional and personal.

The greatest number of voters were commanded by FUNCINPEC, but as a party it was a corps of would-be generals with few troops. The People's party, in contrast, was the mass organization of a typical Communist, one-party state. It had posted its members everywhere, and they had been in place since the Vietnamese organized a countrywide, centralized structure of command and surveillance, working from the center down to the village level. It had been in position since 1979. Party members dominated the army, the police, the administration, the teachers, and, most pervasively, the informers on their neighbors. In a state where corruption and the insolence of office had always been rife, they shared an interest in defending their lucrative jobs against all comers. At the lowest level, their mere livelihood depended on it, and the higher they rose, the greater grew the illicit perquisites.

The ministers and top aides of FUNCINPEC were put in place in Phnom Penh and in the provinces in which they were given the governorships. (The People's party kept the most populous and economically profitable provinces, Battambang and Kompong Cham, although FUNCINPEC had won the elections in both.) But the royalists had few qualified people to staff the positions below the top. Those remained in People's party hands. Insofar as the government could ever be said to be functioning to any degree of efficiency, a risky assumption in Cambodia at any time, it was People's party jobholders who made it run, even under a FUNCINPEC first prime minister, the king's son.

And there were decisive personal differences between the two prime ministers. Ranariddh, fifty-three years old, enjoyed his office hugely, visibly, ostentatiously. The junior French academic relished being received as a head of government in foreign capitals and being able to receive foreign dignitaries in pomp and circumstance. His frequent travels included occasional trips to Aix-en-Provence to continue his university lectures, a pursuit of private interest astonishing for a man nominally at the head of a deeply disturbed nation. Ranariddh fancied the frills and panoply of high office — sumptuous receptions, gala dinners, planes, helicopters, big cars, a battalion of bodyguards. "I always had the feeling that Ranariddh governed between a game of bridge and a game of golf," a resident European scholar of long

Cambodian experience said. And Ranariddh loved talking about all this. What seemed to interest him far less were the affairs of state and the making of decisions about them. He developed high-flying tastes and found the money to satisfy them. Ambassadors and other foreign visitors considered him garrulous and his conversation self-centered, boastful, and fatuous. There was much in his style that recalled his father's well-developed frivolity, but little in his actions or words that resembled Sihanouk's intense interest in politics, tactical skill, analytical lucidity, and the astuteness that stood him, and more often than not his country, in such good stead in his years in power.

Second Prime Minister Hun Sen, too, clearly loves power and its attributes. Like Ranariddh, he lives ostentatiously and well above his ministerial salary. A Khmer Rouge guerrilla fighter since 1970, he had little time for education and speaks neither English nor French. When I first met him in 1979 he was painfully ill at ease before foreigners and responded hesitatingly to their questions. He spoke in the sterile party language that his Vietnamese patrons, to whose side he had defected to escape a Khmer Rouge purge in 1977, must have taught him in an ideological course after he changed sides. The first thing that one noticed was that he had a very perceptible glass eye. Nowadays Hun Sen is at ease with foreigners and tends to self-assured monologues. But they often focus on the issues of governance. He has clearly studied them and is all too ready to make decisions.

The gawky young country boy in ill-fitting dark trousers and short-sleeved white shirt of 1979 has put on flesh and wears well-cut suits and sober ties. A glass eye of more sophisticated design is barely noticeable. The appearance of naïveté has been replaced by evident political cunning and enjoyment of the game. And he, too, has a battalion of bodyguards. Hun Sen has become a formidable politician in the Cambodian setting, and he is studying English. Despite all his educational and social advantages, Ranariddh was a rank political dilettante next to his rival.

20

Back to Square One: 1994–1998

I RETURNED IN 1994, about a year after the beginning of the post-UNTAC era, to a Cambodia under a freely elected government, voted in thanks to the extravagant international enterprise to bring about peace and national reconciliation. After a slow start, the two prime ministers, Hun Sen and Prince Norodom Ranariddh, seemed to have learned to live with each other, sharing power and its spoils. But Ranariddh's share of power in the running of Cambodia was tiny compared to that of the man whom he had defeated at the polls. Cambodia remained mired in warfare, its administration was chaotic, and corruption reigned everywhere. And hardly anyone on the political scene even talked about Cambodia's real problems: social chaos, rampant lawlessness, and endemic poverty that continued to breed malnutrition, illness, and ignorance. This necessary discussion was left to one of UNTAC's commendable by-products, a handful of private human-rights organizations. They are courageous but are confined to protests that the politicians ignore and noble efforts to instill among the humble basic ideas of respect for human dignity that the power elite of all descriptions defile daily.

The joint prime ministers shared no political principle then or now. Ranariddh is a royalist and possible future king. Hun Sen has run a wider political gamut: a radical Khmer Rouge Communist since 1970, he converted to more conventional communism in 1977 after escaping to Vietnam to save his skin from a Pol Pot–ordered purge of Khmer Rouge ranks. He declared himself a free-enterprise democrat when the Vietnamese occupation army left Cambodia in 1989, and converted his Communist country into a nondogmatic state and his Communist party into the People's party. The first and second prime ministers were united by only one common quality — greed for power. But then, ideology has played no part on the Cambodian scene since open politics was introduced under United Nations tutelage in 1992–93. Quarrelsome as political life has been since then, the disputes have rarely involved political principles. Personal power and a share of the spoils have been the issues.

The absence of commitment to identifiable tenets made possible the return of Sihanouk to the throne, surprising temporary alliances of such opposites as Ranariddh and Hun Sen, and a shameful race between both to win over factions of the surviving Khmer Rouge remnants. The political scene since the 1993 elections has been marked by astonishing marriages and divorces, explicable only by the absence of any principle motivating the holders of power.

A parliament, the National Assembly, had been freely and honestly elected, and the international community had congratulated itself on the achievement. It was, after all, the only one of the main objectives of the Paris Agreement that had been attained. But less than a year later, this summmum bonum with a two-billion-dollar price tag had established itself as a dormant body of time-servers, an assembly of no consequence, a gathering lacking even minimal will to exercise the legislative and checking and balancing powers of a democratic parliament. Those were the powers that it had properly assigned to itself in the constitution that it had framed. Its first debate showed remarkable agreement among its 120 members, astonishing after so violent an election campaign. They agreed that they should draw salaries and other benefits amounting to two thousand dollars or more a month, an astronomic demand in a country where the average civil servant earns around twenty dollars a month. They were persuaded by Hun Sen and the financial authorities, who know that Cambodia depends heavily on foreign aid, to scale down their demands. They did, but not by much.

The National Assembly was nine months old when I asked Son Soubert, its second vice president, how many laws it had enacted. He could recall only two, the budget and a reorganization act to modernize government finances and taxation. He winced in embarrassment when I asked how many days the assembly had sat in session. "Maybe one week in '93," he said, and less than twenty days altogether. Under its rules, the parliament is to hold three three-month sessions a year.

"We won, but we don't have the keys to the house yet," said Om Radsady, a FUNCINPEC leader who headed the Foreign Affairs Committee. Senior officials of FUNCINPEC and the Liberal Democrats were receiving threats from People's party activists. Opposing Hun Sen's policies puts your life at risk, said Say Bory, secretary of state for relations with Parliament. I asked him whether he meant his political life. "No," he replied firmly. The spread of corruption had quickly infected the new men from FUNCINPEC, adding material interest to political conflict. Sam Rainsy, FUNCINPEC's finance minister, conceded his party colleagues' fallibility bluntly. "Corruption touches the whole country," he said. "Everybody." This greatly added to violence in local conflicts, and much of the violence was traceable to People's party officeholders protecting their positions. But at the top, adversaries were capable of making common cause in despoiling their country for party or personal benefit. A scandal was simmering just below the surface that showed how far Ranariddh and Hun Sen had progressed in finding common interests.

Rainsy and his FUNCINPEC colleague, Prince Norodom Sirivudh, the foreign minister and a much younger half-brother of Sihanouk, had obtained facsimile copies of a letter signed on June 17, 1994, jointly by the two prime ministers. It was addressed to the Thai prime minister and left little doubt over Hun Sen's and Ranariddh's collaboration in underhanded action against Cambodia's interest. The letter stated that with immediate effect the Defense Ministry, and no other organization, was authorized to export timber. This was a flagrant breach of government policy in favor of a ministry that, together with the Interior Ministry, is headed in the same way as is the government as a whole — by coministers from both parties. Whatever profits resulted from the authorized exports could thus be shared by the parties — or by the two signers.

Worse, earlier in the year, the government, rightfully concerned over the vast ecological damage from rapid deforestation, had promulgated a decision that as of April 1, 1994, all timber exports were "prohibited under any circumstances." The ruling was aimed largely at the beneficiary of the overriding order, the Defense Ministry. It was the military, whose national, regional and local commanders were pocketing huge profits through illegal private sales of the main national resource to Thai officers with close ties to business interests. The two prime ministers by their letter had secretly countermanded the ban on exports. They had communicated this vital decision only to Thailand's head of government, not to the government of Cambodia, which had not been consulted. The letter giving a monopoly on timber exports to the Defense Ministry was also a clear violation of the new financial law, which specified that all state revenues must be paid into the national treasury and accounted for in the budget.

Deputies whom I questioned expressed dismay, but the issue was not raised in the National Assembly. Elected members told me that the legislature functioned mainly when the government submitted draft bills. It did so rarely. The Japanese embassy, in defense of the interests of Japanese customers for Cambodian timber, sent a protest to Foreign Minister Sirivudh. But the People's party faithful who continued to surround the royalist minister and filtered access to him saw to it that the protest was blunted. It took six days for the note from Cambodia's most important source of essential foreign aid to reach the minister's desk.

Meanwhile, the war against the Khmers Rouges continued. It was conducted by a government army in which some progress in integrating Hun Sen's large army and Ranariddh's smaller forces had been made. That is, the small royalist and other non-Communist guerrilla groups had been added to the large State of Cambodia forces, but a disproportionate number of royalists had been given high rank. The total troop strength was officially put at 145,000 men, but foreign military attachés had discovered that, as in Lon Nol's days, large numbers were "phantoms." They existed only on paper, allowing their officers to pocket their pay and the funds for their food rations. The attachés said that officers and noncommissioned officers far outnumbered ordinary soldiers. They estimated the number of generals at a laughable, Ruritanian two thousand or more, and there were several colonels for each general. A number of five-star generals were the icing on the confection; they included the two prime ministers.

General rank did not require most of its holders to do actual military service or ever wear a uniform, but it conferred considerable business privileges. It made it possible, for instance, to command private armies of enforcers and to detain civilian competitors. Particularly in the western province of Battambang, the focus of much contraband trade with Thailand, such private armies were engaged in mafia-like gang wars. Asian criminal syndicates soon discovered that Cambodia had become, in Sam Rainsy's words, "a paradise for money launderers." "It is a cash economy, and the legal framework is weak," the finance minister said. Narcotics traders found Cambodia a splendid transshipment center.

The government army, showing unusual temerity, had driven the Khmers Rouges in a surprise offensive in 1994 from their most precious bastion, Pailin, the center of sapphire mining. The conquest did not last. Cambodian officers descended upon the town, claimed houses for themselves by scrawling their names on the doors and, in the words of a French officer who was allowed to visit the captured town, "stole like rats." What they failed to do, however, was to secure their conquest by setting up defensive positions. A counterattack by a much smaller Khmer Rouge unit drove out the government troops in panic with hardly a fight. The officers loaded their vehicles with their booty, leaving their troops to fend for themselves. The Khmers Rouges kept advancing until they reached the outskirts of Battambang, Cambodia's second city. Fortunately, the monsoon rains stopped them six miles from the town, and they retreated to their Pailin base.

In 1994, nine months after UNTAC had withdrawn, leaving Cambodians in the hands of their own constitutional government with a king and two prime ministers, I found bitterness about the present and scant faith in the future among the people. A sense of deception and disappointment was prevalent. The elections had given a strong vote of confidence to FUNCINPEC, the party that depicted itself, in contrast with its opponents, newly converted Communists of Vietnamese coloration, as representative of a free and open Cambodia.

The party had won a surprising plurality; without the strong-arm methods of the People's party and the threats that it brandished against rural people it would have won a triumphant majority. Ranariddh had received the approval of Cambodians, an approval that was buttressed by his appeals to be given power so that he could turn the running of Cambodia over to his father. After twenty-three years of warfare and the varying degrees of dictatorship of Lon Nol, Pol Pot, Heng Samrin, and Hun Sen, the more or less benevolent authoritarianism of Sihanouk's years looked like a golden age to Cambodians. Their hopes were reinforced by Ranariddh's image as a French professor, an exemplar of Western tolerance and democracy. Ideals were held up to a people badly in need of them, and they had responded.

Instead of their fulfillment, Cambodians had seen Sihanouk and Ranariddh bow to the election losers, share power with them, and adopt avidly their undemocratic and corrupt ways. They were disappointed in their absentee king, on whose skill as a conciliator they had built high expectations. And they had been deserted by Sihanouk's son. Ranariddh was never seen to put up a fight for the freedom and tolerance that they thought he represented, nor to advocate the elemental human rights and progress toward material well-being of which they had stood in dire need for so many years. At best, Cambodians thought their first prime minister was a playboy, at worst an unprincipled seeker of power and gain. They felt betrayed.

And once again, leading politicians began to wish for help from beyond the borders. Om Radsady, the royalist parliamentary committee chairman, combined a frank admission of the failure of the political class to realize the promises of the Paris Agreement with a demand that the international community take on Cambodia as a permanent charge. To him, there was nothing transitional about the United Nations Transitional Authority; he wanted Cambodia to be its permanent ward. "The big powers should take responsibility," he said. "When you buy a car, you get a service guarantee. Maybe we drove the car badly, but you should share responsibility."

Discontent among FUNCINPEC leaders rose. Sam Rainsy, reputed among the international community as the most competent and uncorrupted of the country's leaders, was stripped of his office as finance minister for his constant, outspoken criticism of corruption at all levels and was expelled from FUNCINPEC. First Prime Minister Ranariddh had Rainsy expelled also from

the National Assembly, a procedure not foreseen by the constitution. Foreign Minister Sirivudh resigned in sympathy. Following a trumped-up charge by Second Prime Minister Hun Sen
of having plotted to assassinate him, FUNCINPEC in a particularly cowardly act voted to lift Sirivudh's parliamentary immunity from prosecution. A mild-mannered and unaggressive
man, Sirivudh had shown competence as secretary general of
FUNCINPEC and Ranariddh's campaign manager, which made
him a potential rival of both prime ministers. As a prominent
member of the royal family — Sihanouk's half-brother is a child
of the later years of Sihanouk's father, King Norodom Suramarit — Sirivudh's removal also disposed of a potential rival for
the throne. Only Sihanouk's intervention on behalf of his half-
brother saved him from being imprisoned by a judiciary firmly in
Hun Sen's hands. Sirivudh left for exile in France, where he had
spent the Lon Nol and Pol Pot years. In his absence, he was condemned to ten years in prison for illegal possession of arms.

The ousters of Rainsy and Sirivudh left Ranariddh in charge
of his party; it also left the party without two of its rare effective
and, in the case of Rainsy, popular leaders. The former finance
minister reacted to his purging from FUNCINPEC by forming
his own party, never legally recognized, the Khmer Nation party.
A fierce Khmer nationalism, not free of the customary anti-
Vietnamese overtones, as well as his eloquence and personal integrity, make Rainsy a political actor to be reckoned with.

The Hun Sen–Ranariddh entente began to crumble as the
solidarity of their common enemy, the Khmers Rouges, showed
serious strain. Rival appeals for Khmer Rouge leaders to rally to
the government, together with their troops, began to show remarkable results. The parties vied with each other to draw the defecting
Khmer Rouge units into their military camps. In the expectation
of the electoral battle that was shaping up for May 1998, the contest for defections quickly turned into a political struggle for alliances with Khmer Rouge leaders and the civilian populations
under their thumb. The feared and hated remnants of Pol Pot's

forces, who had been FUNCINPEC's uncomfortable foe-ally in the former Coalition Government, were seen capable of providing the winning margin in the next round of national voting.

The fraying People's party–FUNCINPEC coalition snapped at a convention of the royalists in March 1996. At the opening session, Ranariddh greeted his guest of honor, Hun Sen, with warm words of welcome and a tribute to their cooperation. But the following day, in his keynote speech to an audience of party stalwarts, Ranariddh berated his subsidiary prime minister and spoke as though a truth evident to everyone around him for years had struck him overnight.

"I think we cannot continue to betray the will of the people, which was expressed in 1993, nor can we continue like this until 1998," Ranariddh declared before his startled party. He raised the possibility of breaking up the coalition and dissolving the National Assembly. "To be a puppet prime minister, a puppet deputy prime minister, a puppet minister, a puppet provincial governor or deputy governor . . . is not too good," he confessed. It was an open declaration of hostility to his coalition partner, ending in effect meaningful cooperation within the government. The break encouraged all opponents of Hun Sen to regroup their forces in a common front against the People's party. Sam Rainsy and Son Sann, who had fallen out with Ranariddh, put aside their differences with the first prime minister. So strengthened, Ranariddh intensified his overtures to lure individual Khmer Rouge commanders to his side.

Ieng Sary, Number Two in the Pol Pot government, Number Six in the Communist Party, was the first to break with the Khmers Rouges. The most politically agile of the principal Khmer Rouge chiefs and the least fanatical — which does not diminish his significant share of guilt for the genocidal crimes — he denounced Pol Pot, his brother-in-law and companion since the beginning of the revolutionary struggle and rallied in 1996 to both prime ministers, leaving his options open. Pol Pot, the defector told me in 1997, had sidelined him years earlier. But Ieng

Sary further hedged his bets and linked himself with neither of the governmental parties. Instead, he formed his own party, the National Movement of Democratic Union. His reward was twofold — a royal "amnesty" from the death sentence that the Vietnamese-installed government had imposed on him and Pol Pot in 1979, and de facto control amounting to autonomy over the Pailin region, long a Khmer Rouge stronghold, and its lucrative connections with Thai business, links that reach deep into Thai government circles. Ieng Sary's defection and the establishment of his personal hold over Pailin and surrounding areas on the western border reduced the Khmers Rouges to their redoubt on the northern frontier with Thailand, around the small town of Anlong Veng.

Mysterious events took place there, far from the view of any objective witness. A minority view questions whether the split among the Khmer Rouge leaders was real or a charade staged by Pol Pot to take the curse off the makers of the genocide and launder them to be fit partners for alliance with other parties, like FUNCINPEC. In this view, the leaders tried to clean up their image by a staged rebellion to make it appear that the most odious of them, Pol Pot himself, had been ousted by force and punished. In reality, Pol Pot had agreed to retire for ill-health and had handpicked his successor. In late 1997 I questioned Ieng Sary, the only top-level Khmer Rouge who has taken sufficient distance from his former comrades to qualify as an expert and, perhaps, objective commentator. He believed the division between Pol Pot and the other ranking leaders — Nuon Chea and Ta Mok — to be real. Perhaps.

In the first half of 1997, constant dickering proceeded between FUNCINPEC emissaries and leading Khmer Rouge figures to detach them and their troops and civilian followers. Pol Pot, the majority view holds, bitterly opposed any rapprochement. In February, Ranariddh sent a group of fifteen emissaries to Anlong Veng, the Khmer Rouge headquarters. Nothing was heard from them, but Ranariddh, to give the illusion that he controlled the situation, assured questioners that they remained in contact with him. He was embarrassed when in April it was disclosed that at least ten had been murdered by Khmers Rouges loyal to Pol Pot immediately on their arrival; the others were taken captive. Nonetheless, contacts between some at the Anlong Veng redoubt and FUNCINPEC military representatives continued, amid mounting signs of a deepening split within the Pol Pot movement.

In June 1997 news of the most dramatic event in the fragmentation of the Cambodian Communist party reached Phnom Penh. Pol Pot had had Son Sen, one of his most faithful lieutenants since their Paris days, murdered, together with his wife, Yun Yat, and at least ten others of his family. Son Sen had been Pol Pot's feared defense minister and security chief, his wife the minister of culture, and, according to Ieng Sary, a hardline Communist who exercised strong political influence at the top of the Khmer Rouge pyramid. Nate Thayer, an American reporter who in many years in Phnom Penh made himself a specialist on the Khmers Rouges and maintained close professional contacts with them, reported that the murder of Son Sen marked the beginning of a violent attempt by Pol Pot to scuttle any negotiations.

Fighting broke out between Pol Pot loyalists and those who were enlisted by the man who appears to have seized Pol Pot's place as leader of what is left of the hard core of the Khmer Rouge movement. He is Ta Mok, a one-legged military chief, whose name within the party is synonymous with extreme brutality. As paranoiac as Pol Pot was about Vietnamese penetration of the Khmers Rouges, Ta Mok distinguished himself before the fall of the regime by purging at Pol Pot's orders great numbers of fellow Khmers Rouges suspected of pro-Vietnamese leanings. He did so with a ruthlessness that was deemed extreme even under the Khmer Rouge regime. It is possible that Ta Mok's motivation for his readiness to negotiate an agreement with FUNCINPEC derived from a shared hatred of Hun Sen, who is indeed a Khmer Rouge renegade and a defector to the hated Vietnamese.

The fighting at Anlong Veng ended with Ta Mok in command and Pol Pot, who had fled into the jungle with only a handful of supporters, his prisoner. He was confined to a simple hut, ill but unrepentant, and apparently resigned to his downfall. In July, a "trial" was elaborately staged for the benefit of Thayer as representative of the press, who would carry the news to the world. A "court" of Ta Mok's devising sentenced Pol Pot to life imprisonment for the murder of Son Sen, attempted murder of Ta Mok and Nuon Chea, and "destroying the policy of national reconciliation." "Democracy" was the new battle cry raised by the fanatical Khmers Rouges of Anlong Veng, and they wanted the world to believe that only the "traitor" Pol Pot had kept them from following that cry in the past.

Progressive defections and internal rivalries, no doubt fermented by lucrative offers from Hun Sen's military, reduced Ta Mok's remaining forces to a few hundred and doomed his hold over the last redoubt of the Khmers Rouges. Government troops occupied the abandoned town of Anlong Veng in April 1998. Ta Mok and the last of the Khmers Rouges fled into the Dungrek Mountains on the Thai border, taking with them the fallen leader, their prisoner, Brother Number One.

Pol Pot's end was tawdry, denying the comfort of a concluding act of justice to the Cambodian people, the victims of one of history's most destructive tyrants. Hiding in the malaria-infested mountains was the only defense left to the last of the Khmers Rouges. For how long? Pol Pot's capture and trial before a Cambodian or international court for his crimes against humanity loomed as a real possibility. Was there a more authoritative witness against Ta Mok, Nuon Chea, Khien Samphan, and the other holdouts than Pol Pot himself? What he could tell before a tribunal about their certain role in the genocide of the Cambodian people would be enough to doom each of them many times over. What sweeter revenge against the traitors who had turned against him and humiliated their leader in the eyes of the world! If ever there was a witness whom his captors would want to silence forever it was Pol Pot.

Then, on April 9, the United States let it be known that President Clinton had ordered plans to be made by his military to capture Pol Pot and with the help of Thailand deliver him for trial by an international tribunal. No judge could have handed down a surer warrant of death. Within a week, Pol Pot's end was announced. He died of a heart attack, those who held him prisoner reported. Phnom Penh's request for his body to be turned over for identification and determination of the cause of death was ignored. Without ceremony, crammed into a hastily carpentered crate, posed on a stack of long-burning used tires, Pol Pot's remains were set aflame. Not even his wife and their young daughter were allowed to be present. They might have blurted out to the invited foreign press photographers what had caused that cruel heart to stop beating.

In Phnom Penh, Cambodian democracy all but vanished during 1997. The more intensely Hun Sen and Ranariddh concentrated their thought on the democratic exercise of national elections to come, the more democracy was diminished. Both leaders worked at forming electoral alliances with the surviving smaller parties of the twenty that contested the 1993 voting. Son Sann and Sam Rainsy joined their followers with FUNCINPEC in a National Union Front. It proclaimed a program for democracy, in which Ranariddh succeeded in moderating the ultra-chauvinist views of his partners. As the political discourse heated up, both Hun Sen and Ranariddh began to threaten each other with the use of the tanks or big guns that formed part of the armament of their mutually provocative battalions of personal security forces. Hun Sen drew first blood.

On March 30, 1997, Sam Rainsy and about two hundred of his followers staged a peaceful demonstration in front of the National Assembly to demand the long overdue creation of an independent judiciary. The People's party had never yielded its control over a Communist-style, highly politicized court system, in which accusation is tantamount to conviction. Clearly this was more democracy than the second prime minister was prepared to permit. Four grenades were lobbed into the crowd, killing at least fifteen and wounding more than one hundred. Demonstrators pursued two men whom they had observed throwing grenades but were stopped from giving chase by People's party troops, who made no move to seize the grenade throwers. Sam Rainsy blamed Hun Sen for the murderous attack, a view shared by most international observers; Hun Sen blamed Sam Rainsy for staging the mayhem as a provocation to discredit the People's party.

The grenade attack in front of the very center of a democratic state was the opening salvo of a militarization of the political conflict and the total breakdown of the "comprehensive political settlement of the Cambodia conflict." In May 1997 Hun Sen officially augmented the contingent of bodyguards under his exclusive command from eight hundred to fifteen hundred. He accused Ranariddh of having secretly called into the capital one thousand Khmer Rouge defectors to augment the battalion of eight hundred bodyguards already under his personal orders. The allegation that the reinforcements that Ranariddh undoubtedly brought to his camp were Khmers Rouges has never been sustained by evidence.

Both prime ministers conducted their political campaigns from their mansions, which were turned into fortresses permanently surrounded by their armies, and left them only in armed convoys. No one governed. The two private armies became, in effect, the main forces of political confrontation in the absence of a functioning parliament. FUNCINPEC refused to let the National Assembly resume its sessions when a number of its deputies demanded Ranariddh's removal as party leader and were drummed out of the party by him. FUNCINPEC's demand that they also be dropped from parliament was rejected by the People's party, and the National Assembly went into paralysis. The king, ignoring his constitutional role as arbiter in time of crisis, remained in Beijing, a symbol of futility.

On May 26 customs officials in the port of Sihanoukville, renamed from Kompong Som, opened cases listed as "spare parts" and discovered two tons of arms intended for Ranariddh's bodyguards. The first armed clash followed in June. The personal armies of the leaders threw Phnom Penh into panic by exchanging fire in the very heart of the capital for about an hour. Two of Ranariddh's men were killed. While Ranariddh conducted negotiations with Khieu Samphan to bring the hard-core Khmer Rouge elements, after the fall of Pol Pot, into his anti–Hun Sen National Union Front, Hun Sen renewed his accusations against the first prime minister for negotiating with the Khmers Rouges on his own, raising the level of armament of his guards and reinforcing them with Khmer Rouge troops. Hun Sen threatened military action. In the first days of July, troops of both parties began maneuvering around Phnom Penh and brief clashes took place. With tension mounting by the hour, the two adversaries mysteriously disappeared from the capital. Ranariddh left on a "private visit" to France, Hun Sen on a "holiday" in Vietnam.

On July 5, 1997, Hun Sen threw Cambodia into the brief and decisive civil conflict that had been made inevitable by the bellicose actions and words of both sides. His aim was clear: to seize the vestiges of power remaining in royalist hands. Given the disproportion of forces, his success was foreordained. The dénouement of the unequal partnership began at dawn on July 5, and by dusk the next day, when Hun Sen's troops seized Ranariddh's residence, FUNCINPEC's headquarters and the main FUNCINPEC military base near the airport, the Paris Agreement had been buried. Many homes of FUNCINPEC leaders were vandalized; so was Sam Rainsy's residence. The headquarters of FUNCINPEC and the Khmer Nation party were ransacked and the party archives stolen.

Fighting took place largely around the residences of

FUNCINPEC leaders, security officials, and military officers. Artillery shelled the Tang Krasaing camp near the airport, the main base of troops loyal to Ranariddh. At midday of the first day, Hun Sen, back from a southern Vietnamese beach resort, appeared on television in combat uniform to denounce Ranariddh and the "irregular" forces that he had brought to Phnom Penh. "Too late," he replied when he received a message from Sihanouk in Bejing, where he spends most of his time, requesting a cease-fire. He left the king in no doubt who would, from then on, be the ruler of Cambodia. The second prime minister declared the first a "traitor" who would be put on trial if he returned to Cambodia and demanded that FUNCINPEC leaders who had not been arrested choose a new first prime minister. No formal action was taken to strip Ranariddh of his position.

By the evening of July 6, 1997, the status quo that prevailed before the much-heralded eighteen-nation accord and the UNTAC deployment was in effect restored. Hun Sen and the People's party ruled Cambodia, this time not in an openly one-party Communist state but behind the deceptive trappings of a restored constitutional monarchy and nominally democratic institutions.

The death toll was officially announced at fifty-seven; nearly two hundred were listed as wounded. Unofficial estimates range much higher. Hundreds of wooden houses in the western suburbs of the city, the main theater of fighting, were set aflame and thousands left homeless. It was all over but the looting, an orgy that occupied the victorious troops and much of the population for a day or two. Pochentong Airport, including the duty-free shops, terminal furnishings, the control tower, and repair shops, was particularly ravaged. So were shops selling cars, motorcycles, mopeds, television sets, and electronic gear of all kind. The official accounts cite around twelve thousand motorcycles and mopeds gone as booty of war, certainly an underestimate.

In August 1997 the United Nations special representative for human rights in Cambodia reported to the government details of forty-one cases of summary executions, mainly of FUNCINPEC security officials during and immediately after Hun Sen's coup d'état, with a demand for investigation and action against the perpetrators. Extraordinary cruelty and torture marked most of these political murders. The most prominent victims were Ho Sok, a state secretary in the Interior Ministry, and General Chao Samboth, a high-ranking intelligence officer. At least four other FUNCINPEC generals in high Defense Ministry posts were murdered in cold blood after their arrest by People's party troops. The People's party reported 564 arrests of FUNCINPEC military and security men in the wake of the coup. Dozens of FUNCINPEC, Khmer Nation party, and Liberal Democrat members of the National Assembly and other leading politicians took refuge abroad. Many were conducted to the airport by officials of foreign embassies to assure their safety up to the tarmac. And once again, thousands of ordinary Cambodians crossed the Thai border in search of safety.

Many FUNCINPEC deputies and party officials wasted little time in siding with the coup. On July 16, 1997, Ung Huot, who had already proved his sense of personal loyalty by replacing Prince Norodom Sirivudh as foreign minister, put himself forward as candidate for Ranariddh's post. On August 6 he was elected first prime minister. Since Ranariddh has no intention of renouncing the office, Ung Huot's elevation gave Cambodia three prime ministers. Eighty-six deputies voted for him; at least thirty of those who voted, in effect, to replace Ranariddh in the office from which he had been removed by military force, were members of his party. By a secret voice vote, the same session lifted the prince's parliamentary immunity and made him liable to prosecution if he returned to Cambodia.

The new first prime minister, an Australian citizen who has never laid claim to primacy over his nominal "second," showed the flexibility of his political allegiances in a newspaper comment after his election. "Samdech [Mylord] Hun Sen is a good man," he said. "He is a straightforward, honest man. But you know, lately, in the past almost two years, he became very mean, very bad, because Ranariddh made him so. It was engineered by Ranariddh. He made Hun Sen a devil." All the customary inanity of the Cambodian political discourse is contained in this analysis from the man who holds Cambodia's highest, and hollowest, office.

Before the year was out, the time-honored sequel to a coup d'état was announced by the virtual one-man government and endorsed by the abject National Assembly — the next elections, due in May 1998, were postponed. A kangaroo court subservient to Hun Sen completed the farce in March 1998 by sentencing Ranariddh, who remains in exile, to thirty years in prison for plotting with the Khmers Rouges against the government. His father followed up with a royal pardon, which was part of a Japanese-brokered charade to try to give the elections, if they are held, a democratic face.

Afterword

Only by comparison with the worst that Cambodia has suffered since it was plunged into the Indochina War in 1970 can the notion of progress be applied at all to this tormented country. The four calamitous years of Pol Pot's rule by maniacal murderers, who extinguished or damaged forever the lives of untold numbers of their own people, blighted the nation's social fabric and culture and shattered the bases of its economic survival. They established a nadir so low that any change meant an improvement. But nearly two decades have passed since those brief days of hope, when Cambodia emerged from the Khmer Rouge nightmare, thanks to a Vietnamese invasion and conquest. And today, where stands the nation, now numbering more than ten million?

Today's Cambodia is a basket case. It is a country that hardly nourishes and barely teaches its ever-increasing people, nor does it bind its multiple wounds or cure its many ills. In large measure its workers are exploited, its women ill-used, its children unprotected, its soil studded with treacherous land mines primed to kill. No equitable rule of law or impartial justice shelters Cambodians against a mean-spirited establishment of political and economic power, a cabal that is blind and deaf to the crying needs of an abused people. Their leaders' passions are private: to expand their might and riches. Unlike most politicians else-where, they do not even profess high ideals that they then betray. The betterment of the lot of the people whom they govern is rarely even the object of the customary lip service paid by hold-ers of power all over the world. Cambodia's politicians scarcely pretend to serve the Cambodian people.

While those who rule over Cambodians still professed com-munism their dogma obliged them to mouth the beautiful eter-nal verities of that religion, sadly far more honored in the breach than in the observance. Since their respective Chinese and Rus-sian patrons deserted them, they have forsworn the creed in fa-vor of greed, open, unvarnished avidity. But they have retained the crude methods by which they ruled in the Communist years — terror, torture, and the gun. The democratic innova-tions that the United Nations installed or encouraged have worn so thin that they no longer serve even as a threadbare cover for the rulers' unconscionable disdain for the people or their ruth-less resort to brute force against each other. The political settle-ment to which they committed themselves before the world in 1991 is a dead letter.

The well-being of Cambodians, their constant struggle for food and shelter, health and education, is left in their own hands. Their government ignores their plight without apology. What little help and protection reaches Cambodians comes mainly from outside sources — aid of all kinds from foreign govern-ments, international organizations, and private volunteer groups. Few countries are host to so complete an array of the world's or-ganizations of benevolence as Cambodia, and they attend help-fully to a wide range of needs. That this only scratches the surface is not their fault.

For there is one fundamental need to which outsiders can-not minister — Cambodia's need of leaders, a class of politicians whose concern it is to guide their nation out of the depths of misery into which it was cast in 1970. Cambodia needs not one man on horseback who will be the savior but an elite of aware men and women of goodwill and creative energy to whom the fate of fellow Cambodians matters.

The world had its opportunity to help bring this about when it assigned, with Cambodian consent, the ultimate responsibility for temporarily governing Cambodia and setting it on a path toward a better future to an impartial international authority. It missed its chance of dismantling an illicit regime of brute force and disarming an even more illegitimate and brutal rival. It yielded its mandate to the implied threat of force and took satisfaction instead in an exercise, moving and impressive, in letting the people speak their minds in conditions of severely limited freedom.

The people's message was clear; it would have been clearer yet had the fear of the ruling powers been neutralized. Cambodians wanted leaders who did not rule by fear, a government that held out a hope of freedom from all that had oppressed them for so long, materially and spiritually. They were given instead the shadow of democracy, devoid of substance. The leaders who between them gathered almost all their votes cheated them the moment the polls had closed, and the world chose to applaud the shadow and shut its eyes to the absence of substance.

Will there be another chance? I doubt it. Cambodia is no longer a stumbling block to smoother relations between confrontational major powers. No longer do larger interests of nations that matter globally give urgency to a desire to resolve an issue that needlessly complicates important relationships. Cambodia today is nothing but a pathetically weak, ill-governed, and unproductive country that has vanished from the radar screen that emits signals warning of impending international crises. Cambodia's enduring crisis is strictly its own, that of its survival. Nations do not become extinct; there will always be Cambodians. But their lives can become so impoverished of everything that makes a human being, their leaders so arbitrary, corrupt, and indifferent to everything but their egoism that a people founders and loses the struggle for national survival.

This struggle is not for its survival against a demonic neighbor bent on exterminating the "Khmer race," as is paranoically bemoaned by the pernicious advocates of Cambodian chauvinism, from Lon Nol to Pol Pot. Unfortunately it is also bemoaned by men and women of moderation, who are instantly possessed by a raging furor when Vietnam is mentioned. The threat to Cambodia's survival lies in the fatal incompetence of its political class, in the indifference of its leaders to the parlous descent of their people over nearly three decades into ever deeper illness, ignorance, and demoralization.

Meanwhile, Cambodia's western and eastern neighbors, Thailand and Vietnam, vigorous nations of expanding population and an energetic will to rise rapidly to greater heights of prosperity and well-being, may suffer temporary setbacks but can be relied on to grow steadily in strength. Therein, in the yawning disproportion between bubbling buoyancy and listless lassitude, resides the threat to Cambodia's survival as a sovereign nation.

It is not that Thailand and Vietnam are girding to renew the rivalry of earlier centuries of the kingdoms of Siam and Hue for possession of Khmer soil. Times have changed, and as Vietnam has experienced, conquest by arms of a neighbor bears the price of international revulsion, even if it overthrows one of the worst rulers in history. But states have not been converted to a religion of international beneficence. Would Cambodia's neighbors resist penetrating into a disintegrating country of regions that look ready to fall into a waiting lap?

Cambodia, I fear, is past helping itself. Its future, if it is to have one, cannot be entrusted to the hands of its present leaders, most of their opposition, and the class that they represent. The country has lost its international importance and possesses only its own worth, the life of a nation of ten million. Over the past century its life has been grossly tampered with by many outsiders. By France, for the sake of colonial possession. By Japan, as a piece in its "Greater Asian Co-Prosperity Sphere." By the

United States, to facilitate its withdrawal from a losing war in Vietnam. By China, because having a friend in Cambodia gave it a foothold on the Southeast Asian continent and a thorn in the side of Vietnam, a client of the Soviet Union. By Vietnam, to establish its preeminence over an Indochinese bloc of its design. By the Soviet Union, because those who opposed Vietnam in Cambodia were China's clients.

Will the world for once act in Cambodia for the sake of Cambodians? Can it set aside, for the sake of the survival of a people that has gone in one generation through too many variations on the theme of Hell, its slavish adulation of the principle of national sovereignty as an unquestionable good? It drew close to doing so in the Paris Agreement but fell short in its application. Cambodia looks mortally ill, and experience has shown that its own doctors are not up to the task of curing it. When a powerful Cambodian falls ill he goes abroad to be treated. I fear "abroad" would have to come to Cambodia to try to pull the stricken nation through. I see no other way but to place Cambodia's people into caring and disinterested hands for one generation, administer it for its own sake, and gradually hand it back to a new generation of Cambodians, who will have matured with respect for their own people and are ready to take responsibility for them.

Unrealistic? Of course. Unrealizable? No.

Index